Lecture Notes of the Institute for Computer Sciences, Social Informatics and Telecommunications Engineering 503

The LNICST series publishes ICST's conferences, symposia and workshops.

LNICST reports state-of-the-art results in areas related to the scope of the Institute. The type of material published includes

- Proceedings (published in time for the respective event)
- Other edited monographs (such as project reports or invited volumes)

LNICST topics span the following areas:

- General Computer Science
- E-Economy
- E-Medicine
- Knowledge Management
- Multimedia
- Operations, Management and Policy
- Social Informatics
- Systems

Muthoni Masinde · Antoine Bagula
Editors

Emerging Technologies for Developing Countries

5th EAI International Conference, AFRICATEK 2022
Bloemfontein, South Africa, December 5–7, 2022
Proceedings

 Springer

Editors
Muthoni Masinde 🆔
Central University of Technology, Free State
Bloemfontein, South Africa

Antoine Bagula 🆔
University of the Western Cape
Cape Town, South Africa

ISSN 1867-8211   ISSN 1867-822X (electronic)
Lecture Notes of the Institute for Computer Sciences, Social Informatics
and Telecommunications Engineering
ISBN 978-3-031-35882-1   ISBN 978-3-031-35883-8 (eBook)
https://doi.org/10.1007/978-3-031-35883-8

This Springer imprint is published by the registered company Springer Nature Switzerland AG
The registered company address is: Gewerbestrasse 11, 6330 Cham, Switzerland

Preface

We are delighted to introduce the proceedings of the fifth edition of the European Alliance for Innovation (EAI) International Conference on Emerging Technologies for Developing Countries (EAI AFRICATEK 2022). This comes against the backdrop of technological disruptions associated with the fourth industrial revolution (4IR) era. This revolution seems to be threatening traditional jobs and may exacerbate the unemployment problem besieging many developing countries. It is against this background that the EAI AFRICATEK 2022 Conference was held. During the Conference, presentations by scholars, researchers, developers and practitioners around the world awakened the consciousness of the research community to the need for the adoption of various 4IR technologies in enabling a transformation of African cities and communities in a manner that supports socio-economic advancement therein.

The proceedings contribute towards increasing awareness of the utility and impact of 4IR technologies in stimulating economic growth and also showcase various 4IR-related technologies which are currently in play within the African context. To this end, the proceedings report on studies which focus on the nexus between the under-listed and 4IR technologies, among others. These facets are (1) (Un)Employment and the Future of Work; (2) Society, State and Citizen Welfare, (3) Education in the 4IR Era, (4) Opportunities for Driving Efficiencies and Effectiveness; (5) The 4IR Baseline Architectures and (6) The 4IR in Environment and Agriculture Monitoring.

The technical program of EAI AFRICATEK 2022 consisted of 14 full papers, including 4 invited papers in oral presentation sessions organized in one main conference track. The Conference also featured a Masters and Doctoral Symposium with oral presentations as part of the main conference track. Besides, the Conference was run over 2 days in hybrid mode, with most of the authors presenting in person at the venue. The Conference Programme was structured under 6 themes: (1) Education in the 4IR Era; (2) the 4IR as a Driver of Efficiencies and Effectiveness; (3) Masters and Doctoral Symposium Part I; (4) the 4IR Baseline Architectures; (5) the 4IR in Environment and Agriculture Monitoring; and (6) Masters and Doctoral Symposium Part II.

Working in close coordination with the steering chair, Ivana Bujdakova, Pieter Potgieter (Local Chair), Adeyinka Akanbi (Web Chair) and Leandra Jordaan (Publicity and Social Media Chair) ensured the success of the conference. We would like to express our sincere gratitude to the dedicated organizing committee members: Paul Kogeda, Elisha Markus, Hossana Twinomurinzi, Regina Pohle-Fröhlich, Ntima Mabanza and Joyce Nabende. Our sincere gratitude also goes to all the Technical Program Committee members who, through their hard work, ensured successful completion of the peer-review process of technical papers and resulted in the high-quality technical program, and the proceedings. We acknowledge the financial and logistical support of the Central University of Technology, Free State. Apart from sponsoring the Gala Dinner, the University also offered the Conference Venue and generous support through the Department of Information Technology.

We are confident of the proceedings' contributions to the agenda towards a common programme of action to leverage 4IR technologies to drive socio-economic advancement within the African context. The proceedings awaken the consciousness of the research community to the need for the adoption of various 4IR technologies. Furthermore, the proceedings contribute towards the increased awareness of the utility and impact of 4IR technologies in stimulating economic growth and also showcase various 4IR-related technologies currently in use in Africa.

December 2022   Muthoni Masinde
                                                                Antoine Bagula

Organization

Steering Committee

Ivana Bujdakova
Conference Manager
European Alliance for Innovation

Organizing Committee

General Chair

Muthoni Masinde   Central University of Technology, Free State, South Africa

Technical Program Committee Chairs

Muthoni Masinde   Central University of Technology, Free State, South Africa

Antoine Bagula   University of the Western Cape, South Africa

Web Chair

Adeyinka Akanbi   Central University of Technology, Free State, South Africa

Publicity and Social Media Chair

Leandra Jordaan   Central University of Technology, Free State, South Africa

Workshops Chair

Paul Kogeda   University of the Free State, South Africa

Sponsorship and Exhibits Chair

Elisha Markus   Central University of Technology, Free State,
                                  South Africa

Publications Chair

Muthoni Masinde   Central University of Technology, Free State,
                                  South Africa

Panels Chair

Hossana Twinomurinzi   University of Johannesburg, South Africa

Tutorials Chair

Regina Pohle-Fröhlich   Niederrhein University of Applied Sciences,
                                  Germany

Demos Chair

Ntima Mabanza   Central University of Technology, Free State,
                                  South Africa

Posters Chair

Joyce Nabende   Makerere University, Uganda

Local Chair

Pieter Potgieter   Central University of Technology, Free State,
                                  South Africa

Technical Program Committee

Amon Taruvinga   University of Fort Hare, South Africa
Bankole Osita Awuzie   Central University of Technology, Free State
Emmanuel Tuyishimire   Dakar American University of Science and
                                  Technology, Senegal
Ferdinand Kahenga   Higher School of Computer Science Salama,
                                  Democratic Republic of Congo

Contents

Application of 4IR in Environment and Agriculture Monitoring

Education in the 4IR Era

Reinforcement Learning in Education:
A Multi-armed Bandit Approach

Herkulaas MvE Combrink[1]([⊠]) [iD], Vukosi Marivate[1] [iD], and Benjamin Rosman[2] [iD]

[1] Department of Computer Science, University of Pretoria, Pretoria, South Africa
u29191051@tuks.co.za
[2] School of Computer Science and Applied Mathematics, University of the Witwatersrand, Johannesburg, South Africa

Abstract. Advances in reinforcement learning research have demonstrated the ways in which different agent-based models can learn how to optimally perform a task within a given environment. Reinforcement leaning solves unsupervised problems where agents move through a state-action-reward loop to maximize the overall reward for the agent, which in turn optimizes the solving of a specific problem in a given environment. However, these algorithms are designed based on our understanding of actions that should be taken in a real-world environment to solve a specific problem. One such problem is the ability to identify, recommend and execute an action within a system where the users are the subject, such as in education. In recent years, the use of blended learning approaches integrating face-to-face learning with online learning in the education context, has increased. Additionally, online platforms used for education require the automation of certain functions such as the identification, recommendation or execution of actions that can benefit the user, in this sense, the student or learner. As promising as these scientific advances are, there is still a need to conduct research in a variety of different areas to ensure the successful deployment of these agents within education systems. Therefore, the aim of this study was to contextualise and simulate the cumulative reward within an environment for an intervention recommendation problem in the education context.

Keywords: Autonomous Learning · Education · Reinforcement Learning · Multi-Armed Bandits

1 Introduction

1.1 Recommender Systems

The fourth industrial revolution (4IR) is a disruption and augmentation to real-time processes interwoven with the digital domain [1]. In the context of South Africa, innovation in 4IR technologies is still in its inception as compared to first world countries [2]. Furthermore, 4IR disruptions are mostly observed within industrial mechanical processes, but there are certain domains that might not have benefitted from the full adoption of

M. Masinde and A. Bagula (Eds.): AFRICATEK 2022, LNICST 503, pp. 3–16, 2023.
https://doi.org/10.1007/978-3-031-35883-8_1

these disruptive 4IR technologies, such as in first world education [3]. In the context of education, great strides have been made in terms of developing information and communication technologies (ICTs) that can enable the storage and retrieval of learning material such as learning management systems, through to ICTs that can connect people on digital platforms from anywhere in the world [4]. As the software and autonomous learning components within systems increase, there is a growing need to understand the adaptive automation elements within such a system [5]. Adaptive automation as a concept refers to the locus of control between humans and machines, and where these boundaries reside. An example of an adaptive automation theory used was developed by D'Addona *et al.* (2018). In this framework, where automation is needed, and human decision making is outlined is illustrated using an industrial process (Fig. 1) [6]. Most adaptive automation frameworks are used in industrial processes, but these frameworks can also be applied to other contexts, such as education [3].

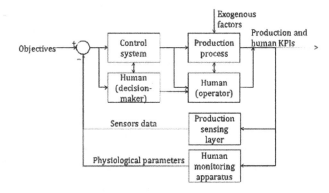

Fig. 1. Framework for human-in-the-loop factory adaptive automation[1]

However, there is still unexplored potential regarding the integration of autonomous learning systems in all spheres of the education domain [7]. One such example is recommender systems [8]. A recommender system is a dynamic machine learning filtering algorithm that uses data and a context to recommend an outcome to a user within a specific system [9, 10]. For example, some of these algorithms include collaborative filtering (context about the user to make the recommendation) to content-based filtering (context about the item that is being recommended) [11, 12]. Companies such as Google and Netflix have made use of these kinds of algorithms to recommend content to users browsing for content on these platforms [13, 14]. As promising as these algorithms are, they also have pitfalls in their implementation.

---

[1] Source: https://www.sciencedirect.com/science/article/pii/S00078 specifix50618301471.

In the education context, collaborative filtering relies on the average student's (user) input to recommend an intervention (the item). This approach runs the risk of applying generic and generalisable interventions to students that require nuanced approaches [14]. On the other hand, content-based filtering places an emphasis on the specific student's (user) own experience of the intervention (item) – but unfortunately this does not scale well in the South African context as students, their cultures and contexts differ [12]. In recent years, a hybrid approach has been adopted, using a combination of elements from both of these to make a sufficient recommendation [15].

As great as these systems are, they too fall short with reference to a few fundamental problems. Firstly, recommender systems suffer from the cold start problem [16]. The cold start problem refers to a situation that occurs when no information is available about a user or the item in the system (student or the required intervention). There are three types of cold start problems that can be classified based on where in the system the data are missing [17]. Type one occurs when a new student (user) enters the system without any prior knowledge on the user, type two when a new intervention (item) enters the system, and type three when the system starts for the first time. This means that recommender systems that are implemented suffer from this problem when the system starts for the first time. Secondly, recommender systems suffer from issues related to data sparsity. This means that not all the relevant information is collected about all the users within a given system. As a result, mislabelling of the interventions (items) is possible in the education context, given that sparsity challenges such as missing data about a specific item or set of users might occur. Thirdly, scalability is a major concern with these systems. The issue of scalability arises on the premise of whether or not the system will be able to cope as the number of students and interventions grows [18]. In studies about recommender systems, it was found that the moment a certain threshold or sample size is reached (depending on the algorithm and system) the results might not be desirable [19]. The fourth major problem relates to the lack of data within a given system [20]. If the system does not have at least enough data from the latent variables used associated with the different users, then the system cannot effectively make any recommendations. The final set of problems relate to a change in data and user preferences. In the education context, students (users) have different needs, and therefore require different interventions (items) to be recommended to them. As time continues, the needs of the same student might change, and as a result, the recommendation should subsequently support this change as well (Fig. 2).

In addition to this, learning design to recommend a specific intervention for a specific student based on their specific needs is a common problem with recommender systems. It is a common problem because the challenge lies in when to recommend what intervention would fit the needs of the student. Not all students would require a recommendation at the same time, and the same recommendation would not have the same impact for all students. Although recommender systems show a lot of promise to provide a solution in a variety of contexts in higher education, unfortunately, there are several technical, philosophical, and pedagogical hurdles that need to be overcome before a scalable solution to recommending interventions to students can be identified. Finding new information about students in real-time might not be a viable solution because these systems might only learn what was valuable to implement retrospectively [21]. To learn in real-time

Fig. 2. Research problems associated with recommender systems[2]

and work with data that is novel and not collected prior, unsupervised learning might be a possible solution. In machine learning, the algorithms' function using context learned from structured data [22]. In unsupervised learning, the approach fundamentally differs from supervised learning as an agent, which is an autonomous decision maker in the form of an algorithm, needs to make choices based on actions and be rewarded in relation to the choices it made within a specific environment [23]. This type of approach is known as reinforcement learning, which is a computer simulation based on principles similar to those found in classical conditioning but applied in the context of a decision-making framework [24].

1.2   Multi-armed Bandits and Markov Decision Processes

Let us propose that an agent is an autonomous decision maker within a specific context. The multi-armed bandit (MAB) problem is a type of reinforcement learning algorithm where the agent needs to make one of two choices per 'arm' in the system [25]. The purpose of the MAB is to solve the problem of choosing the arm within a given context that gives the overall highest rewards [26]. The challenge with traditional MAB problems was that it was applied to very specific situations where the fundamental scenario remained the same, leaving no room for a situation where the actions taken have an influence on future actions [27]. As a result of these shortcomings, Markov Decision Processes (MDP) were introduced to MAB to simulate more complex situations where the environment takes into account the influence current actions have on determining the best future action [28].

This type of autonomous decision making can be represented as a tuple, whereby the MDP state-action-reward loop can be denoted by $\mu = (S, A, T, R, \gamma)$ [29]. In this tuple, S represents conventional states, A signifies the finite actions to be taken by the agent, T denotes the transition from one state to another, R being the reward function, and γ the specific discount factor within the MDP. Within this tuple, the T, R, and γ

---

[2] Source: https://iopscience.iop.org/article/10.1088/1742-6596/1717/1/012002.

are interdependent on conditions for them to function within the MDP. The T element within the tuple can be represented as the placement from S_t to S_{t+1} given a certain A so that T: S_t x A x S_{t+1} → [0, 1] from state 0 to 1 can be denoted as a function of T (s, a, s') representing the probability of transitioning from state s to state s', given a specific A. The R element within the tuple can be denoted as R (s, a, s') for the same state action pairs. The context of the MDP is within a specific set of task instances, which can be denoted as X. This representation allows for the γ to be denoted as $\gamma \in [0, 1]$ given a set of task instances within the MDP space (M). Within the MDP, all state action pairs, including the T (s, a, s') and R (s, a, s') will be referred to as episodes, bound by a specific time context. The probability distribution of taking a specific action based on certain states is called a policy, and is denoted by π. When a policy is tracked over several episodes, the cumulative discounted reward can be calculated as a function of the R at a specific T for each state-action-reward loop. Given these annotations, the problem that an agent is trying to solve is to choose an A, between different S, within several instances of T, to maximize the cumulative reward based on the highest R for each episode [29].

Reinforcement learning does not suffer from the cold start problem and depending on how the reinforcement learning environment is designed, the context from which the agent takes an action and the types of interventions such a system could recommend, are fully customizable and do not suffer from the change in data problem [30, 31]. Lastly, reinforcement learning can transfer knowledge and context learned based on the specific problems that were solved [27–31]. Given this, reinforcement learning has great potential as an alternative for student intervention recommendations [32]. Therefore, the aim of this study was to contextualise and simulate the cumulative reward within an environment for an intervention recommendation problem in the education context.

2 Methods

2.1 MAB Student Intervention Recommendation Framework

To build a system for student intervention recommendations, the environment must be custom made to simulate specific actions taken by the agent and assess how the overall cumulative reward will be impacted by decision making and context in the education simulation. What we should not do within this environment is decide on the specific interventions as this is reserved for domain specific experts. In addition to this, the autonomy an agent has over deciding what type of intervention is best suited for a specific student will be stratified based on hypothetical interventions that are recommended by the agent. In this simulated environment, there should be broad enough categorization of the outcome of a specific intervention, assuming that the emphasis is not on the details of the specific intervention, but rather what constitutes success in implementing such an intervention. For example, if intervention X is recommended to the student and the student follows through on this, then the student has a certain percentage of passing based on the intervention proposed. In other words, the agent will make a choice based on the impact the recommendation will have. Given that the agent can make mistakes (choosing a hypothetical intervention that will not assist the student), the experiments need to include scenarios that illustrate the impact of making mistakes within a given context as well. Furthermore, it is pivotal that each specific student is contextualized in the framework of this problem. To achieve this, an assumption is made that there is a process prior to the MAB problem which correctly categorizes a student based on the problems the students face. The emphasis of this work is on the intervention recommendation component of such a complex system, and not the identification of the plethora of challenges that may exist within this context or how to correctly classify a student based on the interventions they need. Lastly, we assume that each student is a state, the action is the recommendation (or how effective the recommendation is in the context of this simulation), and the reward is assumed (although in a real-world system, this will be learned by the agent). The assumption of the reward is primarily for the purpose of evaluation so that the decision the agent made can be tested against the reward functions for those specific situations (Fig. 3).

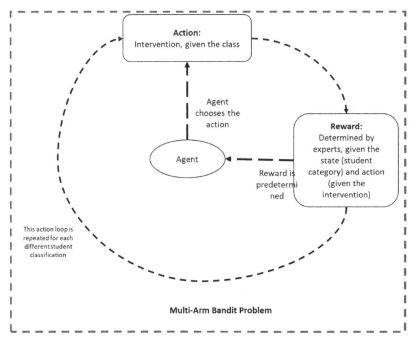

Fig. 3. Schematic representation of the student intervention MAB environment

2.2 Simulation Parameters

We are basing our assumptions on four different reward probabilities given to the environments, based on the type of student classification made. There are hundreds of different student classifications that can be given, each with their own unique interventions. We are only concerned with whether the correct recommendation is made, and not what the recommendation is. We assume that the students were correctly classified. In other words, we are assuming that the classification was perfect for the given student. The agent can also take one of four actions. The first action signifies an incorrect intervention; action two is an intervention with an unknown consequence; action three represents the ideal intervention; and action four represents an intervention that may work, but not for all instances.

We are assuming that all the intervention distributions per class are labelled by experts, and that the interventions are perfect. For our experiments, four different categories of student were used. These four groups or classes of student represent conditions for interventions that are given within education, dependent on the student needs and the problems they face [33–35]. The first class is a student that will pass, no matter the intervention. The second category is a student that will fail but will only pass if the correct intervention is given and stand a 70% chance of passing if the intervention that may work is recommended, and 50% if an incorrect intervention or an intervention with an unknown consequence is given. The third student will fail but will only pass if the correct intervention is given and stand a 50% chance of passing if the intervention that may work is recommended, and 25% chance that an unknown intervention is recommended. The fourth and last student is a student that will fail and will only pass 50% of the time if the correct intervention is given.

On average, the majority of the students who met the entry requirements for a specific degree need minimal to no input to pass their qualification. The exact number has not been agreed upon yet as a domain standard, but the majority of students that will pass, without intervention – roughly 55%. We will classify these as category 1 students [36, 37]. In our example, approximately 20% of students are likely to pass if a specific or specialized intervention is given, and without such an intervention, they are 50% likely to fail, we will constitute this as category 2 [33–38]. Furthermore, 10–20% of students will fail within a given system if the right intervention is not given, and if the right intervention is given, are still likely to fail. We will group this as category 3. Additionally, 5–10% of students will fail within a system due to reasons outside the control of the system. If an intervention is given to these students, they are still likely to fail with little to no chance of success. We will group this as category 4 [33–41]. All the action pairs and their associations with the different categories are summarized in Table 1 below.

Table 1. Summary of simulation parameters in the experiment

Name of Category	The % distribution within cohort	Likelihood to pass for recommendation 1	Likelihood to pass for recommendation 2	Likelihood to pass for recommendation 3	Likelihood to pass for recommendation 4
Category 1	~55% of cohort	100%	100%	100%	100%
Category 2	~20% of cohort	50%	50%	100%	70%
Category 3	~10% of cohort	0%	0%	100%	25%
Category 4	~5% of cohort	0%	0%	50%	0%

Within the confines of the experiment, each category of student will represent its own environment, that is, a simulation will be performed for each environment as outlined in Fig. 3.

2.3 MAB Algorithms

We used three different algorithms to simulate their impact on the proposed education environment. The first algorithm is a random agent. That is, an agent that takes a random A based on the available actions. The purpose of including this was to show the impact of taking random non-informed actions in the form of recommending random interventions within this environment. The second Algorithm was an epsilon greedy algorithm. The epsilon greedy algorithm makes decisions based on the trade-off between exploration and exploitation. Exploration in this instance can be defined as taking an action with an unknown return, and exploitation can be defined as making a decision based on known circumstances and known outcomes. Epsilon can be characterized as the percentage of times decisions are made from an exploration perspective. In the context of this study, epsilon greedy was explored because there are risks associated with exploration when dealing with human subjects. Within the design of the algorithm, epsilon was set to 1%, that is, to explore 1% of the decision made.

The third and final algorithm used in the experimentation was upper confidence bound (UCB). This algorithm works by implementing an exploration and exploitation approach, but unlike epsilon greedy, the exploration-exploitation trade-off is updated as the agent learns more from its environment. This algorithm was included as UCB is an illustration of an agent that has been used in other autonomous learning systems. There are several algorithms that have been used to solve a MAB problem such as temporal difference learning and Bayesian Policy reuse, but for the purpose of this paper, the emphasis is on the evaluation of the cumulative reward within an environment simulating an education student intervention recommendation problem, and not which specific algorithm works best for this environment. To visualise the data from the experiments, the distribution of the recommended interventions as well as the cumulated rewards over the number of episodes were shown. As mentioned prior, each episode is representative of a specific class of student that requires a specific intervention. Within each experiment, each of the four types of categories of student were represented within their own environment, that is, for each of the four categories of student, a different environment was used. Each simulation was repeated 10,000 times, and a confidence interval of 95% was adjusted around the results. Lastly, the distribution of the choices made per environment were illustrated to show how the various agents made decisions across the distributions of the types of interventions that were recommended (Table 1).

3 Results

The first experiment outlines what would happen if a non-smart agent is used to randomly make decisions (Fig. 4). As expected, students who will pass no matter the intervention (Environment 1) reached the maximum rewards after 16 episodes (students). The reward function for students who would only pass 50% of the time if the correct intervention is given (Environment 4) had an average reward of ~10% (CI 8–12%). This illustration outlines that no matter the recommended intervention, students who will pass will not suffer from random interventions recommended to them, whereas the consequences of not recommending the right intervention to students at risk of failing is quite high.

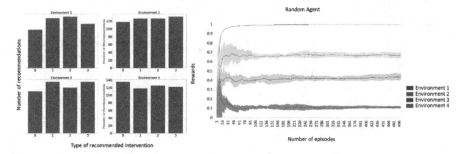

Fig. 4. Random agent recommending intervention simulation

The second experiment outlined what would happen if an agent had to implement decisions, given a certain level of exploration. In this experiment, the most important difference in Environment 4 was the average cumulative reward of ~20% (CI 5–35%). In this simulation, students who require a specific intervention to pass (Environment 2 & Environment 3) overall had an ~80% (CI 75–90%) reward, indicating that a system implementing MAB will be able to provide a high level of accuracy at learning which intervention to implement for a specific class of student if the impact of the interventions recommended is known (Fig. 5). What this approach also illustrated is that there are more risks associated with implementing an autonomous learning system that continuously explores as compared to an agent that randomly makes recommendations as seen with the lower limits of Environment 4 being 0% in several instances.

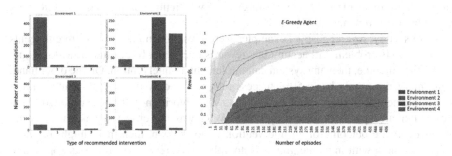

Fig. 5. Epsilon greedy agent recommending intervention simulation

In the last experiment, UCB was used as an illustration of how a better kind of autonomous algorithm can be used to make recommendations within an autonomous learning system. In this simulation, all the overall average rewards were higher than the previous experiments, with lower confidence intervals for each of the cumulative rewards in each environment (Fig. 6).

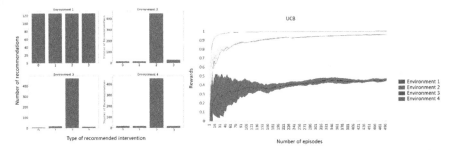

Fig. 6. UCB agent recommending intervention simulation

4 Discussion

Within institutions of higher learning, student retention and student dropout remain a problem [33]. Student retention refers to the students remaining within the institution despite their academic outcome the previous year, whereas student throughput refers to whether or not a student progresses through the system to make it to graduation. Several student support strategies and mechanisms have been explored to identify if they contribute toward the improvement of both student retention and throughput [34]. Some of these student support strategies include social support for students provided by the institution, academic support strategies facilitated by the institution, and high impact practices fostering a sense of learning in the students implemented by the institution [34, 36, 37, 39, 40]. The types of interventions that best fit the challenge a student faces is dependent on a variety of different factors, such as the needs of the student, which interventions are available by the institution, and which intervention is the best fit to aid in solving the problem [40, 41].

In this study, several abstract examples were given to simulate how different agents within a MAB problem will accumulate rewards over time. If the student will pass, no matter the outcome, then any system can implement an intervention. On the other hand, if an intervention only has a 50% success rate, if and only if the correct intervention was implemented to the correct student, then the algorithm will not learn beyond the current human capacity to solve the problem. What was also observed was that in certain instances, if the outcome of an intervention is not known, then there might be more risks associated with implementing a system that explores interventions as opposed to a system randomly recommending interventions. What these systems do really well, as illustrated in the simulations (Figs. 3, 4, 5 and 6) is learn to what extent we can build a system, based on prior knowledge, and how well these systems can potentially recommend an intervention to a student if we have that knowledge and understanding. What these simulations also illustrated are the consequences of not knowing the extent to which interventions can benefit the students. The ethical dilemma is that if a system implements an intervention that could potentially cause harm to a student, is it the fault of the engineers implementing the systems, the policy makers approving the systems, or the lack of understanding experts in the education domain have regarding which interventions work to improve education outcomes? How will a combination of these issues be dealt with, and what fundamental policies need to be in place to assist decision making in this domain? That is why adaptive automation is still important because, at present, the knowledge gap is too wide to implement these systems autonomously, as the study illustrated. The purpose of systems autonomously implementing interventions based on the needs of students is vital but depends on our fundamental understanding of what interventions work for which students, and not how well the algorithms work at solving fundamentally unsolved human problems.

Although there are universal overlaps in schools of thought about the fundamental needs of a student, there are nuanced differences depending on the context from which the student functions [40]. These differences are affected by a variety of factors including socio-economic status, financial situation, home language, the institution's language of instruction, general support structures available to the student, as well as the general drive, persistence, and resilience of the student [36, 42]. Despite these complexities, there is a shift toward the use of systems, such as recommender systems for the higher education context. In the context of higher education recommendation, specifically with reference to student interventions, the purpose of the system is to identify the correct need of the student and recommend a solution to the student that could potentially motivate the student to pass if they are at risk of failing because the correct intervention may be recommended. However, as outlined prior, how well a system recommends a solution is still dependent on our understanding of the problem, and at present, the science is not of such a nature that the system can suggest a recommendation outside the scope of the designed environment and outside the scope of our current understanding of the problem.

What is further complicated about these types of systems is that they should comprise a series of different algorithms so that they can recommend the correct intervention to the correct problem. This makes student intervention systems difficult to implement because students are not homogeneous and the student population, cohort, and society as a whole change over time. The interventions available by the institution and the type of support strategies that will best fit the problem are dependent on the academics, support staff, and student support framework policies of the institution. Complications arise when scaling student support strategies because student needs are vast and complex. In addition to this, the cost and time required to drive real-time analytics to identify, recommend and evaluate the effectiveness of these interventions to students is high if these processes are driven by staff, even if there is a dedicated staff compliment fulfilling this function within a higher education institution [36, 43]. Therefore, despite the potential unintended consequences of these systems, they are significant and potentially instrumental in recommending interventions to students within education. Lastly, the simulations within the experiments were intended to show empirically the consequences if the outcomes of interventions are not known, as to illustrate a need for further research from experts who are working in the education domain.

5 Conclusion

It is essential to design smart systems within higher education institutions that are generalizable and can adapt to both similarities and differences between students. To create such a system, a series of analytical and computational models need to be evaluated as the fundamental process of establishing such a system should rely on a combination of education theory, human intervention, adaptability, and human-machine interactions embedded within a system. Such a system will require a series of analytics, machine learning, and potentially reinforcement learning algorithms, all applied within a student support framework and working in conjunction with people within the system to serve the students and truly assist them. Understanding how to implement interventions within complex systems is fundamentally important as technology alone cannot define the boundaries and scope of what interventions and what processes will be used and will not be used within the education context. The science of systems learning is expanding at a rapid rate, but this type of development will be truly beneficial if coupled with systems-based domain specific knowledge for it to be successful. As disruptive as 4IR might be, our fundamental understanding of concepts remains a top priority if we want autonomous learning to be implemented responsibly to benefit the education domain.

References

1. Coetzee, J., Neneh, B., Stemmet, K., Lamprecht, J., Motsitsi, C., Sereeco, W.: South African universities in a time of increasing disruption. South African J. Econ. Manage. Sci. 24(1), 1–12 (2021)
2. Rashied, N., Bhamjee, M.: Does the global south need to decolonise the fourth industrial revolution? In: Doorsamy, W., Paul, B.S., Marwala, T. (eds.) The Disruptive Fourth Industrial Revolution. LNEE, vol. 674, pp. 95–110. Springer, Cham (2020). https://doi.org/10.1007/978-3-030-48230-5_5
3. Oke, A., Fernandes, F.A.P.: Innovations in teaching and learning: exploring the perceptions of the education sector on the 4th industrial revolution (4IR). J. Open Innov. Technol. Market Complex. 6(2), 31 (2020)
4. Gamede, B.T., Ajani, O.A., Afolabi, O.S.: Exploring the adoption and usage of learning management system as alternative for curriculum delivery in South African higher education institutions during COVID-19 lockdown. Int. J. High. Educ. 11(1), 71–84 (2022)
5. Bortolini, M., Faccio, M., Galizia, F.G., Gamberi, M., Pilati, F.: Design, engineering and testing of an innovative adaptive automation assembly system. Assembly Autom. (2020)
6. D'Addona, D.M., Bracco, F., Bettoni, A., Nishino, N., Carpanzano, E., Bruzzone, A.A.: Adaptive automation and human factors in manufacturing: An experimental assessment for a cognitive approach. CIRP Ann. 67(1), 455–458 (2018)
7. Dwivedi, S., Roshni, V.K.: Recommender system for big data in education. In: 2017 5th National Conference on E-Learning & E-Learning Technologies (ELELTECH), pp. 1–4. IEEE (2017)
8. Obeid, C., Lahoud, I., El Khoury, H., Champin, P.A.: Ontology-based recommender system in higher education. In: Companion Proceedings of the The Web Conference 2018, pp. 1031–1034 (2018)
9. Li, Q., Kim, J.: A deep learning-based course recommender system for sustainable development in education. Appl. Sci. 11(19), 8993 (2021)

10. Nouh, R.M., Lee, H.H., Lee, W.J., Lee, J.D.: A smart recommender based on hybrid learning methods for personal well-being services. Sensors **19**(2), 431 (2019)
11. Zheng, Z., Ma, H., Lyu, M.R., King, I.: Wsrec: a collaborative filtering based web service recommender system. In: 2009 IEEE International Conference on Web Services, pp. 437–444. IEEE (2009)
12. Geetha, G., Safa, M., Fancy, C., Saranya, D.: A hybrid approach using collaborative filtering and content based filtering for recommender system. In: Journal of Physics: Conference Series, vol. 1000, no. 1, p. 012101. IOP Publishing (2018)
13. Gaw, F.: Algorithmic logics and the construction of cultural taste of the Netflix Recommender System. Media Cult. Soc. **44**(4), 706–725 (2022)
14. Anwar, T., Uma, V.: A review of recommender system and related dimensions. Data, Engineering and Applications, pp. 3–10 (2019)
15. Afoudi, Y., Lazaar, M., Al Achhab, M.: Hybrid recommendation system combined content-based filtering and collaborative prediction using artificial neural network. Simul. Model. Pract. Theory **113**, 102375 (2021)
16. Lika, B., Kolomvatsos, K., Hadjiefthymiades, S.: Facing the cold start problem in recommender systems. Expert Syst. Appl. **41**(4), 2065–2073 (2014)
17. Natarajan, S., Vairavasundaram, S., Natarajan, S., Gandomi, A.H.: Resolving data sparsity and cold start problem in collaborative filtering recommender system using linked open data. Expert Syst. Appl. **149**, 113248 (2020)
18. de Graaff, V., van de Venis, A., van Keulen, M., Rolf, A.: Generic knowledge-based analysis of social media for recommendations. In: CBRecSys@ RecSys, pp. 22–29 (2015)
19. Chen, L.-C., Kuo, P.-J., Liao, I.-E.: Ontology-based library recommender system using MapReduce. Clust. Comput. **18**(1), 113–121 (2014). https://doi.org/10.1007/s10586-013-0342-z
20. Ma, C., Gong, W., Hernández-Lobato, J.M., Koenigstein, N., Nowozin, S., Zhang, C.: Partial VAE for hybrid recommender system. In: NIPS Workshop on Bayesian Deep Learning, vol. 2018 (2018)
21. Gräßer, F., et al.: Therapy decision support based on recommender system methods. J. Healthcare Eng. (2017)
22. Hu, Y., Chapman, A., Wen, G., Hall, D.W.: What can knowledge bring to machine learning?—a survey of low-shot learning for structured data. ACM Trans. Intell. Syst. Technol. **13**(3), 1–45 (2022)
23. Dayan, P., Balleine, B.W.: Reward, motivation, and reinforcement learning. Neuron **36**(2), 285–298 (2002)
24. Ludvig, E.A., Bellemare, M.G., Pearson, K.G.: A primer on reinforcement learning in the brain: psychological, computational, and neural perspectives. In: Computational Neuroscience for Advancing Artificial Intelligence: Models, Methods and Applications, pp. 111–144. IGI Global (2011)
25. Even-Dar, E., Mannor, S., Mansour, Y., Mahadevan, S.: Action elimination and stopping conditions for the multi-armed bandit and reinforcement learning problems. J. Mach. Learn. Res. **7**(6) (2006)
26. Koulouriotis, D.E., Xanthopoulos, A.: Reinforcement learning and evolutionary algorithms for non-stationary multi-armed bandit problems. Appl. Math. Comput. **196**(2), 913–922 (2008)
27. Wang, K., Liu, Q., Chen, L.: Optimality of greedy policy for a class of standard reward function of restless multi-armed bandit problem. IET Signal Proc. **6**(6), 584–593 (2012)
28. Krishnamurthy, V., Wahlberg, B., Lingelbach, F.: A value iteration algorithm for partially observed markov decision process multi-armed bandits. Math. Oper. Res. 133–152 (2005)
29. Rosman, B., Hawasly, M., Ramamoorthy, S.: Bayesian policy reuse. Mach. Learn. **104**(1), 99–127 (2016). https://doi.org/10.1007/s10994-016-5547-y

30. Agarwal, S., Rodriguez, M.A., Buyya, R.: A reinforcement learning approach to reduce serverless function cold start frequency. In: 2021 IEEE/ACM 21st International Symposium on Cluster, Cloud and Internet Computing (CCGrid), pp. 797–803. IEEE (2021)

31. Tabatabaei, S.A., Hoogendoorn, M., van Halteren, A.: Narrowing reinforcement learning: overcoming the cold start problem for personalized health interventions. In: Miller, T., Oren, N., Sakurai, Y., Noda, I., Savarimuthu, B.T.R., Cao Son, T. (eds.) PRIMA 2018. LNCS (LNAI), vol. 11224, pp. 312–327. Springer, Cham (2018). https://doi.org/10.1007/978-3-030-03098-8_19

32. Zou, L., et al.: Pseudo Dyna-Q: a reinforcement learning framework for interactive recommendation. In: Proceedings of the 13th International Conference on Web Search and Data Mining, pp. 816–824 (2020)

33. MacGregor, K.: Access, retention and student success–a global view. Student Affairs and Services in Higher Education: Global Foundations, Issues, and Best Practices Third Edition, vol. 107

34. Rajagopalan, R., Midgley, G.: Knowing differently in systemic intervention. Syst. Res. Behav. Sci. 32(5), 546–561 (2015)

35. Burns, M.K., Deno, S.L., Jimerson, S.R.: Toward a unified response-to-intervention model. In: Jimerson, S.R., Burns, M.K., VanDerHeyden, A.M. (eds.) Handbook of Response to Intervention. Springer, Boston, MA (2007). https://doi.org/10.1007/978-0-387-49053-3_32

36. Zhao, C., Watanabe, K., Yang, B., Hirate, Y.: Fast converging multi-armed bandit optimization using probabilistic graphical model. In: Phung, D., Tseng, V., Webb, G., Ho, B., Ganji, M., Rashidi, L. (eds.) Advances in Knowledge Discovery and Data Mining. PAKDD 2018. LNCS, vol. 10938. Springer, Cham (2018). https://doi.org/10.1007/978-3-319-93037-4_10

37. Leitner, P., Khalil, M., Ebner, M.: Learning analytics in higher education—a literature review. Learning analytics: Fundaments, applications, and trends, pp.1–23 (2017)

38. Gupta, S.: Higher education management, policies and strategies. J. Bus. Manage. Qual. Assur. (e ISSN 2456–9291) 1(1), 5–11 (2020)

39. Kuh, G.D., Kinzie, J.: What really makes a "high-impact" practice high impact. Inside Higher Ed (2018)

40. Organ, D., et al.: A systematic review of user-centred design practices in illicit substance use interventions for higher education students. In: European Conference on Information Systems 2018: Beyond Digitization-Facets of Socio-Technical Change. AIS Electronic Library (AISeL) (2018)

41. Cupák, A., Fessler, P., Silgoner, M., Ulbrich, E.: Exploring differences in financial literacy across countries: the role of individual characteristics and institutions. Soc. Indic. Res. 1–30 (2021)

42. Lacave, C., Molina, A.I., Cruz-Lemus, J.A.: Learning Analytics to identify dropout factors of Computer Science studies through Bayesian networks. Behav. Inform. Technol. 37(10–11), 993–1007 (2018). (Fundaments, applications, and trends, pp.1–23)

43. Scanagatta, M., Salmerón, A., Stella, F.: A survey on Bayesian network structure learning from data. Progress Artific. Intell. 8(4), 425–439 (2019). https://doi.org/10.1007/s13748-019-00194-y

Assessing Institutional Readiness for the Fourth Industrial Revolution: Using Learning Analytics to Improve Student Experiences

Silence Chomunorwa[✉][iD] and Carolien van den Berg[iD]

Information Systems Department, University of the Western Cape, Cape Town, South Africa
silchom@gmail.com

Abstract. The Fourth Industrial Revolution (4IR) brought disruptive technologies, dramatically changing the way businesses operate. Higher education institutions make use of learning management systems (LMS) primarily for teaching, learning and assessment. The COVID-19 pandemic has pushed the use of technology for academic continuity, resulting in institutions using LMS for virtual engagements with students, student collaborations, assessments, and as a repository for resources. Student behaviour on the LMS can be tracked, giving useful learning analytics which may be used to improve student success, retention, experience, and institutional performance. This paper is an exploration of institutional readiness for learning analytics. We adopted a qualitative approach, using purposive sampling to select the institution and initial participants. We used the snowball technique to recruit further participants. The personality traits stated in the Technology Readiness Index model were used to formulate interview questions. The findings show that the institution has systems in place to support students, which were launched to address insights from LMS-based learning analytics. The institution is ready for using learning analytics, with participants innovatively using the LMS, showing enthusiasm, and optimisation of the full potential of learning analytics. We recommend the use of learning analytics to come up with effective student support.

Keywords: Fourth Industrial Revolution (4IR) · Data-Driven · Decision-Support · Higher Education · Learning Analytics · Technology Readiness

1 Introduction

The Fourth Industrial Revolution (4IR) has significantly contributed to the improvement of the quality of education. However, 4IR comes with both challenges and opportunities, according to Elayyan (2021), with some institutions lagging in embracing it. According to the United Nations (UN), attaining inclusive and equitable quality education is necessary for sustainable development, making it a sustainable development goal (SDG)

The first author received funding from the NRF.

M. Masinde and A. Bagula (Eds.): AFRICATEK 2022, LNICST 503, pp. 17–32, 2023.
https://doi.org/10.1007/978-3-031-35883-8_2

(Mori Junior, Fien & Horne 2019). This can only be realised if fair, accountable, and informed decisions are made. Decision-making is at the core of higher education, with decisions made varying on impact. Decisions in higher education are aimed at improving student retention, success and experiences, and overall institutional performance. There is a growing need to make accountable decisions, and additional defined approaches used to make decisions, however, most of the approaches lack fairness and account-ability (Bull 2014). Cox et al. (2017), Liu et al. (2017), Kovač & Oreški (2018), Nouri et al. (2019) concur that data-driven decisions are accountable and fair, and often lead to improved institutional performance. Using student learning data is recommended for improving student experience, retention, and chances of success to equip students for the 4IR era.

Learning analytics is an emerging field of study, gaining popularity for its effective-ness in improving institutional performance. Higher education institutions can derive multiple benefits from the use of appropriate data analytics strategies, providing insights that help with decision-making. With the advancement in technology brought about by 4IR, student experiences may be improved through timely decisions, facilitated by real-time analysis and feedback on student learning behaviour (Adams et al. 2020; Elayyan 2021). Artificial intelligence (AI) and machine learning (ML) can optimise and auto-mate several analytics processes, bringing changes to business processes (Elayyan 2021). Studies suggest that learning analytics has the potential of changing higher education (Siemens & Gasevic 2012; Leitner et al. 2017; Wong 2017; Viberg et al. 2018; Sousa et al. 2021). The success of learning analytics in supporting decision-making depends on various factors, which need to be considered and addressed by the institution. With institutions operating differently, it is important to develop a customised framework for learning analytics, instead of using a one-size fits all approach.

Higher education institutions make use of learning management systems (LMS), which are designed to support hybrid teaching and learning (Joo, Kim & Kim2016; Alzahrani et al. 2021). In an LMS, students interact with learning content, resources, and assessments and collaborate in completing academic projects. The use of LMS has grown significantly during the COVID-19 pandemic, supporting remote teaching, learning and assessments by providing virtual engagements, either synchronously or asynchronously (Zhao & Watterston 2021). LMS may be considered the most common source of learning analytics in higher education. As students navigate through an LMS, their behaviour is recorded, leaving a "digital footprint" which may be analysed to give insights on student engagements, predictions on future trends and chances of success and make decisions accordingly, as ascertained by Leitner et al. (2017).

This study aims to assess institutional readiness for using learning analytics to support decision-making. There are various decision-support systems in use in higher education, most of which focus on enhancing the student experience and improving institutional performance (Leitner et al. 2017). This paper was done to explore institutional readiness for learning analytics. The paper commences with a review of the literature on decision-making in higher education as well as the challenges thereof. This is followed by a review of decision-making approaches including data-driven decision-making, decision support systems and learner analytics. The paper subsequently proposes the application of the Technology Readiness Index (TRI) and the methodology applied. This is followed by a discussion of the results and concluding remarks.

2   Decision-Making in Higher Education

Higher education institutions collect and generate huge amounts of data intended to advise decision-making and improve institutional performance. Schildkamp & Datnow (2020) posit that vast amounts of data can be overwhelming if not handled and used appropriately, leading to adverse effects. Furthermore, strategies must be implemented to safeguard these data to comply with policies (Nouri et al. 2019). South African universities face several challenges, according to DHET (2019), centred on decision-making. These include lack of accountability, underperformance, and compromised student and staff experiences. Lepri et al. (2018) and Schildkamp et al. (2017) contend that human challenges in decision-making may be overcome by using a data-based approach, of which learning analytics is an example.

In outlining the importance of methodology in strategic decision-making in higher education, Kadoić, Reðep & Divjak (2017) cite the significance of making effective decisions. Their study suggests a data-driven strategic method for decision-making in the context of higher education. Learning analytics data provide valuable insights that may be utilised to support decision-making. In the study carried out by Seale (2015), which focused on capacity building for Deans to ensure effective leadership in South African higher education institutions, the importance of decision-making was emphasised. There is an organisational shift in management and decision-making, which is in line with global trends (Seale 2015). In this vein, it can therefore be argued that efforts should be made to ensure institutional readiness for the use of data to make decisions, in line with global trends. The editorial (Lytras et al. 2018) on learning analysis posits that the use of data to make decisions has received growing attention in recent years. While empirical evidence shows that processing data can be complex and sophisticated, the adoption of emerging technologies in higher education can be optimised [13]. Empirical evidence shows that the availability of data is not enough for decision-making requiring organisational readiness and user adoption of a data-driven decision-making approach (Bouwma-Gearhart & Collins 2015). There is compelling empirical evidence to emphasise the importance of effective decision-making in higher education, with learning analytics recommended for effective student-support decisions (Leitner et al. 2017; Wong 2017).

3   Challenges with Decision-Making

Executives, academics, and admin staff at institutions of higher learning make decisions that impact students. Vanlommel et al. (2020) posit that teachers often rely on intuitive processes to make decisions that affect their pupils' academic and future trajectories. Although intuitive decision-making may save time and provide creative solutions, there are risks involved. Intuitive decision-making may not consider all alternatives, thereby leaving out the best solution (Okoli & Watt 2018). There is a greater risk of making a decision based on incomplete or inaccurate information (Vanlommel et al. 2020).

Although (Okoli 2020) claims that experience and intuitive expertise improve the effectiveness and efficiency of decision-making in times of crisis, empirical evidence shows that intuitive decision-making lack consistency, fairness and equality (Vanlommel et al. 2017; Visscher 2020; Lasater, Bengtson & Albiladi 2021). Therefore, using such an approach at higher learning institutions may compromise student experiences, success, and retention, as well as institutional performance. According to (Cai et al. 2018) data may be used to understand and improve the student experience.

South African higher education is increasingly becoming a regulated sector with political influence (Mngomezulu & Maposa 2017). Policies and regulations are implemented and constantly reviewed, and decision-makers have to comply to ensure inclusion (Dalton et al. 2019). However, such decisions may not be in the best interest of the institution, as (Bull 2014) argues that decisions made in compliance with policies and regulations are often rigid, and accountable, but may not always be effective. Unfortunately, these decisions may be non-negotiable even though their effectiveness may be questionable. It may be argued that some policies are designed for ideal institutions, and may not be applicable in reality (Engelbrecht et al. 2016). The Authority Principle is highly applicable in education (Bull 2014), where decision-making is done by relying on authority figures. These may be experts in a specific field, executives, or heads of departments. This approach shifts ownership and responsibility from the decision maker, and if the desired outcome is not achieved, no one assumes responsibility (Bull 2014; Mngomezulu & Maposa 2017). Furthermore, the importance of ethics cannot be overemphasised. Some decisions may be effective and logical but may not be ethical. Apart from the strategies above, huge amounts of data gathered and generated may be used to make decisions.

Academic institutions build reputations based on several factors (Yadufashije 2017), including student success rate, research output, and contribution to addressing skills needs, among others. Decision-making is a process of evaluating and identifying the best option or course of action, based on the values and objectives of the organisation (University of Massachusetts 2018). Moreover, while different approaches may be used for decision-making, many lack consistency and accountability (Lepri et al. 2018). Decisions on instruction and intervention are particularly important for teaching and learning experiences, and therefore directly impact throughput rate (Kovač & Oreški 2018), student experiences, and institutional performance. It is therefore recommended to make such decisions based on student learning data.

4   Decision-Making Approaches

Decision-making involves choosing a course of action, from identifying the decision to be made, gathering information, weighing the alternatives and finally making a choice (University of Massachusetts 2018). The urgency of the decision to be made, as well as the impact it will likely have, are the most crucial factors to consider before making a decision (Batteux, Ferguson & Tunney 2019). There are several approaches used for making decisions, and in most cases, a combination of approaches is used. These approaches include careful consideration of both internal and external factors. According to (Bull 2014), some decisions are made based on what is currently trending. Personal preferences, convenience, intuition, tradition, and indifference are some of the strategies that lack consistency, fairness, and accountability.

4.1 Data-Driven Decision-Making

There are several types of data that institutions gather and use to inform their improvement plans, including demographic, school processes, and student-learning data (Prenger & Schildkamp 2018). Decisions made based on data are considered fair, consistent, and accountable (Lepri et al. 2018). Such data may be collected from stakeholders, generated by algorithms and other intelligent systems including learning analytics or as a result of research (Liu et al. 2017; Kovač & Oreški 2018; Nouri et al. 2019). Data are necessary to make strategic decisions and measure organisational performance concerning student throughput, retention, and staff turnover, among others. Organisations face challenges in adopting a data-driven approach to decision-making. Schildkamp et al. (2017) posit that organisational data use depends on the characteristics of the data, the user motivation levels, and the organisation at large.

Data-driven decision-making is increasingly becoming popular in education and other sectors where accountability is expected. This approach is used for university admittance, as well as for making predictions on the probability of success of students (Asif, Merceron & Pathan 2014) in certain courses. Kovač & Oreški (2018) ascertain that there is a need to use data at all levels of education to develop systems that help improve the chances of student success. This is further supported by the findings of Nouri et al. (2019), who conclude that despite a lack of policies and national guidelines, data-driven systems have improved teaching and learning experiences in Europe. Institutions are more likely to succeed in the adoption and successful use of data-driven approaches if teams get support, as concluded by Schildkamp & Datnow (2020).

4.2 Decision-Support Systems

According to (Kashada, Li & Kashadah 2016) decision support systems refer to anything that can be used to provide rational and measurable scientific data on which decisions may be based. Such systems can be manual, hybrid, or specialised computer software. Manual decision support systems have been in use for decades, including SWOT analysis, cost-benefit analysis, Pareto analysis and decision matrixes, among others (Abdel-Basset, Mohamed & Smarandache 2018; Leiber, Stensaker & Harvey 2018). Due to the huge amount of data and the advent of new technologies, hybrid systems and specialised software are becoming popular. The 4IR brought a new era of technology and innovation, enhancing human-computer relationships, making data capturing and processing easy (Ramlall 2020). Technology has the capability of analysing huge amounts of data in a short time, making them more efficient and effective (Cid-López et al. 2015; Francis & Babu 2019). However, these systems have not been fully adopted in most developing countries (Kashada, Li & Kashadah 2016), including the South African Higher Education System. Kashada, Li & Kashadah (2016) posit that user awareness, among other factors, greatly influences the adoption of new technology by individuals. Some of these factors may be explained using models and theories for technology acceptance and adoption. Organisational readiness is of utmost importance in the adoption and use of any new technology and innovation (Nusir, Law & Aldabbas 2012; Kaushik & Agrawal 2021). Readiness may be measured quantitatively using the technology readiness index (Parasuraman 2000; Mufidah, Husaini & Caesaron 2022), and qualitatively by assessing organisational capabilities including the availability of resources, human capacity with skills and knowledge, weighing individual awareness, motivations and inhibitors (Christensen & Knezek 2017; Alzahrani et al. 2021; Kaushik & Agrawal 2021).

4.3   Learning Analytics

Learning analytics refers to the analysis and reporting of measured and collected learner data about learning, as defined by Siemens & Gasevic (2012). The purpose of learning analytics is to understand and optimise learning and learning environments to enhance student experiences and improve success and retention rates. Wong (2017) ascertain that the use of computational techniques and artificial intelligence offers new opportunities for dealing robustly with huge amounts of data that are collected and generated by institutions. Research has shown that learning analytics is crucial for academic planning, lifelong learning skills and strategies, learning resource allocation, curriculum renewal and supporting quality teaching and learning through analysis of the impact of different pedagogical innovations (Siemens & Gasevic 2012; Leitner et al. 2017; Wong 2017; Viberg et al. 2018; Jalil & Wong 2021). Provision of timely, personalised feedback to learners and supporting 21st-century skills such as critical thinking, communication creativity and collaboration makes learning analytics practical and significant in higher education today.

Researchers and data analysts often categorise learning analytics into three categories, depending on how they are used. While predictive analytics uses collected data to establish trends and predict possible future outcomes (Liu et al. 2017; Kovač & Oreški 2018), prescriptive analytics goes deeper, giving potential outcomes of different actions by combining the power of algorithms, machine learning, computational modelling, and business rules to recommend decision choices, leading to possible autonomous systems (Liu et al. 2017). Further from these two, descriptive analytics provides insight into the past by using data mining and aggregation techniques. This past data may be used to reflect on past practices and improve in future. For instance, student feedback surveys may be used to improve pedagogy. Diagnostic analytics is often used to find cause and effect (Asif, Merceron & Pathan 2014; Kovač & Oreški 2018; Alyahyan & Düştegör 2020; Sousa et al. 2021).

Learning management systems (LMS) have tools to track learner behaviour. Analytics from an LMS can be used to design strategies to improve learner engagement, and quality of teaching and learning, offer appropriate intervention, and provide timely feedback to students (Joo, Kim & Kim 2016; Mufidah, Husaini & Caesaron 2022), thereby improving chances of success and retention. Without learning analytics, such decisions are made without any evidence, and their effectiveness is questionable (Kovač & Oreški 2018). Research proved that decisions made on data are fair, accountable, and effective. With the rate at which LMS learning analytics may be generated, the feedback loop can be closed quickly, offering students timely, actionable feedback which is personalised and precise. All institutional stakeholders stand to benefit from the use of learning analytics, especially students, academics, curriculum developers, instructional designers, and student support services personnel.

5 Theoretical Framework

Institutional readiness for learning analytics depends on various factors based on both individuals and the institution. There are many models and theories to predict the likelihood of technology acceptance, including the Technology Acceptance Model in its various forms (TAM, TAM-2, e-TAM), the Theory of Reasoned Action (TRA), and the Unified Theory of Acceptance and Use of Technology (UTAUT and UTAUT 2), among others. While these models and theories are useful and have been extensively used to study technology domestication (Lai 2017; Putra Kusuma 2019; Nugrahani & Wahid 2021), they fall short on assessing the readiness to adopt new technology. Parasuraman developed the Technology Readiness Index, which is a paradigm that focuses on personality dimensions to assess the ability to accept and use new technology (Parasuraman 2000).

The TRI gives optimism, innovativeness, discomfort, and insecurity as the four personality traits that influence an individual's technology use (Parasuraman 2000; Mwapwele et al. 2019). These personality traits do not focus on knowledge and skills, but rather on the individual's beliefs and state of mind. Optimism refers to an individual's belief that technology has positive benefits, while innovativeness is an inherent tendency to explore and experiment with technology. These two constructs are motivators for technology use. Discomfort and Insecurity are inhibitors of technology use. Discomfort is the perceived fear of being overwhelmed by technology and lack of control thereof, while insecurity refers to the perception that the technology may not work as expected and may result in adverse effects (Parasuraman 2000; Mwapwele et al. 2019; Shonhe 2019; Warden et al. 2020; Kaushik & Agrawal 2021; Mufidah, Husaini & Caesaron 2022). An individual can have both motivators and inhibitors. However, motivators should overcome inhibitors for one to be ready to use technology.

The TRI is mostly used quantitatively by using Likert scale surveys. However, in this study, we decided to use it qualitatively to explore institutional readiness based on staff optimism, innovativeness, discomfort, and insecurities about learning analytics.

6 Methodology

6.1 Participants

The sample was drawn from a preselected institution using purposive sampling. The institution was selected for convenience since it is among many other institutions that fit the selection criteria. Purposive sampling ensures that data is collected from all key stakeholders. Initial participants were identified by their positions at the institution and approached for consent. The Snowball method was then used to select more participants. The sample represented academic, support, and administrative staff as well as executive management.

Bryman (2012) posits that interpretivism holds that reality is subjective, socially constructed, and a composite of multiple perspectives. Interpretivism enables a deep understanding and exploration of lived experiences of a complex world from the perspectives of those who live in it (Saunders, Leweis & Thornhill 2009). In this study, adopting an interpretivist approach enables us to explore, interrogate and understand the perceived benefits of learning analytics by stakeholders in the higher education sector. Intepretivism is characterized by subjective deviations, and as such, should be considered in interpreting the findings of this study as well as for future research.

6.2 Procedure

The study was approved by the institutional Social Sciences Research Ethics Committee, and institutional permission was granted to collect data. Two initial semi-structured interviews were carried out first with data analysts/architects. The purpose of this interview was to identify the status of learning analytics; finding out what systems are in place, how learning data is analysed and who has access to what data. A total of 24 participants were interviewed using semi-structured interviews. The duration of the interviews was significantly different- ranging from a minimum of 23 min to a maximum of close to 1 h 30 min. Interviews with Data Analysts (or related) and directors were much longer compared to Admin staff (secretaries) and academics. Data saturation was reached after 19 participants, after which a further 5 interviews were conducted to ensure that no new data emerge.

Interviews were conducted virtually and recorded. Subsequently, thematic analysis was used to analyse the responses. Interviews were transcribed and coded using open-coding. The codes were then grouped into categories, which were then used to come up with themes. Interview questions were guided by literature on technology acceptance models and the technology index model (TRI), which states that an individual's personality influences their potential acceptance of technology, citing optimism, innovativeness, discomfort, and insecurity as the four personality traits that impact acceptance of new technology (Parasuraman 2000). We were interested in identifying optimism through responses with a positive belief of the capabilities of technology, knowledge of systems in place and their perceived potential; innovation by how one's understanding of how learning analytics systems work, how they experiment, navigate and explore learning analytics. Discomfort and insecurity were identified through one's fears of using learning analytics, lack of knowledge of systems in place at the institution, and uncertainty of how to analyse and interpret learning data (Table 1).

Table 1. Participants' breakdown

Position	Number of people
Data Specialist (Analyst, Instructional Designer or related)	8
Managers/Directors	4
Academics	7
Admin/Other Support	4

7 Results and Discussion

Successful adoption and use of any new technology or innovation depend on individuals' beliefs and perspectives, as well as organisational support. Several systems are in place at the institution, and learning analytics is an active source of data that is used to support decision-making for enhancing the student experience and institutional performance. Access to data is provided to authorised stakeholders. However, this came up as a challenge due to the need for privacy in compliance with policies and legislation.

7.1 Personal Beliefs and Perspectives

All participants agree that there is a need to regularly analyse, review, and reflect on how students are performing, and make decisions on intervention, assessment, resource allocation, curriculum renewal and level of support needed, among others. While some participants admit that they cannot analyse data on their own, they highlight that they are willing to get training that will enable them to use data to support decision-making. Participants acknowledge the importance of data-driven decision-support systems but are only willing to undergo training that will enhance their performance and simplify their work. There is optimism that learning analytics will improve the student experience, retention, and success rate, with all participants acknowledging the need to understand and use learning analytics effectively except for some support staff. Two of the support staff interviewed claim that they do make decisions on their own, but rather take instructions from their line managers. All academics claim that they often *"...click around and explore..." student learning data, "...especially access to resources and assessment marks..."* to establish relationships between performance and engagement with resources. Data analysts claim they are *"...fascinated by data and its meaning...",* and always engage with student learning data, among others.

One therefore may conclude that there is great optimism for the potential of learning analytics, and stakeholders are innovative and enthusiastic about learning analytics. The level of discomfort and insecurity is very low, arising mainly from a lack of sufficient knowledge and skills to analyse data. It is important therefore for training to be offered regularly to stakeholders so that the power of learning analytics may be fully realised.

7.2 Institutional Capabilities/Readiness – Systems in Place

Technology Availability

The institution has a Sakai platform LMS in please, which is branded as iKamva at the institution. Findings show that the platform is well known, well communicated, and utilised by the relevant stakeholders. Academic staff use the LMS for teaching, learning and assessments. Participants highlight that iKamva is very effective and easy to use, and enable them to remotely engage with students, allow students to collaborate, and access resources easily.

The LMS have various functionalities that generate student learning behaviour. Participants use LMS-based learning analytics for decision support. What only differs is the decisions and type of data they use. For example, academic staff highlight that they are most interested in real-time analytics which enables them to give timely feedback, and planned intervention. Data analysts, instructional designers, institutional planners, and directors use real-time, predictive, and summative analytics for broader decisions, leading to equitable resource allocation, appropriate curriculum renewal, and student support services, among other services. However, the LMS alone does not provide enough insights for all decisions to be made, and for that reason, the institution has other decision-support systems in place.

Participants realise the importance of learning analytics in advising student support strategies and acknowledge its potential in improving student success and retention. Participant P1, an academic, said, *"I use iKamva daily since lockdown. I don't know all its functions, but I know what I want, and it works for me. I can see how they[students] perform and give feedback accordingly"*. Similar sentiments being aired by other participants, indicating the levels of optimism and innovativeness among staff.

Further to the LMS, the institution is in the process of developing a central data warehouse, which all institutional systems will draw data from. This level of innovation indicates readiness and commitment to data-driven decision support from the institution. For students, these data will include, among others, learning data and biographical information. A centralised database allows sharing of ideas among analysts, higher level of security, enhances data integrity and reduces data redundancy. These efforts are evidence that the system is ready for data-driven decision-support, which includes using learning analytics to enhance student experiences, and improve chances of student success and institutional performance. While some stakeholders did not know about this move, they all unanimously agree that a central database will improve data-sharing and the use of data to support decision-making.

Staff Availability

Snowballing led to interviews with professionals in the data analytics field. The institution has several staff members who are Data Analysts, Data Architects, Instructional Designers, and Teaching and Learning Specialists, among other Information and Communication Technology specialists. They are responsible for various aspects of ICT systems, including decision support systems. In addition, academic staff and administrators are trained to effectively use the LMS for their day-to-day needs without t the need of a specialised professional. For example, participant P2 highlights that he *"...can track student progress and identify those at risk timeously…"*. It is therefore clear that the institution has adequate staff capabilities to use learning analytics effectively.

Analysing and making sense of data is often a challenge for stakeholders. Academics interviewed pointed out that they can *"understand the data they get from iKamva"* concerning student behaviour. However, they highlighted that they would prefer data to be analysed for them and provided with a summary and recommendations. This was also echoed by all other stakeholders except data specialists, who claim they can extract, analyse, and interpret the data for themselves. For successful use of learning analytics, stakeholders need to be able to understand the data at their disposal, as concluded by Leitner et al. (2017), Tsai & …, (2017). Having data professionals giving support to other institutional stakeholders by giving reports and recommendations from learning analytics shows that the institution has the sufficient human capacity to effectively use learning analytics for decision-support.

Learning Analytics-Based Projects
The institution hosts some projects based on learning analytics. These projects vary in scope, depending on whether they are based on predictive, real-time, and summative. However, one can conclude that running such programs illustrate the high level of readiness for using learning analytics that the institution is at.

The Siyaphumelela project was launched in 2020. Siyaphumelela is an IsiXhosa word meaning "We Succeed". This project focuses on using learning analytics to enhance student support. The project has been launched due to student retention and success challenges faced, identified using learning analytics. Participant P3, a Data Analyst, who is part of the Siyaphumelela projects outlined how learning analytics are used to provide improve student experience through curriculum development, and academic and psychosocial support. According to P3, Siyaphumelela is *"… all about using data to make informed decisions that will lead to student success…."*. P3 further posits that the project was launched after some time of using learning and other data analytics for research into student success and challenges. In essence, the Siyaphumelela project is mainly focused on students who need support to succeed.

Data analytics, including learning analytics, in higher education, focuses on identifying gaps in learning and supporting learning at different levels. This may include supporting students academically, psychosocially, or even guiding and preparing them for workplaces. To support and recognise academically high-performing students, the institution runs the Accelerated and Excellence Project (AEP). AEP focuses on supporting high-performing students with their academics as well as equipping them with essential skills required for the workplace.

Further to Siyaphumelela and AEP, the institution is working on a student success and retention framework, aimed at addressing the low undergraduate throughput rate and curbing the high dropout rate. Using data analytics, academic, well-being and financial need have been identified as key factors contributing to student dropout. The framework aims to address such challenges by advising, mentoring, and supporting students throughout their academic journey. The framework relies heavily on learning analytics, identifying students' deficiencies and needs, and referring them to the services that may ensure an improved experience.

Learning analytics is important in identifying students at risk and coming up with strategies to mitigate the risk timeously. A participant, P4 from student support services claims that students often struggle academically due to language (and accent), pace, and low confidence levels. According to P4 *"...[some students]are scared to ask questions from their lecturers for fear of the reaction from other students"*, and others find it *"...hard to acclimatise themselves to the different accents and pronunciations..."* by their lecturers. The institution runs a Tutor Enhancement Program (TEP), which has been designed to offer peer support to such students. Tracking their progress has proved that they significantly improve their academic performance and chances of success, which is in line with empirical evidence from other studies (Morano & Riccomini 2017; Pugatch & Wilson 2018; Arco-Tirado, Fernández-Martín & Hervás-Torres 2019).

8 Conclusion, Limitations and Recommendations

There are several studies on technology readiness, but few on learning analytics. Furthermore, technology readiness has been broadly studied quantitatively, without a deeper exploration of the meanings attached to the indices provided. To complement quantitative studies and contribute to the body of knowledge, this study qualitatively interrogates readiness from a different perspective, by exploring the systems in place and identifying key uses of learning analytics. This study, therefore, contributes to both theory and practice by enabling policymakers, institutional planners, and curriculum designers to better understand innovative ways of using and improving learning analytics to improve student success, retention, and experience. Furthermore, it contributes to the body of knowledge by providing institutional insights, which may help other institutions in adopting a learning analytics-based decision-support approach to improving institutional performance.

This research should be interpreted with its limitations. This paper is part of a broader study on decision-support systems, and limited questions were focusing directly on learning analytics. This was done to reduce the length of the interviews. However, learning analytics-specific follow-up interviews were conducted with a few individuals which provided deeper insight into the use of learning analytics. Furthermore, to have a full picture of institutional readiness, a survey should be carried out with all stakeholders, including students, to triangulate the qualitative data reported herein. We recommend a quantitative study that includes students, who are also part of the university community. Being an interpretive study, subjective deviations are thus inherent in this study. This should be considered on interpreting the findings.

Our findings show that the institution is ready for learning analytics. However, we cannot ascertain its impact on student success, retention and experience since those aspects are out of the scope of our study. The conclusion that the institution is ready for learning analytics has been reached after the analysis of responses from participants, who all show enthusiasm for using data to make an informed decision, and are optimistic about its potential to simplify their work, improve their performance, enhance their experience, improve student retention, success, experience and consequently improve institutional performance.

References

Abdel-Basset, M., Mohamed, M., Smarandache, F.: An extension of neutrosophic AHP–SWOT analysis for strategic planning and decision-making. Symmetry **10**(4), 116 (2018). https://doi.org/10.3390/sym10040116

Adams, R., Fourie, W., Marivate, V., Plantinga, P.: Can AI and data support a more inclusive and equitable South Africa? Policy Action Network: AI and Data Series (2020)

Alyahyan, E., Düştegör, D.: Predicting academic success in higher education: literature review and best practices. Int. J. Educ. Technol. High. Educ. **17**(1), 1–21 (2020). https://doi.org/10.1186/s41239-020-0177-7

Alzahrani, B., Bahaitham, H., Andejany, M., Elshennawy, A.: How ready is higher education for quality 4.0 transformation according to the LNS research framework? Sustainability **13**(9), 5169 (2021). https://doi.org/10.3390/su13095169

Arco-Tirado, J.L., Fernández-Martín, F.D., Hervás-Torres, M.: Evidence-based peer-tutoring program to improve students' performance at the university. Stud. High. Educ. **45**(11), 2190–2202 (2019). https://doi.org/10.1080/03075079.2019.1597038

Asif, R., Merceron, A., Pathan, M.K.: Predicting student academic performance at degree level: a case study. Int. J. Intell. Syst. Appl. **7**(1), 49–61 (2014). https://doi.org/10.5815/ijisa.2015.01.05

Batteux, E., Ferguson, E., Tunney, R.J.: Do our risk preferences change when we make decisions for others? A meta-analysis of self-other differences in decisions involving risk. PLoS ONE **14**(5), e0216566 (2019). https://doi.org/10.1371/journal.pone.0216566

Bouwma-Gearhart, J., Collins, J.: What we know about data-driven decision making in higher education: informing educational policy and practice. In: Proceedings of International Academic Conferences (2015). https://ideas.repec.org/p/sek/iacpro/2805154.html. Accessed 3 Sept 2021

Bryman, A.: Social Research Methods. 4th edn. Oxford University Press (2012)

Bull, B.: 10 Approaches to Making Educational Decisions (2014). https://etale.org/main/2014/07/14/10-approaches-to-making-educational-decisions/. Accessed 16 June 2020

Cai, J., Morris, A., Hohensee, C., Hwang, S., Robison, V., Hiebert, J.: Using data to understand and improve students' learning: empowering teachers and researchers through building and using a knowledge base. J. Res. Math. Educ. **49**(4), 362–372 (2018). https://doi.org/10.5951/jresematheduc.49.4.0362

Christensen, R., Knezek, G.: Readiness for integrating mobile learning in the classroom: challenges, preferences and possibilities. Comput. Hum. Behav. **76** (2017). https://doi.org/10.1016/j.chb.2017.07.014

Cid-López, A., Hornos, M.J., Carrasco, A., Herrera-Viedma, E.: A hybrid model for decision-making in the information and communications technology sector **21**(5), 720–737 (2015). https://doi.org/10.3846/20294913.2015.1056281

Cox, B.E., et al.: Lip service or actionable insights? Linking student experiences to institutional assessment and data-driven decision making in higher education. J. High. Educ. **88**(6), 835–862 (2017). https://doi.org/10.1080/00221546.2016.1272320

Dalton, E.M., Lyner-Cleophas, M., Ferguson, B.T., McKenzie, J.: Inclusion, universal design and universal design for learning in higher education: South Africa and the United States. African J. Disabil. **8**(1), 1–7 (2019). https://doi.org/10.4102/ajod.v8i0.519

DHET: 2000 To 2016 First Time Entering Undergraduate Cohort Studies for Public Higher Education Institutions (2019). www.dhet.gov.za. Accesssed 15 Jan 2021

Elayyan, S.: The future of education according to the fourth industrial revolution. J. Educ. Technol. Online Learn. **4**(1), 23–30 (2021). https://doi.org/10.31681/JETOL.737193

Engelbrecht, P., Nel, M., Smit, S., Van Deventer, M.: The idealism of education policies and the realities in schools: the implementation of inclusive education in South Africa. Int. J. Incl. Educ. **20**(5), 520–535 (2016). https://doi.org/10.1080/13603116.2015.1095250

Francis, B.K., Babu, S.S.: Predicting academic performance of students using a hybrid data mining approach. J. Med. Syst. **43**(6), 1–15 (2019). https://doi.org/10.1007/s10916-019-1295-4

Jalil, N.A., Wong, M.E.L.: Learning Analytics in Higher Education: The Student Expectations of Learning Analytics. dl.acm.org. (November, 5), pp. 249–254 (2021). https://doi.org/10.1145/3502434.3502463

Joo, Y.J., Kim, N., Kim, N.H.: Factors predicting online university students' use of a mobile learning management system (m-LMS). Educ. Tech. Res. Dev. **64**(4), 611–630 (2016). https://doi.org/10.1007/s11423-016-9436-7

Kadoić, N., Reðep, N.B., Divjak, B.: A new method for strategic decision-making in higher education. CEJOR **26**(3), 611–628 (2017). https://doi.org/10.1007/s10100-017-0497-4

Kashada, A., Li, H., Kashadah, O.: The impact of user awareness on successful adoption of decision support system DSS in developing countries: the context of libyan higher education ministry. Am. Sci. Res. J. Eng. **16**(1), 334–345 (2016). http://asrjetsjournal.org/. Accessed 26 Aug 2020

Kaushik, M.K., Agrawal, D.: Influence of technology readiness in adoption of e-learning. Int. J. Educ. Manag. **35**(2), 483–495 (2021). https://doi.org/10.1108/IJEM-04-2020-0216/FULL/XML

Kovač, R., Oreški, D.: Educational data driven decision making: early identification of students at risk by means of machine learning. In: The Central European Conference on Information and Intelligent Systems, pp. 231–237 (2018)

Lai, P.C.: The literature review of technology adoption models and theories for the novelty technology. JISTEM-J. Inform. Syst. Technol. Manage. **14**(1), 21–38 (2017). https://doi.org/10.4301/S1807-17752017000100002

Lasater, K., Bengtson, E., Albiladi, W.S.: Data use for equity?: how data practices incite deficit thinking in schools. Stud. Educ. Eval. **69**(100845) (2021). https://doi.org/10.1016/j.stueduc.2020.100845

Leiber, T., Stensaker, B., Harvey, L.C.: Bridging theory and practice of impact evaluation of quality management in higher education institutions: a SWOT analysis. Eur. J. High. Educ. **8**(3), 351–365 (2018). https://doi.org/10.1080/21568235.2018.1474782

Leitner, P., Khalil, M., Ebner, M.: Learning analytics in higher education—a literature review. In: Peña-Ayala, A. (ed.) Learning Analytics: Fundaments, Applications, and Trends. SSDC, vol. 94, pp. 1–23. Springer, Cham (2017). https://doi.org/10.1007/978-3-319-52977-6_1

Lepri, B., Oliver, N., Letouzé, E., Pentland, A., Vinck, P.: Fair, transparent, and accountable algorithmic decision-making processes. Philos. Technol. **31**(4), 611–627 (2018). https://doi.org/10.1007/s13347-017-0279-x

Liu, D.-T., Bartimote-Aufflick, K., Pardo, A., Bridgeman, A.J.: Data-driven personalization of student learning support in higher education. In: Peña-Ayala, A. (ed.) Learning Analytics: Fundaments, Applications, and Trends. SSDC, vol. 94, pp. 143–169. Springer, Cham (2017). https://doi.org/10.1007/978-3-319-52977-6_5

Lytras, M.D., Aljohani, N.R., Visvizi, A., Pablos, P.O.D., Gasevic, D.: Advanced decision-making in higher education: learning analytics research and key performance indicators. Behav. Inform. Technol. **37**(10–11), 937–940 (2018). https://doi.org/10.1080/0144929X.2018.1512940

Mngomezulu, B.R., Maposa, M.T.: The challenges facing academic scholarship in Africa in: knowledge and change in African universities. In: Knowledge and Change in African Universities, pp. 175–188 (2017). https://brill.com/view/book/edcoll/9789463008457/BP000011.xml. Accessed 1 Janu 2021

Morano, S., Riccomini, P.J.: Reexamining the literature: the impact of peer tutoring on higher order learning. Prev. Sch. Fail. **61**(2), 104–115 (2017). https://doi.org/10.1080/1045988X.2016.1204593

Mori Junior, R., Fien, J., Horne, R.: Implementing the UN SDGs in Universities: Challenges, Opportunities, and Lessons Learned, vol. 12(2), pp. 129–133 (2019). https://doi.org/10.1089/SUS.2019.0004, https://home.liebertpub.com/sus

Mufidah, I., Husaini, L.R., Caesaron, D.: Improving online learning through the use of learning management system platform: a technology acceptance model-technology readiness index combination model approach. Jurnal Teknik Industri 24(1), 61–72 (2022). https://doi.org/10.9744/JTI.24.1.61-72

Mwapwele, S.D., Marais, M., Dlamini, S., van Biljon, J.: Teachers' ICT adoption in south african rural schools: a study of technology readiness and implications for the south africa connect broadband policy. African J. Inform. Commun. 24(24), 1–21 (2019). https://doi.org/10.23962/10539/28658

Nouri, J., et al.: Efforts in europe for data-driven improvement of education a review of learning analytics research in seven countries. Int. J. Learn. Anal. Artific. Intelli. Educ. 1(1), 8–27 (2019)

Nugrahani, U.R., Wahid, N.A.: Technology acceptance model and motivation-opportunity-ability theory influences on indonesian dota2 gamer customer to customer online know-how exchange. J. Phys. Conf. Ser. 1779(1), 012003 (2021). https://doi.org/10.1088/1742-6596/1779/1/012003

Nusir, M., Law, E., Aldabbas, H.: Evaluating the adoption and acceptance of egovernment in developing countries: a case study of jordan. In: Proceedings of the 12th European Conference on Egovernment, vols 1 and 2 (2012)

Okoli, J.: Improving decision-making effectiveness in crisis situations: developing intuitive expertise at the workplace. Develop. Learn. Organ. (2020). https://doi.org/10.1108/DLO-08-2020-0169

Okoli, J., Watt, J.: Crisis decision-making: the overlap between intuitive and analytical strategies. Manag. Decis. 56(5), 1122–1134 (2018). https://doi.org/10.1108/MD-04-2017-0333

Parasuraman, A.: Technology readiness index (Tri): a multiple-item scale to measure readiness to embrace new technologies 2(4), 307–320 (2000). https://doi.org/10.1177/109467050024001

Prenger, R., Schildkamp, K.: Data-based decision making for teacher and student learning: a psychological perspective on the role of the teacher. Educ. Psychol. 38(6), 734–752 (2018). https://doi.org/10.1080/01443410.2018.1426834

Pugatch, T., Wilson, N.: Nudging study habits: a field experiment on peer tutoring in higher education. Econ. Educ. 62, 151–161 (2018). https://www.sciencedirect.com/science/article/pii/S0272775717303849?casa_token=2KtEgUXFZFcAAAAA:YQKdG6CDzIl-La_zLQ91C Ikp1O1MiJleBiE01UkR2GRJ-6EmThEm1zTA0RLEst00vvcRmbTuiA. Accessed 14 June 2022

Putra Kusuma, G.: Evaluation of e-government use among civil servants using unified theory of acceptance and use of technology model-a case of central mamberamo regency. Int. J. Sci. Technol. Res. 8(09). www.ijstr.org. Accessed 16 Jan 2020

Ramlall, S.: The impact of the Fourth Industrial Revolution on the survival of employee skills sets in the retail environment (2020). http://iiespace.iie.ac.za/handle/11622/460. Accessed 4 Nov 2021

Saunders, M., Leweis, P., Thornhill, A.: Research Methods For Business Students. Fisth ed. Prentice Hall (2009)

Schildkamp, K., Datnow, A.: When data teams struggle: learning from less successful data use efforts. Leadership Policy Schools 1–20 (2020). https://doi.org/10.1080/15700763.2020.1734630

Schildkamp, K., Poortman, C., Luyten, H., Ebbeler, J.: Factors promoting and hindering data-based decision making in schools. Sch. Eff. Sch. Improv. 28(2), 242–258 (2017). https://doi.org/10.1080/09243453.2016.1256901

Seale, O.: Building leadership and management capacity for deans in South African higher education (2015). https://core.ac.uk/download/pdf/188770461.pdf. Accessed 6 Sept 2021

Shonhe, L.: An assessment of the technology readiness of public librarians in Botswana. Global Knowl. Memory Commun. **68**(4/5), 275–287 (2019). https://doi.org/10.1108/GKMC-10-2018-0086

Siemens, G., Gasevic, D.: Guest editorial-learning and knowledge analytics. J. Educ. Technol. **15**(3), 1–2 (2012). https://www.researchgate.net/profile/Mohamed-Mourad-Laf ifi/post/Could_anybody_point_out_good_references_book_or_other_manual_about_SIE MENS_FUM_Card_such_as_FUM_230_FUM_511_and_son_on/attachment/59d64c3f7919 7b80779a6180/AS%3A484047265767424%401492417269115/download/Journal+of+Edu cational+Technology+%26+Society.pdf#page=6. Accessed 4 June 2022

Sousa, E.B.G.D., Alexandre, B., Ferreira Mello, R., Pontual Falcão, T., Vesin, B., Gašević, D.: Applications of learning analytics in high schools: a systematic literature review. Front. Artific. Intell. **4** (2021). https://doi.org/10.3389/FRAI.2021.737891/FULL

Tsai, Y., Gasevic, D.: Learning analytics in higher education—challenges and policies: a review of eight learning analytics policies. In: The Seventh International Learning Analytics, 233–242 (2017). https://doi.org/10.1145/3027385.3027400

University of Massachusetts: Decision-making process (2018). https://www.umassd.edu/fycm/ decision-making/process/. Accessed 25 July 2020

Vanlommel, K., Van Gasse, R., Vanhoof, J., Van Petegem, P.: Teachers' decision-making: data based or intuition driven? Int. J. Educ. Res. **83**, 75–83 (2017). https://doi.org/10.1016/j.ijer. 2017.02.013

Vanlommel, K., Van Gasse, R., Vanhoof, J., Van Petegem, P.: Sorting pupils into their next educational track: how strongly do teachers rely on data-based or intuitive processes when they make the transition decision? Stud. Educ. Eval. **69** (2020). https://doi.org/10.1016/j.stueduc. 2020.100865

Viberg, O., Hatakka, M., Bälter, O., Behavior, A.M.-C.: The current landscape of learning analytics in higher education. Comput. Hum. Behav. **89**, 98–110 (2018). https://www.sciencedirect.com/ science/article/pii/S0747563218303492 . Accessed 31 May 2022

Visscher, A.J.: On the value of data-based decision making in education: the evidence from six intervention studies. Stud. Educ. Eval. **69** (2020). https://doi.org/10.1016/j.stueduc.2020. 100899

Warden, C.A., Yi-Shun, W., Stanworth, J.O., Chen, J.F.: Millennials' technology readiness and self-efficacy in online classes. **59**(2), 226–236 (2020). https://doi.org/10.1080/14703297.2020. 1798269

Wong, B.T.M.: Learning analytics in higher education: an analysis of case studies. Asian Asso. Open Univ. J. **12**(1), 21–40 (2017). https://doi.org/10.1108/AAOUJ-01-2017-0009/FULL/ HTML

Yadufashije, C.: Building reputable university system in Africa. SSRN Electron. J. (2017). (September, 20). https://doi.org/10.2139/ssrn.3032650

Zhao, Y., Watterston, J.: The changes we need: education post COVID-19. J. Educ. Change **22**(1), 3–12 (2021). https://doi.org/10.1007/s10833-021-09417-3

M-learning During COVID-19: A Systematic Literature Review

Esmhan Jafer[1][(✉)] and Hossana Twinomurinzi[2] 📵

[1] Sudan University of Science and Technology, Khartoum, Sudan
smo5101986@gmail.com
[2] Centre for Applied Data Science, University of Johannesburg, Johannesburg, South Africa
hossanat@uj.ac.za

Abstract. Mobile learning (m-learning) offered opportunities for learning before COVID-19 disease (COVID-19) but experienced a significant surge in usage since learning moved to the homes. This systematic review collates studies published between 2020 and 2021 to understand the impact, challenges, opportunities, and gaps in m-learning during COVID-19. The key findings from the 26 papers reveal the extent to which many families, educators, and governments were caught off guard, some glaring family challenges, and social and digital divides inscribed in technology infrastructure, especially in developing countries. M-learning assumes adequate internet and digital technology infrastructure which means that developing countries continue to be affected the most. A research agenda is created for how m-learning can be better leveraged for future disruptions.

Keywords: COVID-19 · Higher education · m-learning · Online learning · Online education

1 Introduction

Digital technologies play a significant role in education today [1], with m-learning enabling education anytime and anywhere. There was as a tremendous increase in the use of digital technologies, especially mobile, since the COVID-19 outbreak around January 2020. COVID-19 affected every sector including education [2–5], from nursery school to university. Most education communities and campuses were forced to shut and suspend classes and scrambled to shift classes from traditional platforms to online formats [2, 6–8] to limit the spread of the virus through social distancing [9]. According to UNESCO, 99.4% of the students in the world were affected by COVID-19 with the economic and societal consequences being far-reaching [10, 11].

The government and private education sectors attempted to use m-learning tools such as the Educator's Room, Learning House, Telegram, Zoom, Kahoot, YouTube, Google Meet [3, 12], and many others. Mobile learning refers to e-learning via portable computing devices, such as Windows CE devices, Palms, or even a digital cell phone. E-learning is a substitute for conventional education and can also be used in conjunction

M. Masinde and A. Bagula (Eds.): AFRICATEK 2022, LNICST 503, pp. 33–49, 2023.
https://doi.org/10.1007/978-3-031-35883-8_3

with it. Both traditional education and e-learning are supplements to mobile learning. M-learning is a subset of e-learning, which is a larger term that encompasses both online and mobile learning environments. Despite the difficulties in implementing it, m-learning is the best alternative now available to ensure that epidemics do not spread because it guarantees spatial distance [13]. This paper focuses on m-learning during COVID-19.

M-learning was already popular especially for higher education due to its ubiquity and effectiveness in enabling learning anywhere and anytime [4]. M-learning allows for collaborative learning where peers can share their learning experience and be a part of the communication of specific practice, have immersive experiences, and offers greater flexibility. M-learning means that every student can access high-quality education at an affordable price [2, 5, 14, 15] and experience education [16], increased family time, personal improvement and gaining new skills [2], autonomy, and self-learning [14, 17].

Nonetheless, the unexpected transition to m-learning for many institutions because of COVID-19 exposed challenges, inequalities, and benefits. One of the challenges was failing to concentrate at home [3, 17]. The home environment has many distractions such as noise, family members, and housework. Also, home is associated with rest, which makes concentration difficult [2]. Other challenges included the lack of resources and internet accessibility in many outlying areas, the unavailability of internet access [2, 18], lack of supporting academic resources [2] inadequate prior training on m-learning for both students and educators [2, 11, 14, 17], fieldwork courses that needed the usage of labs [2, 14], and the sudden heavy demand on internet services [17]. Also, m-learning was difficult [2] as some students experienced less personalized contact with educators and with each other [2, 14].

This paper, therefore, sought to understand how m-learning during COVID-19. Specifically, the study sought to answer the following research question using a systematic review: *"What did COVID-19 reveal about m-learning"*?

The remainder of the paper is formatted as follows: the next section presents the method used to conduct the systematic review and is followed by the classification method used to extract meaning from the identified papers. The last two sections present the analysis of the findings and conclusions and set a research agenda.

2   Methodology

A systematic literature review (SLR) method was adopted for the study using Okoli and Schabram's [19] method. The purpose of the study was to answer the following main question: *What did COVID-19 reveal about m-learning*?

Due to the multidisciplinary nature of the question, and to cover the most extensive scope, the following electronic search engines were used:

- Elsevier Science Direct (https://www.sciencedirect.com)
- Research gate (https://www.researchgate.net/)
- IEEE Explore (https://ieeexplore.ieee.org/Xplore/home.jsp)
- Google Scholar (http://scholar.google.com/)

The search terms which were used in this study include two sets of keywords as shown in Table 1 below:

Table 1. Phrases in the Search Terms

No	Category	Keyword
1	Learning	Online learning E-learning Online Education M-learning Mobile learning
2	Coronavirus disease	COVID_19 Coronavirus disease Coronavirus Pandemic

2.1 First Stage. Collecting the Relevant Papers

The search elements were combined using the logical operator (AND) resulting in the following search string: ("Online learning" OR e-learning OR "online education" OR m-learning OR "mobile learning") AND (COVID-19 OR coronavirus disease).

2.2 Second Stage. Screening Using Inclusion and Exclusion Criteria

COVID-19 is a recent concept and hence there was no need to include data older than 2020 [9, 20]. The inclusion criteria were therefore related to the type of data included in the research papers as Table 2 below:

Table 2. Inclusion & Exclusion criteria

Criterion	Inclusion criteria	Exclusion criteria	Quality criteria
Focus	Peer-reviewed research papers about m-learning during COVID-19 from student's and educator's perspectives	Research papers about m-learning during COVID-19 from parent's perspective	

(*continued*)

Table 2. (*continued*)

Criterion	Inclusion criteria	Exclusion criteria	Quality criteria
Level of Education	All levels from nursery schools to higher education		The educational context for students and educators
Period of Research	Published between January 2020 - July 2021		The period during which Corona disease appeared
Geographical spread	Open		
Sources	Published in journals, scholarly outlets such as conferences, and academic publications	Published in reports, books, or have not been peer-reviewed	Predatory publications were excluded

2.3 Third Stage. Data Extraction

All the titles, abstracts, and keywords of the studies that resulted from the inclusion and exclusion criteria stage were scanned. Articles with no relevance to the scope of the SLR were excluded. For the papers that were included, the introduction and conclusions of each article were reviewed to determine their relevance. The three steps resulted in the hits as described in Table 3 below:

Table 3. Study and report selection process

Electronic database	Initial search (1st order selection)	2nd order selection	3rd order selection
Elsevier Science Direct	25	14	5
Google Scholar	21	20	11
IEEE Explore	13	13	9
Research gate	6	4	0
AIS Electronic Library	1	1	1
Total	66	52	26

3 Classification Framework

A classification framework from Amui et al. [21] was adapted, which uses closed coding to analyze and classify the selected papers. Table 4 shows the classification framework used for the paper.

Table 4. Coding and classification Framework for analyzing the studies

Classification	Context	Codes
Context	Primary schools	1A
	Secondary schools	1B
	Higher education	1C
Opportunities (m-learning resource)	Flexibility in time, place, characteristics, and psychological conditions	2A
	Financial Affordability	2B
	Having the new technology for m-learning	2C
	Accessibility	2D
Opportunities (related to students)	Enhanced Learning Experience	3A
	Develop Future Skills	3B
	Working remotely	3C
	Educational equity	3D
	Communication	3E
Opportunities (related to educators)	Practice technology and gaining skills	4A
	Creating online platforms for educators	4B
	Broadcasting educational lessons on TV and radio platforms	4C
	Working remotely	4D
	Increase educators' role	4E
Opportunities (related to contents of m-learning)	Creating comprehensive m –learning resource sites	5A
	Increase in the use of available resources	5B
	Education system development	5C
Resources challenges	Internet access	7A
	No computers	7B
	Digital devices are not good enough	7C
	Digital skills	7D
	Poor infrastructure	7E
	Inconsistent power supply	7F
Educator readiness challenges	Lack of training in online teaching	8A
	Lack of training in teaching	8B
	difficult to determine the state of students	8C

(*continued*)

Table 4. (*continued*)

Classification	Context	Codes
Challenges Facing Students	Lack of training in online teaching	9A
	Lack of Interaction	9B
	Negative emotions	9C
	Lack of family support	9D
Learning content challenges	Academic Resources	10A
	Coverage of the curriculum	10B
	Security	10C
	Lack of standards for quality content delivery	10D
	Laboratory activities	10E
Origin	Developing countries	11A
	Developed countries	11B

3.1 A Summary of the Selected Papers

Table 5 summarizes each of the resulting 26 papers.

Table 5. Brief Summary of the Selected Papers

NO	Authors & year	Brief Summary
1	Cotero, Karina (2021)	The paper identified and defined those skills which are basic to carry out the teaching-learning process virtually and online. It was found that students did not have the necessary skills to achieve their learning objectives as they had been doing in the face-to-face learning modality
2	Dhawan, Shivangi (2020)	The study focused on the Strengths, Weaknesses, Opportunities, & Challenges (SWOC) of m-learning. The key findings are that the academy experienced greater flexibility with online teaching
3	Humayun, Mamoona (2020)	The article offers guidelines to practitioners in the selection of suitable M-learning equipment and furnishes a tightly closed framework for the safety of M-learning records and the environment. The proposed framework is expected to furnish a promising answer for developing trustworthy and open instructing online instructing surroundings and may prefer to overcome the deficiencies delivered about by university closures for the duration of COVID-19
4	Suryaman, et al. (2020)	This article aimed to obtain and identify knowledge about the effect of the COVID-19 disease on the educational method. The findings point to several obstacles experienced by learners, and educators in learning activities and online teaching namely mastery of technology is still lacking, additional internet quota costs

(*continued*)

Table 5. (*continued*)

NO	Authors & year	Brief Summary
5	Surendra, et al. (2020)	This study explored the factors that predict the use of e-learning during COVID-19 among students of sports science education in institutions of higher education in Indonesia, the study identified aspects of access where many students do not have sufficient resources for mobile technology associated with facilitating learning, especially Internet access
6	Section, Early Career (2020)	The paper described the capabilities, implementation, and challenges of virtual learning for cardiology fellows-in-training (FITs) and fellowship programs in the COVID-19 era and beyond. Many novel tools had been used in the education of trainees. For example, the group chats application WhatsApp by Facebook was, and continued to be, used by many trainees for both sharing of medical knowledge and collaboration
7	Joko, Joko (2020)	The study analyzed supporting and inhibiting factors, the effectiveness of m-learning, and preventing the spread and impact of COVID-19 among students. The results refer to M-learning can prevent the spread and impact of COVID-19, 100% of students are not exposed and are not affected by COVID-19
8	Al-okay, et al. (2020)	There is a dilemma in accepting the new educational system "e-learning" by students within educational institutions. The result has confirmed the positive of direct effect variables (subjective norm, perceived ease of use, and perceived usefulness) on the student's intention to use the e-learning system
9	Harida, Eka Sustri (2020)	This paper explored the confidence of the students in m-learning in the Covid-19 situation. It found that some students did not feel confident with this kind of learning, some are enthusiastic, and others felt bored
10	Luh, et al. (2020)	The goal of this study was to describe how primary school m-learning solutions for COVID-19 pandemics worked. One of these solutions is to provide programming on a television station in areas where internet access is limited. Another option is to provide education via radio
11	Adnan, et al. (2020)	This research study examines the attitudes of Pakistani higher education students toward compulsory digital and distance learning university courses amid COVID-19. The findings of the study highlighted that a majority of students are unable to access the internet due to technical as well as monetary issues
12	Anderson, Nicole (2021)	The study investigated if some of the assumptions established regarding online learning remained true. While the COVID-19 responses showed that m-learning is feasible on a large scale, the study found there was still much room for improvement
13	Maulana, et al. (2020)	The study analyzed the COVID-19 impact on Islamic Higher Education (IHE). The finding revealed that Prior to COVID-19, the majority of Indonesian educators lacked significant mobile learning experience, although they were prepared for it
14	Jima'Ain, et al. (2020)	COVID-19 was studied in relation to the Industrial Revolution 4.0 (IR 4.0), and the associated teaching style. The finding revealed that extensive preparation on the part of both the educator and the student is required. For education to continue, educators innovation and students' tenacity are absolutely essential, and it's time to demonstrate how IR 4.0 can improve education

(*continued*)

Table 5. (*continued*)

NO	Authors & year	Brief Summary
15	Murad, Dina Fitria (2020)	The study looked into how organizers, conferences, and students were prepared for the current conditions, their readiness to go through the learning process while keeping educational quality, and how satisfied users (trainers and students) were with their learning. The findings suggested that online education has improved the preparation of education professionals in Indonesia
16	Wan Hassan, et al. (2020)	This article aimed to identify the challenges students face when using Google Classroom as a T&L method amid the COVID-19. The study showed that the average level of challenges students face when using Google Classroom
17	Liu,Zhen (2021)	This study identified user requirements to experience the online scene,and that students with poor self-control cannot complete their study plans effectively
18	Mishra, et al. (2020)	This article aims to process the fundamentals required for educational learning and m-learning amid COVID-19. It offered comprehensive picture of the continuing online teaching activities amid the lockdown, including the relationship between the change management process in the education system and the online education process during the COVID-19 epidemic
19	Awan, Muhammad Ta veer (2020)	The study aimed to elucidate the effect of virtual classrooms on student learning outcomes. More than 67% of participants felt they were negatively affected by the closure of schools, universities, and colleges in the education sector
20	Edy, Leksono (2020)	The study found that m-learning activities using different mediums such as Google Meet, WebEx, and Google Zoom. During COVID-19, influence learner motivation differently
21	Oyedotun, Temitayo Deborah (2020)	The paper provided suggestions for improving learning and teaching using online facilities in times of turmoil and epidemics, especially in developing and least-developed countries. During a crisis, comfort must be the priority for both students and staff
22	Agung, et al. (2020)	This study is a cohort case study about perceptions of their m-learning amid COVID-19. The result refers to the main factor that affects the success of m-learning is accessibility
23	Toquero, Cathy Mae (2020)	This study suggests preparing studies from educational institutions to document and reduce the impact of COVID-19.The paper also provided policy implications of formulating environmental policies that can strengthen university health management systems
24	Aguilera-hermida, A Patricia (2020)	The article detected perceptions of students' colleges of their use, acceptance, and adoption of m-learning in emergencies. The results refer to how attitude, self-efficacy, motivation, and technology usage of play a significant role in students' cognitive engagement and academic performance
25	Pratama, et al. (2020)	This study investigated the feasibility of an online class based on Edmodo. The findings show that the online class instead of class meetings was well advertised by the students
26	Xie, Xin Siau, Keng (2020)	This study found that students who experiment with m-learning experience a change in their perception are more likely adopt it after the panademic

3.2 Structuring the Findings

The coding was done using the classification framework and placed in Appendix A (https://data.mendeley.com/datasets/v5p9wh9hfj/draft?a=3f2049ea-1bbc-48a8-9650-b29daf250edf). The results are then discussed in the following section.

4 Analysis and Discussion of Findings

4.1 Context

Figure 1 shows the context in which the research was done.

Fig. 1. The Context of the Research

The findings suggest that majority of the research has been done in higher education contexts. There is little research on m-learning during COVID-19 in primary and secondary schools. This could be a result of many factors including the age group which requires much more strict ethics requirements. Within the scope of this study m-learning during the pandemic has mainly been studied from a Higher Education perspective and much less at the primary and secondary levels.

The way that students and educators at the primary and secondary levels interact with m-learning is different. Even though students at younger ages are regarded as digital natives, it was found that they too needed to learn to use m-learning in the same way as digital illiterates. There is therefore a gap in research on m-leaning at the primary and secondary levels during the pandemic.

4.2 Opportunities (M-learning Resources)

The descriptions below show the most important characteristics that mobile devices contribute as a resource to m-learning (Fig. 2).

Fig. 2. Opportunities Related To M-learning Resource

Most of the research papers indicated flexibility (the ability to engage with learning from any location and at any time, and in any manner required) and accessibility (enabling students to attend lectures and seminars from anywhere at any time and access m-learning resources and can even be accessed in rural and remote areas) as the most important characteristics that mobile devices contribute as a resource to m-learning.

4.3   Opportunities (Related to Students)

Figure 3 below shows the m-learning opportunity for the students

■ Enhanced Learning Experience.

■ Develop Future Skills.

▨ working remotely.

■ educational equity.

▨ communication

Fig. 3. Opportunities Related To Students

The majority of the research papers (14 papers) mentioned m-learning as a big opportunity for students to enhance the learning experience. M-learning presents an opportunity to change the existing learning strategies to give students a flexible approach to managing their learning experiences most of the students become self-directed learners. It also provides course scheduling flexibility that enables students to plan their time for completion of courses available online and encourages and enhances peer learning. Nine papers revealed that m-learning provides more opportunities for online students to participate in real-time interaction and to communicate with off-online students as there is satisfactory interaction too among educators and students. The students can share their opinions and provide peer learning opportunities with communication capabilities via email and social media such as WhatsApp for inquiries, and feedback. Only two papers mentioned that m-learning provides opportunities for students to work remotely.

4.4   Opportunities (Related to Educators)

Figure 4 below shows how m-learning is an opportunity for educators.

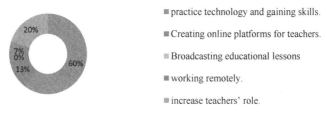

■ practice technology and gaining skills.

■ Creating online platforms for teachers.

▨ Broadcasting educational lessons

▨ working remotely.

▨ increase teachers' role.

Fig. 4. Opportunities Related To Educators

Educators as the main element in formal education are encouraged to adapt to the implementation of learning that originally used conventional face-to-face methods and switched to m-learning. The opportunity is for educators to practice with technology to acquire the necessary technical skills. Digital technologies enable educators and mentors to blend m-learning with traditional learning and ensure face-to-face and easy access to online content. Rather than only facilitating communication, educators could be coaches, mentors, and evaluators and enable them to share materials and videos for the benefit of educators by colleagues and university administration. M-learning also enables educators to create online platforms. No research papers mentioned broadcasting educational lessons via radio or TV.

4.5   Opportunities (Related to Contents of M-learning)

The descriptions below show that m-learning a big opportunity for content (Fig. 5).

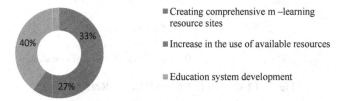

Fig. 5. Opportunities Related To Contents Of M-learning

The content of m-learning as one of the main pillars of the success of m-learning. 40% of the papers indicated an opportunity to make the curriculum responsive to the needs of the changing times. The content is then more persuasive because it makes the learner more interested in the material provided by the lecture, for example through creative video. 33% indicated an opportunity for creating a comprehensive m-learning resource site with live cloud recordings of teachings, meetings, lectures, and other interactions. 27% indicated an opportunity for an increase in the use of available resources.

4.6   Resources Challenges

The descriptions below indicate resources challenges (Fig. 6).

Thirty-four percent mentioned the challenges facing m-learning during COVID-19 related to limited internet access, slower internet speeds at home, heavy internet bills, and students do have not good internet data at home. 28% also indicate poor infrastructure additionally to the inconsistent power supply. 26% indicate the unavailability of computers, laptops, and/or tablet facilities for all participants in the educational process.

- Internet access
- No computers
- Digital devices are not good enough
- Digital skills
- Poor infrastructure
- Inconsistent power supply

Fig. 6. Challenges Related to Resources

4.7 Educator Readiness Challenges

The descriptions below reveal the challenges facing educator readiness (Fig. 7).

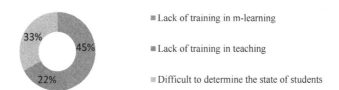

- Lack of training in m-learning
- Lack of training in teaching
- Difficult to determine the state of students

Fig. 7. Challenges Related to Educator Readiness

Forty-five percent found that educator readiness was missing, and the educators lacked training in m-learning. 33% indicates the difficulty that educators find in determining the status of students at the other end of the network. For example, educators were unable to read the face and moods of students and thus found it difficult to change the teaching pattern. They were also not sure whether the students switched on the mobile device for the sake of it, were actively learning, or not doing anything at all. 22% indicated that educators are not aware of the existing solutions; therefore, they are not able to choose a suitable solution according to their needs or to find solutions that encourage participation in the live classroom that works with the educators teaching ability and style.

4.8 Challenges Facing Students

The descriptions below show the challenges facing students (Fig. 8).

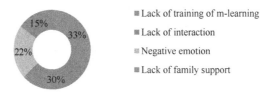

- Lack of training of m-learning
- Lack of interaction
- Negative emotion
- Lack of family support

Fig. 8. Challenges Facing Students

The key challenges related to the students included a lack of training in m-learning (33%), a lack of social interaction between students, and a lack of direct contact between students and educators, especially in practical training (30%). 22% represent students with negative emotions as the result of sudden life changes, financial hardships, stress balancing life, and lack of motivation.

4.9   Learning Content Challenges

The descriptions below indicate the challenges facing the content of m-learning (Fig. 9).

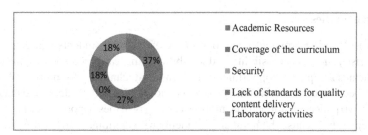

Fig. 9. Challenges Facing Content

Most of The challenges facing the content of m-learning are related to the lack of Supporting Academic Resources, no research papers mentioned unauthorized access to the personal information of the students in the m-learning system (Security). It is likely that security from mobile devices poses less of a threat to institutional infrastructure.

4.10   Origin

The descriptions below show the region where research paper done (Fig. 10).

Fig. 10. Origin

Most research was from the context of developing countries. Developed countries had only five research papers. The phenomenon could be a result of the m-learning maturity in many developed countries or even the infrastructural maturity in developed countries being prepared for disruptive phenomenon.

5   Research Agenda

The above findings lead to further research required in terms of learning during the time of crisis.

5.1 Context

There were gaps in understanding m-learning at primary and secondary levels of education. The following are some research questions that need to be answered, therefore:

- What has been the impact of m-learning at primary and secondary levels of education post-COVID?
- What are the challenges facing m-learning implementation at primary and secondary levels of education post-COVID?
- What are the critical success factors (CSFs) for m-Learning in higher education?

5.2 Opportunities

Although m-learning provided many opportunities for both students and educators in times of crisis, such as accessibility and flexibility of m-learning resources, the current study indicates a gap in the opportunities to own new technology for mobile education, and this is because of the accessibility to the technology for both students and educators. Also, only two papers mentioned that mobile learning provides opportunities for students to work remotely because the number of students who combine study and work is low. M-learning also provided opportunities for educators to practice technology and acquire skills, but the current study indicates a lack of opportunity to broadcast educational lessons on TV and radio platforms. The following are some research question that needs to be answered, therefore:

- What are the student and educator's experiences and attitudes toward m-learning in times of crisis?

5.3 Student Challenges

The result of the current study suggests that accessibility is still the major challenge facing the success implement m-learning during the time of crisis most students have limited internet access, slower internet speeds at home, heavy internet bills, and students do have not good internet data at home, especially who live in which are in rural areas. Additionally, lack of training in m-learning is another challenge facing student. However in the current study there is a gap in the lack of family supports for students, especially students who belong to under privileged families and where the responsibility lies on family members to assist in routine tasks. For example, if parents are not educated enough, how will m-learning be possible for younger learners? Most research papers indicated that m-learning is one of the solutions to ensure the continuity of education during times of crisis, despite the presence of many challenges that can face its implementation. An most important question for further research is therefore:

- What are the government policies that must be implemented to overcome the challenges of accessibility and lack of training in m-learning ?

5.4 Educator Readiness

For the educator to become an electronic educator, an intellectual reformulation is needed where the educator is convinced that traditional teaching methods must change to match the amount of knowledge that exists. The education also need to learn modern methods of teaching and effective strategies. The results of the current study indicate there is a gap in educator readiness is lacking, and educators lack training in teaching. Including training in interactive online teaching methods, the formation of an individual learning trajectory, and online multidisciplinary course development. The training for educators can improve student learning in educational programming for the instructors to facilitate the goals aligned with the learning goals of higher education institutions. The following are some research questions that need to be answered, therefore:

- What is the readiness of educators for m-learning post-COVID?
- How does m-learning influence the role of the educator post-COVID??

5.5 Learning Content

There is a gap in security and privacy around m-learning, there was no research about secure access to the personal information of students in m-learning. The following are questions that can be investigated:

- How can data privacy and data security be maintained in m-learning spaces?
- How can m-learning data be shared without compromising security and privacy?

5.6 Origin

Developed countries had only five research papers likely because of the infrastructural maturity that was prepared for the disruptive phenomenon. In contrast, a mobile device has spread rapidly in both developed and developing countries, so the number of mobile phones in some developing countries exceeds the number of individuals. The following questions can therefore be investigated:

- How can m-learning act as a facilitator beyond the digital divide in developing countries?

6 Conclusions and Implications of the Study

Higher education was affected by the COVID-19 pandemic with thousands of school closures in a very limited period to enforce social distancing measures. However, the global pandemic also opened opportunities for other countries to reconsider their educational mode of delivery and include emerging technologies.

M-learning which allows distributed flexible access to educational content is required at all educational levels, yet there was limited research at the primary and secondary levels. Even though the mobile device was found as the most favorable tool for m-learning, especially for its ubiquity and interactivity, it also presents distractions as the mobile is also used for non-educational purposes. Most mobile devices also have limited capacity and must be forced to either stream content or access previously streamed content. This also has implications in terms of data costs, infrastructure, and physical devices for both the educator and the student.

M-learning also brought parents and guardians closer to their children's education as they were required to assist. Parents, therefore, needed to suddenly learn critical teaching skills, many of whom struggled to adjust, while others found it helpful. The impact of this parent involvement with their children's education through m-learning would also need to be established.

The unreadiness of educators to adapt to m-learning coupled with the inability to read the student's moods was a stressor. There was also stress among students with some going into depression. Educators play a strong role in recommending alternatives for students and were therefore not able to adequately assist in this regard.

References

1. Adnan, M., Anwar, K.: Ed606496, vol. 2, pp. 2–8 (2020)
2. Aguilera-Hermida, A.P.: International Journal of Educational Research Open College students' use and acceptance of emergency online learning due to COVID-19. Int. J. Educ. Res. Open. **1**, 100011 (2020). https://doi.org/10.1016/j.ijedro.2020.100011
3. Awan, M.T.: Covid-19 Pandemic, Outbreak Educational Sector and Students Online Learning in (2020)
4. Biswas, B., Roy, S.K., Roy, F.: Students Perception of Mobile Learning during COVID-19 in Bangladesh: University Student Perspective. Aquademia, vol. 4, ep20023 (2020). https://doi.org/10.29333/aquademia/8443
5. Cotero, K.: Appropriation of skills in students who migrated from traditional education model to an online education model, derivated from COVID-19, pp. 13–16 (2021)
6. Currie, G., et al.: COVID-19 impact on undergraduate teaching: medical radiation science teaching team experience. J. Med. Imaging Radiat. Sci. **51**, 1 (2020). https://doi.org/10.1016/j.jmir.2020.09.002
7. Dhawan, S.: Online learning: a panacea in the time of COVID-19 crisis. J. Educ. Technol. Syst. **49**, 5–22 (2020). https://doi.org/10.1177/0047239520934018
8. Doghonadze, N., Aliyev, A., Halawachy, H., Knodel, L., Adedoyin, A.S.: The Degree of Readiness to Total Distance Learning in the Face of COVID-19 - Teachers' View (Case of Azerbaijan, Georgia, Iraq, Nigeria, UK, and Ukraine) (2020). https://doi.org/10.31578/jebs.v5i2.197
9. Mahalakshmi, K., Radha, R.: COVID-19: A Massive Exposure Towards Web-Based Learning (2020). https://doi.org/10.37896/jxu14.4/266
10. Agung, A.S.N., Surtikanti, M.W.: Students' Perception of Online Learning during COVID-19 Pandemic: a case study on the English students of STKIP Pamane Talino. SOSHUM J. Sos. dan Hum. **10**, 225–235 (2020). https://doi.org/10.31940/soshum.v10i2.1316
11. Humayun, M.: Blockchain-based secure framework for e-learning during COVID-19. Indian J. Sci. Technol. **13**, 1328–1341 (2020). https://doi.org/10.17485/ijst/v13i12.152
12. Sengottaiyan, K., Rathinaswamy, J.: Covid 19 and Its Impact by Lockdown Editor Dr. Zaheda Begum Shaik Dept. of Political Science Co–Editor Ms . Beena Kumari Indira Gandhi University (2020)
13. Kumar Basak, S., Wotto, M., Bélanger, P.: E-learning, M-learning, and D-learning: conceptual definition and comparative analysis. E-Learn. Digit. Media. **15**, 191–216 (2018). https://doi.org/10.1177/2042753018785180
14. Suryaman, M., Cahyono, Y., Muliansyah, D., Bustani, O., Suryani, P., Fahlevi, M.: COVID-19 Pandemic and Home Online Learning System: Does It Affect the Quality of Pharmacy School Learning ? vol. 11, pp. 524–530 (2020)
15. Toquero, C.M.: Challenges and Opportunities for Higher Education amid the COVID- 19 Pandemic: The Philippine Context, vol. 5 (2020)

16. Xie, X., Siau, K.: Association for Information Systems AIS Electronic Library (AISeL) Online Education During and After COVID-19 Pandemic Online Education During and After COVID-19 Pandemic (2020)
17. Oyedotun, T.D.: Research in Globalization Sudden change of pedagogy in education driven by COVID-19: perspectives and evaluation from a developing country. Res. Glob. **2**, 100029 (2020). https://doi.org/10.1016/j.resglo.2020.100029
18. Sukendro, S., et al.: Heliyon using an extended Technology Acceptance Model to understand students ' use of e-learning during Covid-19: Indonesian sport science education context. Heliyon. **6**, e05410 (2020). https://doi.org/10.1016/j.heliyon.2020.e05410
19. Okoli, C., Schabram, K.: A guide to conducting a systematic literature review of information systems research. Work. Pap. Inf. Syst. **10**, 1–51 (2010). https://doi.org/10.2139/ssrn.1954824
20. Lei, P., Tse, R.: Overcoming the Sudden Conversion to Online Education During the COVID-19 Pandemic: A Case Study in Computing Education, pp. 17–22 (2021)
21. Bartocci, L., et al.: Sustainability as a dynamic organizational capability: a systematic review and a future agenda toward a sustainable transition. J. Clean. Prod. **142**, 308–322 (2017). https://doi.org/10.1016/j.jclepro.2016.07.103

Opportunities for Driving Efficiencies and Effectiveness

Archiving 4.0: Dataset Generation and Facial Recognition of DRC Political Figures Using Machine Learning

Ferdinand Kahenga Ngongo[1,2]([✉]) [iD], Antoine Bagula[2] [iD], and Olasupo Ajayi[2] [iD]

[1] Ecole Supérieure d'Informatique SALAMA, Lubumbashi, Democratic Republic of Congo
ferdinandkahenga@esisalama.org
[2] University of Western Cape, Cape Town, South Africa

Abstract. It is widely recognized that digital archiving represents many advantages compared to manually preserved documents. These include i) reduced risk of losing data, ii) eco-friendliness, iii) data security, iv) faster access to data, v) simple data management, vi) overall costs saving, and vii) potential for data recovery. However, in contrast to developed nations, which have experienced a steady maturity in the field, digital archiving is still in its infancy in developing countries, especially in Africa, where years of slavery, colonization, both economic and political issues, and wars have deprived nations of their history. Building around techniques of the fourth industrial revolution (4IR), this paper addresses this gap by proposing a digital archiving model called "Archiving 4.0". The model curates a dataset of images of political figures in the Democratic Republic of Congo (DRC) from different sources and classifies these images using machine learning techniques to achieve facial recognition that will help recognize historical people in photographs and videos. To the best of our knowledge, the proposed dataset constitutes the first attempt at digital archiving in the political space of the DRC and provides an example that can be emulated to spin out related works on the African continent where digital archiving is needed for political research studies and also for the preservation of the history of nations. Through performance evaluation, accuracy, precision, recall, and loss; the paper reveals that Transfer learning outperforms traditional machine learning on different metrics of interest when using the generated dataset: 93% of validation accuracy.

Keywords: Archiving · Deep Learning · Democratic Republic of Congo · Transfer learning · Face recognition

1 Introduction

It is widely recognized that our past shapes our future by defining and redefining our perception of the world. This is a result of our memories being storages of blocks of experiences of the past upon which we construct visions and plan the future. Therefore, a better understanding of the world we live in can be attained from the knowledge of our

M. Masinde and A. Bagula (Eds.): AFRICATEK 2022, LNICST 503, pp. 53–64, 2023.
https://doi.org/10.1007/978-3-031-35883-8_4

past which shapes our present and ineluctably influences our ways of doing things, acting in society, and how identifying ourselves. Archiving is a key process for achieving social and economic development and administrative efficiency, as it encompasses the entire gamut of significant governmental activity from past to present experiences, including its successes and failures. While developed nations have experienced a steady maturity in the field, digital archiving is still in its infancy in developing countries, especially in Africa where years of slavery, colonization, economic and political instabilities, and wars have robbed nations of their history. As largely reported, there are several national archives and records of African countries being held in foreign countries abroad. This is evidenced by the recent repatriation of large amounts of African archival records to western metropolitan cities.

Like in many other African countries, the history of archives in the Democratic Republic of Congo (DRC), has gone through very difficult times. Delphin Bateko Moyikoli in [1] reported that there was the first destruction and looting of the archives of the Belgian colony (Belgian Congo) by Leopold II in the year 1908. This was followed by the looting and destruction of archives around the 1960s period of the country's independence. Added to these, is the looting of the presidential archives by the Alliance of Democratic Forces for the Liberation of Congo and its allies in 1997, archives that had already been neglected during the Second Republic. These repeated archive lootings, theft, and destruction have made it difficult to maintain a proper archiving system of the DRC, which could help in keeping track of the country's history. Today's key archiving issue in the DRC consists of not only building adequate storage and digital repository but also in the reconstruction and documentation of these archives.

This paper contributes to the field of digital archiving by proposing a model called "Archiving 4.0" that relies on Fourth Industrial Revolution (4IR) techniques to i) generate a dataset of political figures of the DRC from different sources and ii) detect and recognize the faces of these personalities by relying on machine learning techniques. The second contribution of this article is to determine, based on experiments carried out, the appropriate machine learning models for the detection and recognition of figures given the small quantity of data and the degraded quality of certain pictures, with some dating as far back as the early 1960s. Several approaches have been used and their results are compared to select the best models and paradigms to be used when dealing with the generated and/or similar archiving datasets. Performance evaluation reveals that a pre-trained model using Transfer learning outperforms traditional machine learning models on different evaluation parameters.

The remainder of this paper is organized as follows: a background and literature review on the topic being studied is presented in Sect. 2, while Sect. 3 reports on the research methodology used and the data generation. A performance evaluation with a comparison of models used is presented in Sect. 4. Section 5 concludes the paper and provides suggestions for future work.

2 Background and Literature

2.1 Face Detection and Face Recognition

There are multiple applications of facial recognition in the fields of security, access control, transport, and healthcare. A significant number of scientific papers have been devoted to face detection and face recognition systems that make it possible to identify or verify the identity of an individual in just a few seconds based on his facial characteristics: e.g. distance between the eyes, bridges of the nose, corners of the lips, ears, chin, etc.

Many of the techniques used in facial recognition are based on models of convolutional neural networks trained on several images containing figures. Several frameworks and results of these works are accessible. Haar [2], DeepFace [3] from Facebook, FaceNet [4] from Google, Dlib [5], Multi-task Cascaded Convolutional Networks (MTCNN) [6], Retina-Face [7] are some of the most popular ones. Face recognition can be divided into 3 steps: (1) face detection, (2) feature extraction, and (3) classification. Dlib CNN, MTCNN, and Retina-Face are networks used for face detection and facial landmarks. Feature extraction in the case of face recognition can be done in different ways. FaceNet, for example, is a deep neural network that takes an image of the person's face as input and outputs a vector of 128 numbers, called embedding, which represents the most important features of a face [4].

As part of the "Archiving 4.0" framework, machine learning was used for facial detection on Robben Island Mayibuye Archives in [8]. Dlib HOG, Dlib CNN, OpenCV's Haar cascade, OpenCV's Caffe, and TensorFlow were compared based on the Average Precision, Precision, and Recall metrics with CNN performing the best [8]. Similarly, in [9] Dlib and MTCNN as face detectors were also used to index the faces on the historical photographs of the Stockholm city museum with MTCNN showing better performance.

2.2 Transfer Learning

Motivation. "Transfer learning is the improvement of learning in a new task through the transfer of knowledge from a related task that has already been learned" [10]. The fundamental motivation for Transfer learning was discussed in NIPS-95 workshop on "Learning to Learn" [11] which focussed on the need for lifelong machine learning methods that retain and reuse previously learned knowledge. This has been recently reinforced by Andrew Ng in the tutorial called "Nuts and bolts of building AI applications using Deep Learning" where he stated that Transfer learning will be the next driver of machine learning commercial success [12].

Transfer Learning in Deep Learning. In CNN, the first few layers are used to extract high-level general features, while class-specific features are captured by the last couple of layers. The learned features from the first layers appear not to be specific to a particular dataset or task, but general in that they are applicable to many datasets and tasks [13].

The CNN Transfer learning strategy consists of freezing the first layer's weights of the pre-trained model and only training the newly added dense layers with randomly initialized weights. Figure 1 shows how the parameters learned in Task 1 of the pre-trained model are transferred to Task 2.

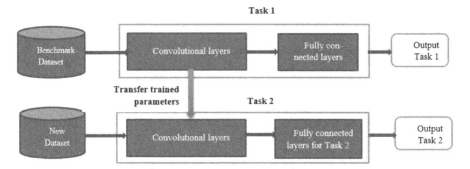

Fig. 1. Transfer of trained parameters in the context of deep learning

2.3 Evaluation Metrics

In machine learning, the accuracy (1), precision (2), and recall (3) metrics respectively indicate what proportions of all positive predictions are actually positive and how many positives the model identifies. In the context of object detection, the intersection over union (IoU), defined in (4) helps to know how accurate the predicted bounding boxes of objects in the image are. It gives the overlap between the ground truth bounding box and the predicted bounding box. For instance, Fig. 2 shows the ground truth and the predicted bounding box of president Mobutu's image.

$$Accuracy = \frac{Number\ of\ correct\ predictions}{Number\ of\ total\ predictions} \tag{1}$$

$$Precision = \frac{True\ Positive}{True\ Positive + False\ Positive} \tag{2}$$

$$Recall = \frac{TruePositive}{TruePositive + FalseNegative} \tag{3}$$

$$IoU = \frac{area\ of\ intersection}{area\ of\ union} \tag{4}$$

Fig. 2. The ground truth bounding box is in yellow and the predicted bounding box is in blue. The area of intersection is the intersection between the yellow and the blue bounding boxes. The detected face at 78% in the image is former president Joseph Mobutu (Color figure online)

3 Methodology and Data Acquisition

3.1 Methodology

The bulk of our methodology is summarized in Fig. 3 and consists of two phases. Phase 1 consists of the dataset generation while Phase 2 brings together the different stages of training machine learning models for the detection, classification, and recognition of personalities in images.

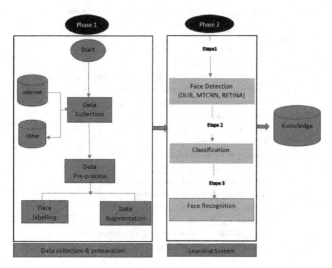

Fig. 3. Main phases of the methodology

An image sent to phase 2 is subjected to face detection step 1, which extracts all the faces present in the image using models such as DLIB, MTCNN, or RETINA-FACE. The faces are then classified using the classification model previously trained with the set of data collected in phase 1. Once classified, the annotation of each face is placed on the initial image.

3.2 Data Collection and Preparation

Our dataset is a collection of old and recent images of well-known political figures from the DRC [17]. This dataset is composed of 3431 images with 4113 annotations of the faces of 19 politicians, including 5 presidents of the republic, 1 vice-president, 7 prime ministers, 1 governor, 2 presidents of the national assembly, a president of the senate, and the others. 30% of the images are old black and white photographs of politicians who fought for the independence of the DRC in the 1960s.

The acquisition of these images was done through the manual and automatic collection (web-scrapping). At least 70% of the data was acquired from the Internet, Google, Facebook, YouTube, and Twitter. The other images were obtained from old newspaper publications and old videos with black and white images. Figure 4 shows the breakdown of the Dataset in terms of images per person.

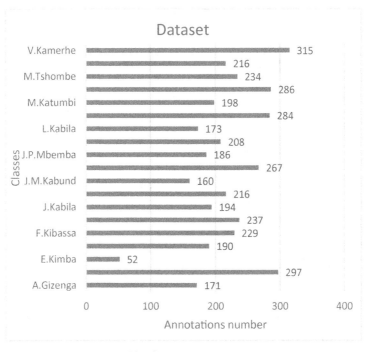

Fig. 4. Dataset balance

The approach taken for data preparation consisted of a minimum of 50 images for people with fewer images, around 150 images for the second category of politicians, and 300 images for those who had more images available through the different media that were considered. The quality of the images was balanced between those of high resolutions and others with very low resolutions. All images were then set to a size of 300 × 300 pixels. Finally, manual labeling was done using Roboflow [14].

The richness of the curated dataset lies not only in the diversity of the quality of the images but also in the fact that we have images of certain people from their youth to old age. Similarly, the images were captured using scanners and cellphone cameras from newspapers (Fig. 5).

Fig. 5. Labelling process

4 Performance Evaluation

4.1 Face Detection

Three different models (MTCNN, RETINA-FACE and DLIB) were used for the face detection. As shown in Figure 6, each of these models gave us the ability to:

- align and detect faces by flipping through 4 points representing facial-area and landmarks
- extract features
- extract facial FaceNet embeddings which are vectors of the characteristics of a face

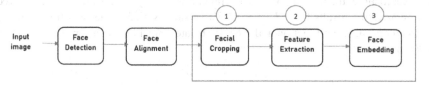

Fig. 6. Steps of face detection

Table 1 summarizes the detection accuracies of each of the three models considered.

Table 1. Accuracy of face detection by model

	Model	Detection accuracy (%)
1	MTCNN	60.5
2	DLIB	75.4
3	RETINA-FACE	92.1

RETINA-FACE gave the highest accuracy and hence was considered for the rest of this work. As mentioned earlier, the dataset is composed of images with various parameters in terms of quality, size, the physical appearance of people, and so on. All models showed a low success rate against very old images.

4.2 Classification

After the face detection step, we placed all the detected faces in sub-folders labeled with the class names. For instance, the Lumumba sub-folder contained all the faces extracted for Lumumba. Three classification approaches were tested to find the best performance on our data. These include:

- a CNN called "Model 1" which takes as input cropped faces as shown in point (1) of Fig. 6.
- A classifier referred to as "Model 2" which takes as input embedding vectors, and
- a deep neural network MobileNetV2 model called "Model 3" which was pre-trained on imageNet [15] and thereafter trained by Transfer Learning on cropped faces.

Model 1. This model is a convolutional network of 3 convolutional layers followed each time by a max pooling and then by a Fully connected layer. The model takes as input a small image of the face resulting from the face detection step. The validation accuracy is around 35%.

Model 2. We compared the results of 4 different classifiers, namely, BoostedTreesClassifier, RandomForestClassifier, DecisionTreesClassifier, and LogisticClassifier. The results obtained after validation allowed us to set our sight on LogisticClassifier as shown in Fig. 7.

Model 3. Obtained after freezing 100 layers of MobileNetV2 model [16] pre-trained on imageNet to allow the training of only the remaining 54 layers. This technique allowed us to improve the results from 71% to 93.7%. MobileNetV2 model was trained using the Adam optimization function and the sparse categorical cross-entropy loss function for 20 epochs.

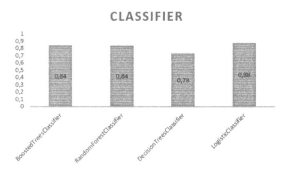

Fig. 7. Classifier validation accuracy comparison

Table 2 compares the results of the three models obtained for three different performance metrics. They reveal that Model 3 outperforms the other two models across all three metrics.

Table 2. Evaluation metrics comparison on the test set

	Model	Accuracy (%)	Precision (%)	Recall (%)
1	Model 1	35.7	32.2	31.4
2	Model 2	88.4	86.3	86.4
3	Model 3	93.7	93.1	92.9

4.2.1 Facial Recognition

Facial recognition is the phase that consists of placing each detected and classified face in the context of its initial image and telling which class the person(s) in the image belongs to. In this work, facial recognition was performed by combining the best performances of the previous steps 1 and 2.

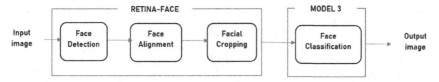

Fig. 8. Facial recognition steps

As shown in Fig. 8, a new input image containing a personality under study undergoes the following operations: face detection, face alignment, and facial cropping with RETINA-FACE; then the extracted face from the image is then used as input to the CNN model Model3 which classifies the face. If the image contains several faces, the classification step will be repeated for each of them. The Output image is the Input image on which bounding boxes are added to identify each known personality.

4.3 Discussion of Results

In this paper, we extracted from our original dataset a portion that allowed us to constitute 10 classes of training and test sets composed of respectively 507 and 127 images. According to the results obtained, it appears that the image type (black and white or color) does not influence face detection. On the other hand, the quality of the pixels and the position of the face on the image have an impact on the detection. Images taken from old newspapers have a low detection rate, as evidenced by the detection accuracy of 79.8% for Kasa-vubu and 90% for Lumumba, the lowest and for the oldest pictures in our illustration study as shown in Fig. 9.

It is also worth noting from this study that photographs with faces in a non-frontal position also presented some difficulties during the face detection step. The classification using cropped faces obtained from the face detection gave a poor result on the small amount of data, however when for the same number of images, the classification was done using the embedding vectors, the results were much better. Ultimately, using Transfer

Fig. 9. Non-detected faces of Kasa-Vubu and Lumumba.

learning with adequate frozen layers yielded the best result of all. Figure 10 shows the benefit of freezing and fine-tuning certain layers of Model 3 network which significantly boosted the accuracy of the model from 70% to 93.7% of accuracy.

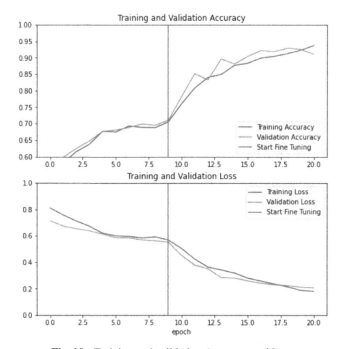

Fig. 10. Training and validation Accuracy and Loss.

All of these executions were performed on Google Colab Pro using the Tesla 100-PCIE GPU Accelerator.

5 Conclusion

In this paper, a curated dataset of several images of different generations of political figures who have played key roles in the history of DRC from her independence to the present day was presented. The particularity of the dataset is that it is made of images from several sources and different qualities. Once curated, the images were passed through different machine-learning models for facial classification and recognition. The obtained results revealed that the models performed better with more recent pictures for image classification, while models that leveraged Transfer learning gave better results in terms of face detection compared to those based on basic machine learning only. There is scope for future extensions of the presented work in the field of deep learning optimization by using automatic layer selection as well as the deployment of the transfer learning model into real-life federated learning infrastructures for museums. Such federated learning infrastructures will benefit from extensions the networking techniques borrowed from [18–20] for the interconnection of participating museums.

References

1. ADIAC: Journée internationale des archives: la RDC en marge de l'événement. Agence d'information d'Afrique Centrale, 14 June 2018. https://www.adiac-congo.com/content/jou rnee-internationale-des-archives-la-rdc-en-marge-de-levenement-84714. Accessed 04 Apr 2022
2. Viola, P., Jones, M.: Rapid object detection using a boosted cascade of simple features. In: Conference on Computer Vision and Pattern Recognition, p. 1 (2001)
3. Taigman, Y., Yang, M., Ranzato, M., Wolf, L.: DeepFace: closing the gap to human-level performance in face verification. In: 2014 IEEE Conference on Computer Vision and Pattern Recognition, pp. 1701–1708 (2014)
4. Schroff, F., Kalenichenko, D., Philbin, J.: FaceNet: a unified embedding for face recognition and clustering. In: 2015 IEEE Conference on Computer Vision and Pattern Recognition (CVPR), pp. 815–823 (2015)
5. Dlib c++ Library. http://dlib.net/. Accessed 09 May 2022
6. Zhang, K., Zhang, Z., Li, Z., Qiao, Y.: Joint face detection and alignment using multitask cascaded convolutional networks. IEEE Signal Process. Lett. 23(10), 1499–1503 (2016)
7. Deng, J., Guo, J., Zhou, Y., Yu, J., Kotsia, I., Zafeiriou, S.: RetinaFace: single-shot multi-level face localisation in the wild. arXiv:1905.00641 (2019)
8. Kern, D., Zweng, M., Sello, S., Bagula, A., Klauck, U.: Archiving 4.0: application of image processing and machine learning for the Robben Island Mayibuye Archives. In: 2020 International SAUPEC/RobMech/PRASA Conference, pp. 1–6 (2020)
9. Poudel, A.: Face recognition on historical photographs (2021). https://uu.diva-portal.org/ smash/get/diva2:1622968/FULLTEXT01.pdf. Accessed 09 May 2022
10. Soria, E., Martín, J., Martinez-Sober, M., Magdalena-Benedito, J.R., et al.: Handbook of Research on Machine Learning Applications and Trends: Algorithms, methods, and techniques: Algorithms, methods, and techniques. IGI Global, Hershey (2009)
11. Learning to Learn: Knowledge Consolidation. http://socrates.acadiau.ca/courses/comp/dsi lver/NIPS95_LTL/. Accessed 01 June 2022
12. Ng, A.: Nuts and bolts of building AI applications using Deep Learning. NIPS Keynote Talk. (2016)

13. Yosinskim, J., Clune, J., Bengio, Y., Lipson, H.: How transferable are features in deep neural networks? In: Advances in Neural Information Processing Systems 27 (NIPS 2014) (2014)

14. "Roboflow. https://docs.roboflow.com/annotate. Accessed 10 June 2022

15. Deng, J., Dong, W., Socher, R., Li, L.-J., Li, K., Fei-Fei, L.: ImageNet: a large-scale hierarchical image database. In: 2009 IEEE Conference on Computer Vision and Pattern Recognition, pp. 248–255 (2009)

16. Chiu, Y.C., Tsai, C.Y., Ruan, M.-D., Shen, G.Y., Lee, T.T.: Mobilenet SSDv2: an improved object detection model for embedded systems. In: 2020 International Conference on System Science and Engineering (ICSSE), pp. 1–5 (2020)

17. Kahenga Ngongo, F., Bagula, A.: J. YOTE, "DRC_POLITICIANS_DATASET," *Mendeley Data,* vol. V1 (2022). https://doi.org/10.17632/dz47c9pnd5.1

18. Bagula, A.B.: Hybrid traffic engineering: the least path interference algorithm. In: Proceedings SAICT 2004, ACM International Conference Proceedings Series, pp. 89–96, October 2004

19. Bagula, A.B.: Hybrid routing in next generation IP networks. Elsevier Comput. Commun. **29**(7), 879–892 (2006)

20. Bagula, A.B.: On achieving bandwidth-aware LSP/LambdaSP multiplexing/separation in multi-layer networks. IEEE J. Sel. Areas Commun. (JSAC) **25**(5), 987–1000 (2007). Special issue on Traffic Engineering for Multi-Layer Net-works

On the Machine Learning Models to Predict Town-Scale Energy Consumption in Burkina Faso

Baowendsomme Armel Yameogo[1], Tounwendyam Frédéric Ouedraogo[1(✉)], and Constantin Zongo[1,2]

[1] Université Norbert ZONGO, BP 376, Koudougou, Burkina Faso
baowendsommearmel@gmail.com, frederic.ouedraogo@unz.bf
[2] Agence Burkinabè pour l'Electrification Rurale, BP 345, Ouaga 01, Burkina Faso
constantin.zongo@aber.bf

Abstract. The lack of forecast of the electricity consumption in Burkina Faso is a great concern. This leads to selective power cut due to insufficient production. This situation leads to selective power cut, which has a negative impact on economic activities. In this paper, we present a model to forecast household energy consumption in the Middle West region of Burkina Faso. We propose three predictive models of energy consumption that we evaluate to select the best one in our context. The proposed models are the Decision Tree Regressor, the Random Forest Regressor, and the Neural Network. We assessed them through three measures, namely the Root Mean Squared Error, the Mean Absolute Error and the R2-Score. We found that the neural networks has more satisfactory performance. The type of meter, the power of the meter, and the month of the year are factors that influence household energy consumption. Our contribution is an important step in the planning of energy production to meet the growing consumption of households.

Keywords: Predictive model · Machine learning · Energy consumption

1 Introduction

The need for electrical energy is growing all over the world. In southern countries such as Burkina Faso, the population frequently suffers power cuts, thus depriving households and large companies of sufficient energy for the development of their activities. Yet, availability of electricity is a condition for the country's economic development. With population growth, the improvement of the standard of living of the population as well as the development of factories, this situation of energy deficit is a great challenge for Burkina Faso which is a developing country [2,5,7].

The planning of energy needs then becomes an important element because it will allow decision-makers to put in place the means of electricity production

© ICST Institute for Computer Sciences, Social Informatics and Telecommunications Engineering 2023
Published by Springer Nature Switzerland AG 2023. All Rights Reserved
M. Masinde and A. Bagula (Eds.): AFRICATEK 2022, LNICST 503, pp. 65–73, 2023.
https://doi.org/10.1007/978-3-031-35883-8_5

to meet those needs. This planning of energy needs cannot be done without a good estimate of the evolution of consumption.

Machine learning offers a number of methods that make it possible to perform predictions [3,9,10]. The purpose of this work is to explore these different means in order to build an accurate model for predicting the energy consumption of a town. We applied our study on the energy consumption data collected from Middle West region of Burkina Faso.

We present in this paper the preliminary results of our research project. The problem addressed in our project is to design standard models that will characterize consumers. The prediction of energy consumption is a first step in this work. This is a regression of household energy consumption, we have chosen to compare the results of three regression models.

The rest of paper is structured as follows. Section 2 presents the related work. In the Sect. 3, we present the data set and exploratory analysis. Section 4 shows the modeling framework. We present and discuss results in Sect. 5. Section 6 gives the conclusion and perspectives.

2   Related Work

A large number of studies have focused on energy prediction using different machine learning methods [8,11–13]. These studies have been done in many areas. [17] used the random forest model and the gradient boosting model to predict the GDP growth. He evaluated the accuracy of the forecast by mean absolute percentage error and root squared mean error and found the gradient boosting model to be better. His approach is close to the one used in [11] which applies the same method to predict home energy consumption.

There are many papers that obtained better prediction results with the neural networks model applied in various contexts [1,4,6,13–16]. The prediction of energy consumption has been deal by different researchers. In [13], the authors devised a recurrent neural network model (RNN) to make predictions (time horizon of week), of electricity consumption profiles in commercial and residential building for many cities in United States of America (USA). They compared the recurrent neural network model with the conventional multi-layered perceptron neural network model. They found the RNN model more accurate to predict the commercial building's load profiles. But in the other hand the conventional multi-layered perceptron neural network is better than RNN to predict aggregate electricity consumption in residential buildings.

We can conclude that in the literature there is no better model as such. The context and data play an important key in the model building [3,10]. Our contribution goes in the same way and propose for the first time a model to predict household energy consumption at town-scale in Burkina Faso. We obtained similar results to previous work.

3   Data and Exploratory Analysis

In this section we present the data collected from households in the Middle West region of Burkina Faso[1]. This region is located 100 km from Ouagadougou, the capital. We present the dataset and give some results of the Exploratory Data Analysis, important for machine learning models training.

3.1   Dataset

In this paper, or study is based on electricity consumption data, measured from households located in different localities(villages and sectors) in the Middle West region of Burkina Faso. The data can be accessed from github[2]. We recorded each household consumption and other information every month for a year. In total, we have 29824 records with 10 columns each. Figure 1 shows the two first records, after cleaning the data.

	Customer full name	Period	Period in Months Years	Meter type	Meter power	Operator name	Serial number	Energy consumption	Unit	Locality
0	CASSOU INSPECTION CEB 2	2021-03-01 to 2021-03-31	Mars 2021	MONOPHASE	3	INCONNU	25112455925	20	KWH	CASSOU
1	CASSOU LYCEE DEPARTEMENTAL	2021-03-01 to 2021-03-31	Mars 2021	MONOPHASE	10	INCONNU	25112455974	140	KWH	CASSOU

Fig. 1. Overview of the data after cleaning step

Table 1 summarizes key statistics of the data.

Table 1. Electricity consumption statistics for households in the center West region over one year.

Number of localities	Consumption(kWh)	Meter	Meter power(Ah)
12	$1 - 7523$	1-phase and 3-phase	$3 - 30$

3.2   Exploratory Analysis

In order to choose the appropriate predictive models for the dataset at our disposal, we proceed to its basic analysis. Visualization of our data through box plots or boxplot revealed the presence of outliers. It also allowed us to better understand the structure of our data. We study in particular the centering, the dispersion and the normality of our data.

---

[1] The country is administratively divided into 13 regions and the Middle West is the third most important.

[2] https://github.com/fredoued/Armel_ml_code.

We present here in particular the energy consumption according to the month. Figure 2 presents the distribution of the energy consumption of the households according to the month of the year. The months are encoded in numbers from 1 to 12 so that January corresponds to 1, February to 2 and so on.

The median values of energy consumption depending on the month are not equal. There is a connection between the amount of energy consumed and the month of the year. Figure 2 also indicates that household consumption in August is lowest. This could be explained by the fact that the month of August in Burkina Faso generally experience heavy rainfall and that energy consuming household equipment and devices such as fans, freezers and air conditioner are rarely used in this period. All this therefore contributes to the decrease in energy consumption observed.

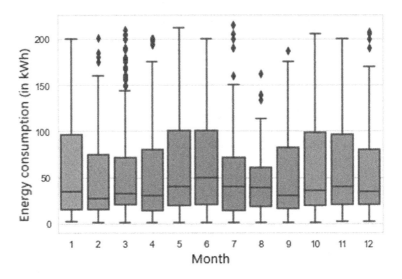

Fig. 2. Energy consumption according to the month

We used the Bartlett test to study the dispersion of the data. It makes it allows to test whether the variances of the samples considered are significantly different or not by making the following hypothesis.:

- H0: The variances of the samples are equal if the p-value > 5%.
- H1: The variances of the samples are not all equal if the p-value < 5%.

We sample the household consumption according to 3 perspectives: the month, the meter type and the meter power. We found the p-value equals to $2.27e - 10$ for the meter power sampling. The hypothesis H0 is therefore rejected so we deduce that the variances are not all equal. Similarly, the p-value of the monthly sampling is greater than 5%. This means that the variances of the monthly consumption are not the same. Contrary to the previous ones, the H0 hypothesis is verified for the meter type sampling. We found the p-value equal to 0.16 which is greater than 5.

In summary, the househ0old energy consumption is related to different factors such as meter power, type of meter and month of the year. Household energy consumption increases when meter power increases. Similarly, it goes up when switching from the 1-phase type meter to the 3-phase type meter.

4 Modeling Framework

There is a panoply of algorithms for prediction in machine learning. We can therefore rightly ask ourselves the question: How to choose the right algorithm for its predictive model ? Several criteria are taken into account for the choice of predictive model. We will mention a few of them.

One of the criteria is the amount of data available. Indeed, in machine learning, there are models adapted to large data sets such as those based on logistic regression algorithms or neural networks [6, 10]. Conversely, there are also models that are not efficient on large dataset such as Support Vector Machines (SVM) or K-Nearest Neighbors [10]. Another criterion relates to the structure of the data. Data like images, sounds, and text are considered unstructured data. Conversely, tabular data such as those contained in excel files are considered structured data. And, in the presence of unstructured data, it is advisable to useneural networks [9]. Certain types of models, in particular decision trees and their derivatives, are not very effective when a lot of quantitative variables are manipulated. On the other hand, when you have a lot of qualitative variables, it is advisable to use decision trees. Figure 3 summarizes the criteria set out to facilitate the choice of the predictive model.

Based on the stated criteria and the background and form analysis of the data collection, we propose three machine learning models that we compare using the performance indicators in order to find the best one. These are decision tree, random forests and neural networks.

In order to assess the accuracy of the three models, we calculate different performance measures after training so that at the end we can compare them.

We use three metrics: Root Mean Squared Error (RMSE), the Mean Absolute Error (MAE) and the coefficient of determination or R2-Score. These metrics are among the most used to evaluate the regression problem's accuracy.

- RMSE provides an indication of the dispersion or variability of the quality of the prediction. RMSE can be related to the variance of the model. For example, an RMSE of 10 is relatively low if the average of the observations is 200. However, a model has a high variance if it leads to an RMSE of 10 while the average of the observations is 15. Indeed, in the first case, the variance of the model corresponds to only 5 of the mean of the observations, whereas in the second case, the variance reaches more than 65 of the mean of the observations.
- MAE is the sum of the absolute differences between our target and the forecast. It therefore measures the average magnitude of errors in a set of predictions, regardless of their directions. Thus an MAE of 5 kWh indicates that on average the model is 5 kWh from the real value.

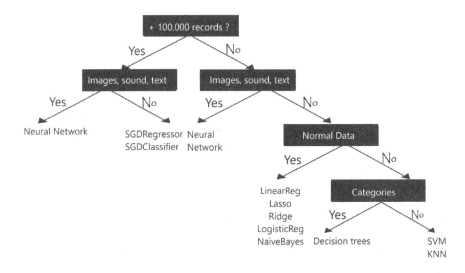

Fig. 3. Decision tree for the choice of predictive model

– The R2-Score metric shows the effectiveness of the adjustment of the regression analysis. The best possible score is 1.0.

After describing the modeling framework, we present in the next section the results of the training and evaluation of models.

5   Results and Discussion

Table 2 summarizes the results obtained by the training and evaluation of the models on the same dataset. It is easily noticed that the neural network has the best score, especially with the MAE metric, we obtained the value 2.64. In other words, the predicted value is −2.64 or +2.64 relative to the value actual power consumption. Moreover, the neural network has a much better R2-score which is 0.93, which means that the linear regression is in line with the collected data. The RMSE metric of 16.31 kWh for the neural network indicates a more or less acceptable variability of the prediction, the average consumption per month being 102 kWh, which needs to be improved.

Table 2. Assessing performance of models through three metrics

	RMS Error	MA Error	R2-Score
Model 1 Decision tree	19.45	5.13	0.89
Model 2 Random forests	20.41	6.74	0.88
Model 3 Neural networks	16.31	2.64	0.93

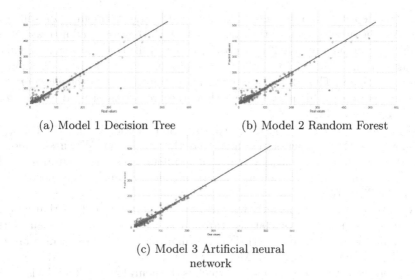

(a) Model 1 Decision Tree   (b) Model 2 Random Forest

(c) Model 3 Artificial neural
network

Fig. 4. Machine learning predictive models of energy consumption.

The results we obtained are different from those of [8] who deal with prediction problem in another context. They compared Neural Network and Random Forest to predict the output current of photovoltaic plant. Figure 4 shows the results of the three machine learning models. The blue dots represent the rightness of the prediction. Each dot has on the horizontal axis the reel consumption of a household and on the vertical axis the model predicted value. The closer the dots are to red line($y = x$), the better the model.

In other words, the red line is the expected values (household energy consumption) and the blue dots are the predictions of the proposed models. We can notice that model 3 based on neural networks manages to have predictions much closer to the real value of the energy consumed compared to models 2 and 3. The latter have predictions much further from the actual power consumption concerning this interval of power consumption, much higher than the average. So, we can say that model 3 manages to have predictions quite close to the real energy consumption despite a much lower number of training samples.

The size of samples according to meter power is not distribute evenly, The meter power 3 and 5 represent more than 90% of the total household. We have very few households with meter power of 15 or 30, less than 5%.

6 Conclusion

Most west africa countries face low power production. Since many years, this problem remains a challenge for the different government in these countries. There are many causes of this lack of energy for household but one is main: a bad forecast of electrical energy needs. The population frequently suffers power cuts, thus depriving households of lighting and large companies of sufficient energy for the development of their activities. With the sustained increase of the population, the energy deficit is a problem that is likely to persist if adequate measures are not taken. Good planning is the first measure that will allow to solve the problem. This planning requires a good prediction of the energy needs. Our contribution in this paper showed how the prediction of need can be done with machine learning tools.

We collected data on household consumption in the center-west region of Burkina Faso. Measurements were made monthly for a year. We chose 3 models of machine learning decision tree regressor, random forest and Neural networks to build the prediction framework. These models are among the most widely used in the literature.

After pre-processing the data, we performed an upfront analysis that allowed us to detect significant correlations through statistical tests. We trained the three models and we compared their performance with 3 metrics which are the Root Mean Squared Error, the Mean Absolute Error and the R2-Score. The results obtained showed that model 3 which is the neural network model is better than the other two models. Nevertheless, we are aware of the smallness of the sample particularly for certain categories of consumers. Future work will consist to increase the data by carrying out more measurement in order to improve the modeling.

References

1. Ahmad, M.W., Mourshed, M., Yuce, B., Rezgui, Y.: Computational intelligence techniques for HVAC systems: a review. Build. Simul. **9**(4), 359–398 (2016). https://doi.org/10.1007/s12273-016-0285-4
2. Brew-Hammond, A.: Energy access in Africa: challenges ahead. Energy Policy **38**(5), 2291–2301 (2010)
3. Burkart, N., Huber, M.F.: A survey on the explainability of supervised machine learning. J. Artif. Intell. Res. **70**, 245–317 (2021)
4. Duong, V.H., Ly, H.B., Trinh, D.H., Nguyen, T.S., Pham, B.T.: Development of artificial neural network for prediction of radon dispersion released from Sinquyen Mine, Vietnam. Environ. Pollut. **282**, 116973 (2021)
5. Hafner, M., Tagliapietra, S., De Strasser, L.: Energy in Africa: Challenges and Opportunities. Springer, Cham (2018). https://doi.org/10.1007/978-3-319-92219-5
6. Johnstone, C., Sulungu, E.D.: Application of neural network in prediction of temperature: a review. Neural Comput. Appl. **33**(18), 11487–11498 (2021). https://doi.org/10.1007/s00521-020-05582-3
7. Karekezi, S.: Poverty and energy in Africa-a brief review. Energy Policy **30**(11–12), 915–919 (2002)
8. Maria, M., Yassine, C.: Machine learning based approaches for modeling the output power of photovoltaic array in real outdoor conditions. Electronics **9**(2), 315 (2020)
9. Muhammad, I., Yan, Z.: Supervised machine learning approaches: a survey. ICTACT J. Soft Comput. **5**(3) (2015)
10. Nasteski, V.: An overview of the supervised machine learning methods. Horizons. b **4**, 51–62 (2017)

11. Nie, P., Roccotelli, M., Fanti, M.P., Ming, Z., Li, Z.: Prediction of home energy consumption based on gradient boosting regression tree. Energy Rep. **7**, 1246–1255 (2021)

12. Olu-Ajayi, R., Alaka, H., Sulaimon, I., Sunmola, F., Ajayi, S.: Building energy consumption prediction for residential buildings using deep learning and other machine learning techniques. J. Build. Eng. **45**, 103406 (2022)

13. Rahman, A., Srikumar, V., Smith, A.D.: Predicting electricity consumption for commercial and residential buildings using deep recurrent neural networks. Appl. Energy **212**, 372–385 (2018)

14. Somu, N., MR, G.R., Ramamritham, K.: A deep learning framework for building energy consumption forecast. Renewable Sustainable Energy Rev. **137**, 110591 (2021)

15. Sözen, A., Arcaklıoğlu, E., Özalp, M., Çağlar, N.: Forecasting based on neural network approach of solar potential in turkey. Renewable Energy **30**(7), 1075–1090 (2005)

16. Tran, T.T.K., Bateni, S.M., Ki, S.J., Vosoughifar, H.: A review of neural networks for air temperature forecasting. Water **13**(9), 1294 (2021)

17. Yoon, J.: Forecasting of real GDP growth using machine learning models: gradient boosting and random forest approach. Comput. Econ. **57**(1), 247–265 (2021)

Application of Latent Dirichlet Allocation Topic Model in Identifying 4IR Research Trends

Muthoni Masinde[(✉)]

Central University of Technology, Bloemfontein, Free State, South Africa
`muthonimasinde@gmail.com`

Abstract. The dynamic nature of the technologies associated with the fourth Industrial Revolution (4IR) presents complex scenarios for researchers, practitioners and policymakers alike. To this end, reaching decisions such as what technology to invest/train in could be made easier through a 4IR technology trend predictive tool. In this paper, we apply Latent Dirichlet Allocation (LDA) topic model to identify and predict trends in 4IR technologies. The LDA models were developed and trained using text composed of abstracts, titles and keywords retrieved from 11,7314-IR related to the 2012 to 2022 publications in the Web of Science database. The effectiveness of the resulting tool was then evaluated using text from email message distributed to subscribers of the IEEE's Tccc-announce mailing list. From the results, our model correctly identifies trends in the following 4IR technologies and applications domains: Internet of Things, Artificial Intelligence/Machine Learning, Big Data/Data Analytics, Augmented Reality, Smart Manufacturing, Supply Chains, Sustainability and Circular Economy. By plotting and visualizing these trends over time (2019 to 2022), the validation text confirms our tool's ability to identify the trajectory developments as identified by other similar tools such as Bibliometric Analysis.

Keywords: Latent Dirichlet Allocation (LDA) · Fourth Industrial Revolution (4IR) · Technology Trends · Bibliometric Analysis and Topic Models

1 Introduction

1.1 An Overview of the Fourth Industrial Revolution

Compared to previous industrial revolutions, the fourth industrial revolution (4IR) has received tremendous attention in its short period of existence [1–3]. The main differentiator of 4IR from the other three industrial revolutions, is the adoption of cyber-physical-systems (CPS) [4]. This is because CPS supports seamless integration of physical and computational worlds, which in turn enables the implementation of features such as adaptability, safety, security and scalability. While the research community has produced large number of publications that documents developments in systems, business models and methodologies, 4IR has received equal attention within the business community seeking to better the world of business through smarter, efficient, adaptive, secure

M. Masinde and A. Bagula (Eds.): AFRICATEK 2022, LNICST 503, pp. 74–94, 2023.
https://doi.org/10.1007/978-3-031-35883-8_6

products/services and environments [3]. Prior to 2020, 4IR was mostly associated with digital integration and intelligent engineering while its top components were CPS, additive manufacturing, virtual and augmented reality, cloud computing, big data analytics and data science.

The core enabling technologies of 4IR include: (1) internet of things (IoT) and related technologies such as Radio-frequency identification (RFID), sensors, actuators, mobile devices (and associated communication technologies such as Wi-Fi, Near-Field Communication (NFC)); (2) cloud computing; (3) CPS; and (4) industrial integration, enterprise architecture and enterprise application integration that every organization requires in order to transit to 4IR. In the latter, new business models are required in order to support the inevitable integration of 4IR. According to Xu et al. [4], these integrations will trigger changes in enterprise architecture, ICT integration and processes.

In terms of 4IR's application domains, smart manufacturing sector has dominated - with applications such as digital twin shop-floor [5], intelligent manufacturing [6, 7] and CPS in manufacturing [8]. There are also many applications in the logistics sector in form of smart supply chain, with examples such as those reported in [9–11]. In the last three years (2020 onwards), the focus of 4IR research includes innovative and business models [12–14], blockchain technologies [15, 16], application of augmented reality [17, 18] in different domains, human factors [17, 19–21] and sustainability [20, 21]. In relation to business models and sustainability, digital platforms [12, 22, 23] and circular economy [24, 25] are two strongly emerging areas.

The use of bibliometric analysis as way to identify trends from literature is widely documented [26, 27], even in the 4IR sub-field [2, 24, 28]. For instance, in Muhuri et al. [2], the authors carried out a bibliometric analysis of publications from the Web of Science (WoS) and Scopus databases using the search phrase "Industry 4.0" based on publications dating until 2017. However, research that uses topic models to assess trends in 4IR are limited [29, 30]. This is the gap this paper aims to fill.

1.2 Topic Modeling

In general, topic modeling aims to demonstrate inter-links in discrete data by discovering structural relations and meaning in voluminous information and data [31, 32]. Application domains for topic modeling span all spheres of life, for example, in political sciences and medical sciences. Others are in source code analysis, opinion and aspect mining [32]. Topic modeling finds its empirical grounding is in computer science's subfields of text mining and natural language processing. Topic modelling tools support statistical analysis of collection of documents [31]. The basic assumption is that a topic is a list of words where the latter refers to unstructured text from sources such as email, tweets and books. Topic models assume any part of the text is combined by selecting words from probable baskets of words – each basket in this case corresponds to a topic.

1.3 Latent Dirichlet Allocation (LDA)

Latent Dirichlet Allocation (LDA) is one of the most popular technique for topic modelling [32]. Furthermore, LDA is a probabilistic model of corpus in which each document is represented as a probabilistic distribution over Latent topics. In other words, each topic is a distribution over words and a document is a mixture of topics. For a given application, the topic distribution in all documents share a common Dirichlet prior. Mathematical representation of the main terms (Corpus, Document, Topic and Number of Words) can be found in publications such as these ones [30–37]. One of the strengths of LDA is its ability to work with very large corpus and to identify sub-topics for technology area composed of many sub-topics. LDA achieves this by first generating terms in a set of documents then going further to generate a vocabulary to discover hidden topics. Given the nested nature of the 4IR topic, LDA was found to be the most appropriate. For parameter estimation inference, LDA applies either expectation propagation, variational method or Gibbs Sampling. Gibbs Sampling is the most commonly used; it employs the Monte Carlo Markov-Chain algorithm. Besides, LDA is supervised learning algorithm [32, 36].

LDA has been widely researched and has found intense application in social media analytics [32]. Different extensions of LDA have also emerged over the years, each with enhanced features. Some of these features include ability to capture correlation among topics, to classify documents, analyse documents in different languages and to analyse the temporal evaluation of topics in very large collection of documents. Some examples of these extensions are: (1) Dynamic Topic Model (DTM), which can vision the topic trend and (2) Labelled LDA (LLDA), which is supervised algorithm. Others are (3) Maximum Entropy Discrimination LDA (Med LDA) [34, 35] which applies hierarchical Bayesian Model concept and (4) Relational Topic Model (TRM) which focuses on networks of text data. Besides, there is a wide range of tools and software for implementing LDA modeling such as those listed in [32]. For this paper, the MATLAB implementation of LDA was used.

1.4   Dynamic Topic Models

Over and above the function of LDA, dynamic topic models capture how the meaningful patterns of words change over time [31]. In the implementation of Dynamic LDA (D-LDA), the use of probabilistic time series allow the topics to vary smoothly over time. The weakness of D-LDA has been reported as its inability to capture rare words as well as long tail of language data [31]. This problem has however been solved through Embedded Topic Model (ETM) where continuous representation of words is made use of [31, 38]. In [31], Dynamic ETM (D-ETM) [31] is introduced to address the problem that ETM cannot analyse a corpus whose topics shift over time. D-ETM works by building on word embedding topic models and dynamic topic models. Given the dynamic nature of 4IR technologies, a variation of D-ETM is considered the best option.

2 Data and Methods

2.1 Data Sources

The following two sources of data were used to extract the text for the LDA topic modeling.

The TCCC-ANNOUNCE Archives. One of the functions of the IEEE's Technical Committee on Computer Communications (TCCC) is to provide the members with a forum for technical discussions and interactions (https://tccc.committees.comsoc.org/) [39]. To this end, the Committee runs mailing lists (https://tccc.committees.comsoc.org/mailing-list/) such as the tccc-announce and tccc-discuss. The tccc-announce is used for announcements related to on-topic call for papers (CFPs) and faculty or research job openings. The key requirement for these announcements is to have a primary focus on networking and communication. Consequently, most of the topics covered by these CFPs cover the 4IR technologies. As of August 2022, the mailing list had 4,599 subscribers. Besides, the author of this paper has been receiving these announcements since 2011. The text data (typically containing emails of announcements) used in this paper was retrieved from tccc-announce archive as follows:

- File 1 – a combination of 5 archive files consisting the List's home at Columbia University from 2001 to 2013
- File 2 – an export of selected (2019 to August 2022) of tccc-announce emails received by the author.

Web of Science Core Collection. In order to identify the kind of research being carried out under the general topic of Fourth Industrial Revolution (4IR), publications were extracted from the Web of Science (WoS) core collection (https://clarivate.com/webofsciencegroup/solutions/web-of-science-core-collection/) using the search phrase: *ALL = (("4th industrial revolution" or "4IR" OR "Industry 4.0") and ("technologies" or "technology")).* After applying filters such publication year (2012 to 2022) and language (English), a total of 11,731 publications were extracted. From these, text strings used for text processing in MATLAB were created by concatenating the following headings: ArticleTitle, SourceTitle, BookSeriesTitle, BookSeriesSubtitle, ConferenceTitle, AuthorKeyword, KeywordsPlus, Abstract and MeetingAbstract. These entries were stored in a comma separated value (CSV) file. A second file was exported in the Research Information System (RIS) format and later used for Bibliometric Analysis presented in Sect. 2.3

2.2 Text Pre-processing

The text data files were pre-processed using existing functions (e.g. *preprocess-Text(inputText)*) in MATLAB. Through this, common pre-processing functions were performed, including: converting data to lowercase, tokenization, erasing of punctuation marks and Lemmatization. The flow of these steps is presented in Fig. 1 below.

As shown in Fig. 1, the text files (e.g. "Tccc2010–2013.txt") were converted to strings of text, which were then passed over to the text pre-processing functions. The 'remove stop words' removes a list of stop words (such as "and", "of", and "the") from the input string. Given that the tccc-announce text files contains email announcements, the frequency of occurrence for common written-speech words (such as "international", "conference", "discussing", "correct", "grammar" "spelling", "indicate" and "contribution") was very high. Further, since such words would affect the results of analysing the text using topic models, these words were manually identified and removed using the function '*removeWords*' as shown in step 4 in the Fig. 1 below.

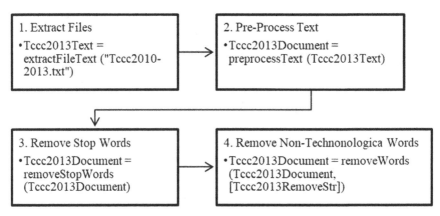

Fig. 1. Text pre-processing steps followed

2.3 Bibliometric Analysis

Bibliometric analysis has been widely used as a quantitative method for studying different aspects of research publications [26, 27]. One of these aspects is the identification of the main research areas within a scientific field. On the other hand, one of the most commonly used bibliometric analysis software is VOSviewer that is capable of creating co-occurrence or co-authorship maps from network text files such Research Information System (RIS) [40, 41]. For this paper, the bibliometric analysis was performed using RIS file containing 11,577 publications from the WoS. The maps generated by the VOS Viewer Software were used to determine the main technologies that were featured under various themes of 4IR. To minimize the number of items included in the map, the minimum number of occurrence for a keyword was set at 10; this resulted in in 961 items clustered in 11 clusters shown in Fig. 2 below. From this, the following themes are identifiable:

2.3.1 System Intelligence Design Aspects of 4IR Technologies

With 225 items, this constitutes the largest cluster and is represented by colour red (in Fig. 2). The identified technologies are algorithms related to Artificial Intelligence, Machine Learning, Deep Learning and Artificial Neural Networks. Further, the applications of these algorithms in domains such as smart manufacturing, digital twin, additive manufacturing, 3-D printing, is depicted. Besides, the application of the algorithms in the following dimensions is illustrated: classification, optimization, simulation, sustainable manufacturing, data analysis, data mining, and predictive maintenance.

2.3.2 Adoption and Innovation in Emerging Technologies

This is the second largest cluster with 210 items and depicted in colour green in the co-occurrence map. The dominant technologies include augmented reality, virtual reality, autonomous vehicles and collaborative robotics. The focus is mostly on application domains such as manufacturing, food industry, health and education. On the other hand, the dimensions highlighted are automation, safety, flexibility, productivity and digitalization.

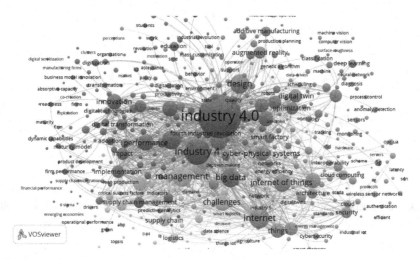

Fig. 2. Bibliometric analysis map for the 2012 to 2022 WoS publications focusing on 4IR

2.3.3 Developments Within IoT

In third position is the blue cluster that has 208 items that relate to the evolution of the core technology – Internet of Things (IoT). The highlighted baseline technologies are cloud computing, wireless sensor networks, wireless communication and radio frequency identification (RFID). Alongside these supporting technologies are the overarching issues of security, privacy and interoperability. The associated emerging technology included are Industrial IoT (IIoT), Blockchain, 5G, edge computing and fog computing. Emerging applications areas identified are smart city, smart grid and factory automation.

2.3.4   Enhanced and Futuristic Business Management

Fourth in popularity is the cluster represented in colour red, which has 159 items. The main management themes covered are smart supply chain management, lean production, digital transformation (including ditigilization), big data analytics, business models (with a focus on small and medium enterprises (SMEs)), e-commerce, performance management, integration, agility and servitization.

2.3.5   Technologies for Supporting Sustainability Agenda

At number 5, and represented by colour purple, are 90 items related to sustainability frameworks and models. The items depict 4IR as a current and future catalyst for implementing and managing sustainability. Some of the aspects include sustainable development, sustainable supply chain, sustainable environment, cleaner production, renewable energy, resilience, efficiency, risk management, reverse logistics, and emission reduction. As can be seen in Fig. 3 below, the theme of circular economy is strongly connected in the map.

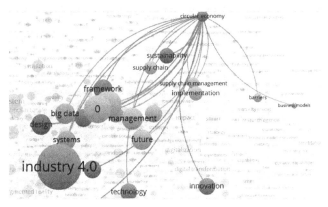

Fig. 3. Bibliometric analysis map for the 2012 to 2022 WoS publications focusing on circular economy

2.3.6   Big Data and Related Systems

The next significant cluster (light blue) with only 39 items represens Big Data, and related technologies and systems such as Data Science, Intelligence and Context and Systems. Due to many articles applying these technologies for studying the Covid-19 pandemic, it is not surprising that 'Cod-19' emerged as term in this cluster. Due to its common application in construction projects related to big data, the Building Information Model (BIM) also featured strongly under this cluster.

2.3.7 Other Minor Technologies

The much smaller Cluster 7 (Orange) had 26 items such as Blockchain Technology, Smart Logistics, Analytics, Evolution, and Opportunities. Clusters 8, 9, 10 and 11 had only one item each, which are chain, digital manufacturing and product life cycle respectively. These five clusters were not included in the subsequent text processing steps. Based on the remaining six clusters discussed above, the identified 4IR technologies and application areas were identified for further trend topic model analysis as discussed in the subsequent sections of this paper.

2.4 Analysis of the WoS Text Data Using Topic Models

Latent Dirichlet Allocation (LDA) [32] model was applied to the pre-processed text as depicted in Fig. 4 below and explained in the following paragraphs.

Step 1: Extraction CSV files from WoS: based on the Publication Year column, the WoS publications were divided into 5 files containing 2211, 2802, 2364, 2669 and 1531 publications for years 2012 to 2018, 2019, 2020, 2021 and 2022 respectively. The percentage distribution of the number publications for each of the five files is shown in Fig. 5 below. This split was meant to create some form of time-series on which to compare the developments in each of the 4IR technologies identified in Sect. 2.3 above.

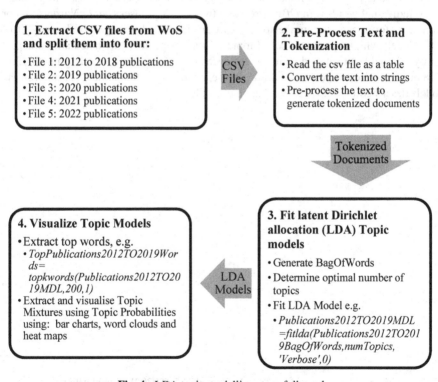

Fig. 4. LDA topic modelling steps followed

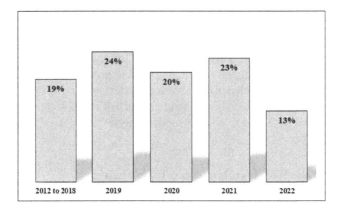

Fig. 5. Distribution of WoS publications by year of publication

Step 2: Text Pre-Processing and Tokenization: Pre-defined MATLAB functions for text pre-processing (*preprocessTex( )* and *removeStopWords()*) were applied to each of the 5 files.

Step 3: Latent Dirichlet allocation (LDA) Topic models: the resulting tokenized documents (one for each publication in each of the 5 files) were then used to generate bag of individual words (*bagOfWords()*) and two-words phrases (*bagOfNgrams()*). For optimal performance, the number of topics were identified through *goodness-of-fit* of LDA models with varying number of topics. This was achieved by calculating the perplexity of a held-out set of documents for each of the four files (excluding the 2012 to 2018 one). The lowest perplexity value was selected [37] as this indicated how well the models described the set of documents in each file.

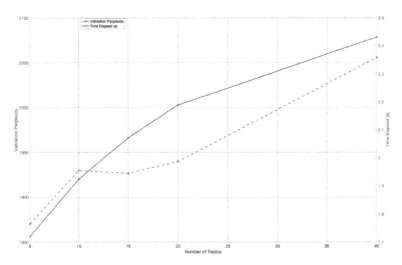

Fig. 6. Goodness-of-fit of LDA topic models for 2020 WoS publications

From Fig. 6 above for example, 10 was the optimal number of topics for the 2020 publications file. Similar number was obtained for the 2019, 2021 and 2022 files. For the 2012 to 2018 file however, different values (ranging from 15 to 25) were obtained using different LDA solvers ("cgs" "avb" "cvb0" and "savb"). The diversity of topics as well as lack of concentration of the 4IR could explain this variance. In line with literature reviewed, which revealed that 2019 was the main year when 4IR publications surged, this file (for 2012 to 2018) was omitted from the subsequent analysis.

Step 4: Visualize Topic Model: based on their probabilities, different topic mixtures were visualized using bar charts, heat maps and word clouds. Further details of this are presented under the results section of this paper.

2.5   Analyze Tccc-Announce Text Using Longer Phrases

To reflect the phrases that represent both the 4IR technologies (e.g. "Internet of Things" and "Machine Learning"), the MATLAB tool for analyzing text data using Multiword Phrases was applied to the tccc-announce files. In this case, two-words phrase was selected using the function *bagOfNgrams()*. An example of the results from this mapping are shown in Fig. 7 below.

Fig. 7. Word cloud for tccc-announce emails for 2021

From Fig. 7 above, the same trends identified from the WoS dataset as subjected to the bibliometric analysis, is also identified from the tccc-announce dataset. This further affirmed the choice of the trends used in the text processing. Similar matching (with the bibliometric analysis) trends were identified for text containing tccc-announce emails sent during the years 2019, 2020 and 2022.

3 Results

3.1 LDA Topic Models for WoS

To enable contextualization of the words included in the LDA topic models for the 4 files (containing WoS publications) considered, 5 and 10 top key words for the 2-word-phrase and single-word LDA topic models respectively, were extracted using the predefined MATLAB function *topkwords( )*. The results are discussed below.

3.1.1 LDA Topic Models Mixtures

In order to compare keywords/phrases from the LDA topic models mixtures with those from the bibliometric analysis, the topic probabilities were plotted using both the two-word and one-word phrases bag of words. Sample results of this are shown in Figs. 8 and 9 below. As shown in Fig. 8, two-word topics mixtures with highest probabilities are 1, 5, 2 and 6 respectively while topics 9, 3, 10 and 8 have the lowest values. On the other hand, topics 10, 6 and 8 (see Fig. 9) have the highest probabilities in the one-word-phrase topics while all the other topics have much lower values of probabilities. An inspection of the top words in these topics, as shown in Tables 1 and 2 below, confirms (see Topics 1 and 5 in Table 1 and Topics 8 and 10 in Table 2) that they are the same top words (in each cluster) as identified through the bibliometric analysis as presented in Sect. 2.3 of this paper. It is also worth noting that some of the words included under Topic 6 in Table 2 are not necessarily 4IR-related but are common words used in publications.

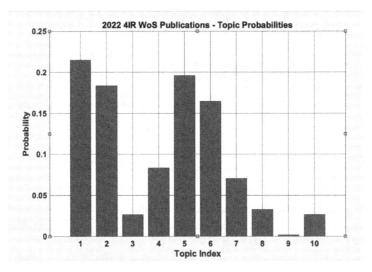

Fig. 8. LDA topic models for two-words mixtures for 2022 WoS publications

Table 1. Top words of the LDA topic models for double words for 2022 WoS publications

1	machine learning, industry 40, computer science, industry 50, sustainable development
2	computer science, smart manufacturing, science engineering, industry 40, c 2022
3	augmented reality, deep learning, quality management, chemistry engineering, operations management
4	internet things, artificial intelligence, big data, industrial internet, blockchain technology
5	industry 40, digital twin, digital twins, automation control, control systems
6	industry 40, supply chain, literature review, industry 4, 4 0
7	industry 40, 40 technologies, circular economy, 4 0, business economics
8	industry 40, smart factory, business model, waste management, international conference
9	digital transformation, industrial revolution, 3d printing, methodology approach, fourth industrial
10	industry 40, artificial intelligence, internet things, materials science, fourth industrial

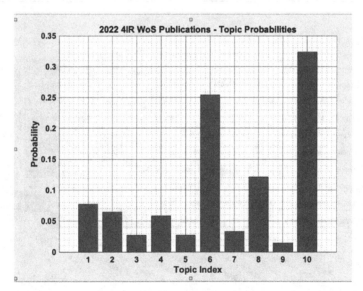

Fig. 9. LDA topic models for single words mixtures for 2022 WoS publications

3.1.2 Correlations for Topic Words Probabilities

Topic words' probabilities were created using the MATLAB function *corrcoef()* and the results presented using heat maps similar to the one shown in Fig. 10 below. From such maps, it is possible to visualize the correlations between the various sub-themes/technologies under 4IR. For instance, there is a high (value of 0.2724) correlation between issues of sustainability and production in manufacturing sector. This indicates high focus on research into ways of making manufacturing more sustainable.

Table 2. Top words of the LDA topic models for single words for 2022 WoS publications

1	research, supply, management, chain, business, industry, study, technologies, literature, 40
2	industry, 40, industrial, technologies, development, revolution, smart, information, intelligence, science
3	industry, 40, digital, manufacturing, technologies, study, transformation, management, companies, implementation
4	systems, system, process, manufacturing, production, data, quality, model, control, proposed
5	environment, technology, design, development, science, application, smart, efficiency, present, product
6	new, time, based, different, results, approach, paper, problem, case, scheduling
7	science, materials, maintenance, reality, computer, c, virtual, human, high, due
8	internet, data, iot, things, network, applications, industrial, blockchain, networks, security
9	food, performance, results, covid19, technology, model, health, waste, factors, analysis
10	learning, education, energy, construction, engineering, 3d, skills, training, additive, printing

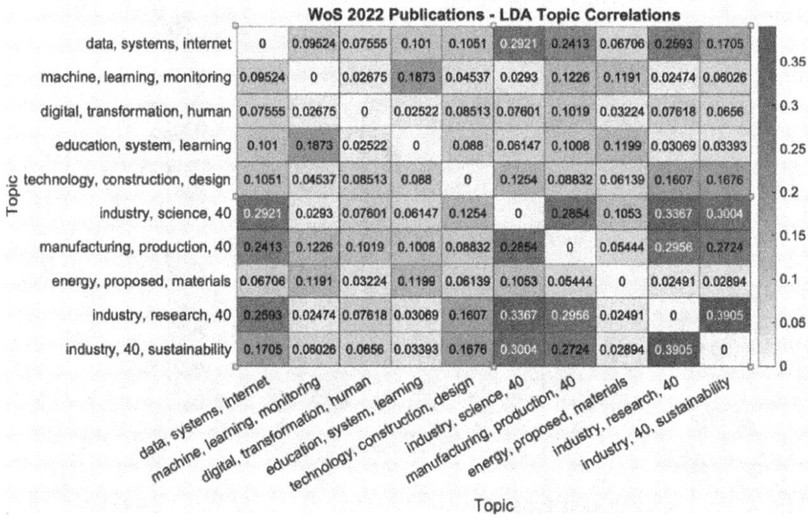

Fig. 10. LDA topic models for single words correlation for 2022 WoS publications

3.2 Fourth Industrial Revolution (4IR) Trends

Based on the top words identified through the LDA Top Models presented in sections above, the following trends were identified and matched with those identified through the bibliometric analysis.

3.2.1 System Intelligence Design Aspects of 4IR Technologies

As reflected by the words and phrases shown in Table 3 below, system intelligence design aspects of 4IR have evolved over the last 4 years and their applications in domain areas such as 3D-printing, energy, education, smart cities and construction has been amplified. Aspects of training/skilling and digital transformation have also come into limelight.

Table 3. Emerging system intelligence design aspects of 4IR technologies

Year	Two-word-phrase bag of words	Single-word-phrase bag of words
2019	machine learning, cloud computing, emerging technologies, decision making, 3d printing	data, machine, method, accuracy, detection, based, learning
2020	digital twin, internet things, business model, smart cities	system, control, sensors, applications, twin, 3d, assembly, robot, technology
	machine learning, artificial intelligence, neural network, cloud computing	learning, engineering, education, skills, technology, reality
2021	data, machine, learning, method, process, model, system, proposed, time, algorithm	
2022	digital twin, automation control, control systems	learning, education, energy, construction, engineering, 3d, skills, training, additive, printing
	digital transformation, 3d printing,	

3.2.2 Developments Within IoT

Over the last 4 years, research into developments within IoT, such as cloud computing and cyber-physical systems (CPS) have stabilized while more focus is now on trends such as industrial internet of things (IIoT) and blockchain technologies. As can be seen from the list shown in Table 4 below, issues of security and privacy still remain a concern and are still heavily researched on.

Table 4. Emerging developments within Internet of Things

Year	Two-word-phrase bag of words	Single-word-phrase bag of words
2019	big data, supply chain, cyberphysical systems	data, internet, industrial, smart, systems,
2020	cyberphysical systems, artificial intelligence, industrial internet	data, internet, things, network, industrial, communication, security, cloud
2021	artificial intelligence, machine learning	network, industrial, security, applications, computing, control
2022	artificial intelligence, big data, industrial internet, blockchain technology	data, network, applications, industrial, blockchain, networks, security
	artificial intelligence, materials science	

3.2.3   Adoption and Innovation in Emerging Technologies

As detailed in Table 5 blow, the adoption and innovations under virtual reality and augmented reality have persisted. Applications domains for 4IR innovations have been extended from smart manufacturing to include education, health (in particular, a surge in research around the Covid-19 pandemic) agriculture and the general food industry.

Table 5. Adoption and innovation in emerging technologies

Year	Two-word-phrase bag of words	Single-word-phrase bag of words
2019	engineering industry, virtual reality, digital economy, conference proceedings	design, manufacturing, process, system, production, systems, control, virtual, product, industry
	augmented reality, cyber physical, physical system, data analysis, sensor networks	
2020	computer science, science engineering, augmented reality, engineering education	
2021	education, learning, work, health, intelligence, new, covid19, human	
	smart manufacturing, augmented reality, manufacturing industry, digital transformation	environmental, science, technology, study, food, analysis, agriculture
2022	augmented reality, deep learning, quality management, chemistry engineering, operations management	science, materials, maintenance, reality, virtual, human
		food, performance, results, covid19, technology, model, health, waste, factors, analysis

3.2.4   Enhanced and Futuristic Business Management

In this sub-sector, 4IR technologies have been largely used in managing supply chains. In the last 2 to 3 years however, there is a huge focus on redefinition of business models both for pre-adoption and post-adoption of 4IR. Newest in this area are topics under circular economy and expansion of the domain to include waste management and construction industry. Some of these words and phrases are listed in Table 6 below.

Table 6. Adoption and enhanced and futuristic business management

Year	Two-word-phrase bag of words	Single-word-phrase bag of words
2019	supply, chain, technology, environmental, study, energy, performance, logistics, impact, risk	
2020	supply chain, digital transformation, internet things	management, research, manufacturing, business, supply, chain
2021	supply chain, big data, supply chains, chain management	supply, chain, technologies, management, data, technology
	deep learning, business economics, business model, construction industry	
2022	supply chain, smart factory, business model, waste management	supply, management, chain, business, industry, technologies
	smart factory, business model, waste management	circular economy, business, economics

3.2.5 Big Data and Related Systems

Similar to the bibliometric analysis, only a few words and phrases were identified through the LDA Topic Models. The list in Table 7 below show that developments in big data and data analytics are in tandem with developments in other sub-fields of 4IR. For instance, its application in industrial IoT (IIoT) and in blockchain technologies.

Table 7. Big data and related systems

Year	Two-word-phrase bag of words	Single-word-phrase bag of words
2019	model, computer, data,	
2020	big data, business economics, data analytics	data, model, machine, method, maintenance, approach, based, system
	iot, data, internet, things, network, industrial, communication, security, cloud	
2021	science, computer, systems, data, emerging, model	
2022	systems, system, process, manufacturing, production, data, quality, model, control,	
	internet, data, iot, things, network, applications, industrial, blockchain, networks, security	

3.3 Predict Top LDA Topics of Tccc Emails Documents

From the results presented in the section above, it can be confirmed that there is a strong correlation between the results of both the bibliometric analysis and LDA Topic modeling of the WoS publications on one hand and the content from the email communication within the Tccc mailing list on the other hand. Subsequently, this section describes how the LDA Topic models of WoS were used to predict the focus of publications that may result from the tccc-announce communications. This was achieved using the *predict( )* function of MATLAB, e.g. *topicIdx = predict(Publications2022MDL,Tccc2021Documents)* which predicts the Topic Model from the 2022 WoS publications that matches the tccc email content contained in the documents named *"Tccc2021Documents"*.

It is a well-known trend that call for papers (conference, journal articles and workshops) published in year^n, will results in publications in year $^{n+1}$. For this reason, emails sent in 2021 were used to predict LDA Topics using the LDA Models generated using 2022 WoS publications. For instance, the text of the email shown in Fig. 12 below was extracted and pre-processed following the steps shown in Fig. 1. The *predict( )* function was then applied on the processed documents; the results are show in Fig. 11 below. The documents were matched with LDA Topic 8 of the 2022 publications. For comparison and verification purposes, the *predict( )* function was also performed using the 2019, 2020 and 2021 WoS publications. A visual inspection of the content of the word cloud shown in Fig. 11 confirms that the email text conforms more to the 2022WoS publications.

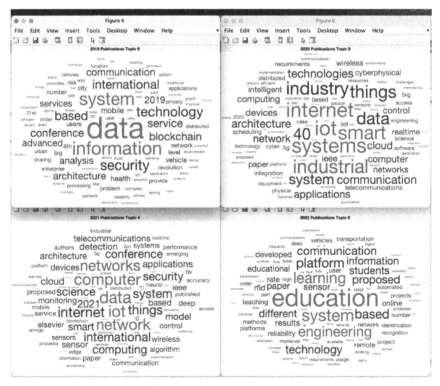

Fig. 11. Sample results of predicting Tccc content using LDA topic models for WoS publications

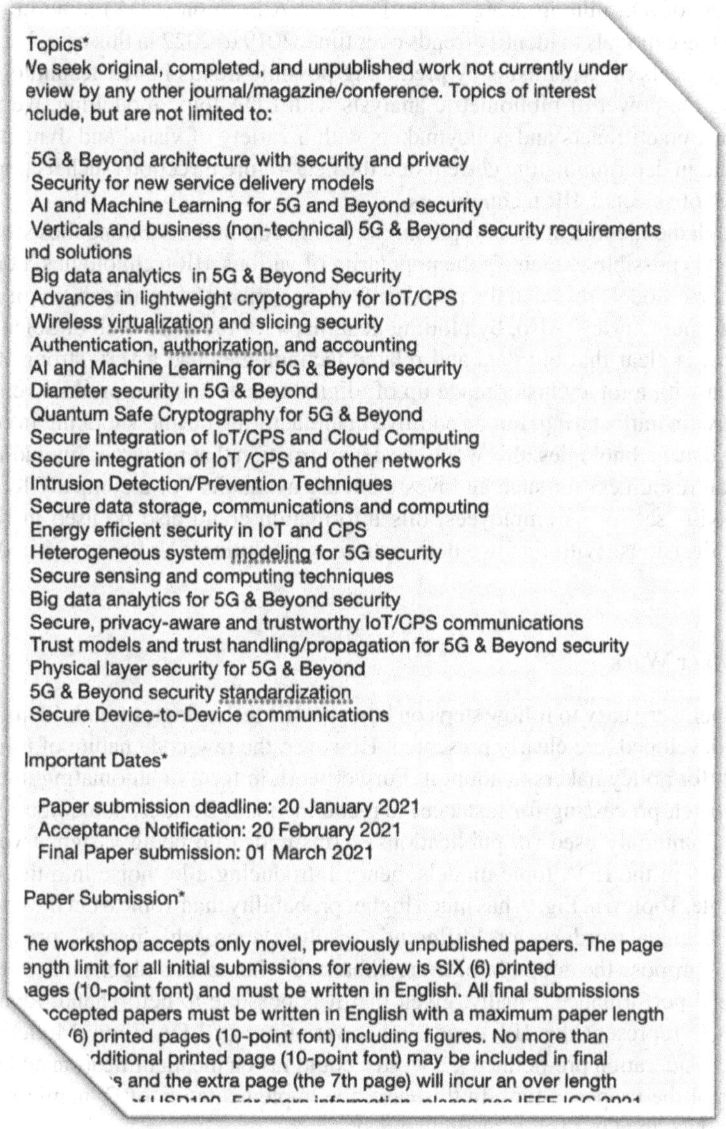

Topics*
Ve seek original, completed, and unpublished work not currently under
eview by any other journal/magazine/conference. Topics of interest
nclude, but are not limited to:

5G & Beyond architecture with security and privacy
Security for new service delivery models
AI and Machine Learning for 5G and Beyond security
Verticals and business (non-technical) 5G & Beyond security requirements
ind solutions
Big data analytics in 5G & Beyond Security
Advances in lightweight cryptography for IoT/CPS
Wireless virtualization and slicing security
Authentication, authorization, and accounting
AI and Machine Learning for 5G & Beyond security
Diameter security in 5G & Beyond
Quantum Safe Cryptography for 5G & Beyond
Secure Integration of IoT/CPS and Cloud Computing
Secure integration of IoT /CPS and other networks
Intrusion Detection/Prevention Techniques
Secure data storage, communications and computing
Energy efficient security in IoT and CPS
Heterogeneous system modeling for 5G security
Secure sensing and computing techniques
Big data analytics for 5G & Beyond security
Secure, privacy-aware and trustworthy IoT/CPS communications
Trust models and trust handling/propagation for 5G & Beyond security
Physical layer security for 5G & Beyond
5G & Beyond security standardization
Secure Device-to-Device communications

Important Dates*

 Paper submission deadline: 20 January 2021
 Acceptance Notification: 20 February 2021
 Final Paper submission: 01 March 2021

Paper Submission*

he workshop accepts only novel, previously unpublished papers. The page
ength limit for all initial submissions for review is SIX (6) printed
ages (10-point font) and must be written in English. All final submissions
  ccepted papers must be written in English with a maximum paper length
   '6) printed pages (10-point font) including figures. No more than
    dditional printed page (10-point font) may be included in final
     s and the extra page (the 7th page) will incur an over length
       of USD100. For more information, please see IEEE ICC 2021

Fig. 12. Sample extract of Tccc email sent in early 2021

4   Discussion and Conclusion

4.1   LDA Topic Models for Decision Support

Numerous studies have used published articles to analyse the trends of the technologies
associated with the fourth industrial revolution (4IR). However, most of these studies
take static and quantitative approaches such as bibliometric analysis [2, 42] and literature reviews [3, 7, 8, 11, 19, 21]. In this paper, we build on this approach through the

introduction of text mining using Latent Dirichlet Allocation (LDA) topic modelling. We apply these models to identify trends over time, 2019 to 2022 in this case. We further introduce aspects of dynamisms by predicting possible trends in 4IR technologies. By combining the power of bibliometric analysis with LDA topic modelling, we provide researchers, practitioners and policymakers with a variety of visual and dynamic tools that can aid in determining the current and the near-future direction (such as popularity or decline) of selected 4IR technologies.

Through the identification of topic mixtures and correlations among these topics for instance, it is possible to identify the popularity of various 4IR technologies. For example, our LDA models revealed the popularity of the concept of sustainability in relation to smart manufacturing. Also, by plotting heat maps for the 2021 Web of Science publications, it is clear that big data and related technologies had a very strong (0.6603) correlation with a topic cluster made up of: digital transformation, productive systems and additive manufacturing. For an additive manufacturing business looking into investing in big data technologies, this would be a confirmation that resources (including tools and human resources) for such an investment are available. For a company looking to identity skills set for its employees, this information could also be used in reaching informed decisions. With this, we demonstrate our solution's ability to aid in decision making.

4.2 Further Work

In this paper, very easy to follow steps on how the 4IR technologies trends identification tool was developed, are clearly presented. However, the raw-code nature of this makes it difficult for policymakers to adopt it. Further work in form of automating these steps (in form batch processing for instance) is recommended. Besides, some non-technical and very commonly used (in publications) terms ended up being assigned very high probabilities in the LDA topic models, hence introducing a lot noise into the models. For example, Topic 6 in Fig. 9, has much higher probability than Topic 8 but the earlier has non-4IR-technical words such as 'different', 'results', 'approach', 'paper', 'problem' and 'case'. We propose the adoption of more enhanced tokenization algorithms to improve the models' performance. Finally, given that it is possible to beforehand, identify the keywords to represent the 4IR trends, other variations of LDA Topic Modelling that put into consideration pre-defined keywords, could fasten the identification and training processes of the proposed tool. In this case, the implementation of Dynamic ETM (D-ETM), as described in [31], is recommended.

References

1. Lu, Y.: Industry 4.0: a survey on technologies, applications and open research issues. J. Ind. Inf. Integr. **6**, 1–10 (2017)
2. Muhuri, P.K., Shukla, A.K., Abraham, A.: Industry 4.0: a bibliometric analysis and detailed overview. Eng. Appl. Artif. Intell. **78**, 218–235 (2019)
3. Oztemel, E., Gursev, S.: Literature review of Industry 4.0 and related technologies. J. Intell. Manuf. **31**(1), 127–182 (2018)

4. Da Xu, L., Xu, E.L., Li, L.: Industry 4.0: state of the art and future trends. Int. J. Prod. Res. **56**(8), 2941–2962 (2018)
5. Tao, F.: PM10 - Digital Twin shop-floor: a new shop-floor paradigm towards smart manufacturing. Robot. Comput. Integr. Manuf. **61**, 10 (2017)
6. Kang, H.S., et al.: Smart manufacturing: past research, present findings, and future directions. Int. J. Precis. Eng. Manuf. Green Technol. **3**(1), 111–128 (2016)
7. Zhong, R.Y., Xu, X., Klotz, E., Newman, S.T.: Intelligent Manufacturing in the Context of Industry 4.0: a review. Engineering **3**(5), 616–630 (2017)
8. Monostori, L., et al.: Cyber-physical systems in manufacturing. CIRP Ann. **65**(2), 621–641 (2016)
9. Hofmann, E., Rüsch, M.: Industry 4.0 and the current status as well as future prospects on logistics. Comput. Ind. **89**, 23–34 (2017)
10. Ivanov, D., Dolgui, A., Sokolov, B.: The impact of digital technology and Industry 4.0 on the ripple effect and supply chain risk analytics. Int. J. Prod. Res. **57**(3), 829–846 (2019)
11. Ben-Daya, M., Hassini, E., Bahroun, Z.: Internet of things and supply chain management: a literature review. Int. J. Prod. Res. **57**(15–16), 4719–4742 (2019)
12. Maquera, G., Costa, B.B.F., Mendoza, Ó., Salinas, A., Haddad, A.N.: Intelligent Digital Platform for Community-Based Rural Tourism — A Novel Concept Development in Peru, pp. 1–18 (2022)
13. da Rocha, A.B.T., de Oliveira, K.B., Espuny, M., da M. Reis, J.S., Oliveira, O.J.: Business transformation through sustainability based on Industry 4.0', Heliyon, vol. 8, no. July, p. e10015 (2022)
14. Kitsantas, T.: 'Exploring blockchain technology and enterprise resource planning system: business and technical aspects, current problems, and future perspectives. Sustainability **14**(13), 7633 (2022)
15. Kumar, S., Raut, R.D., Agrawal, N., Cheikhrouhou, N., Sharma, M., Daim, T.: Technovation Integrated Blockchain and Internet of Things in the food supply chain: adoption barriers. Technovation **118**, 102589 (2022)
16. Yetis, H., Karakose, M., Baygin, N.: Blockchain-based mass customization framework using optimized production management for Industry 4.0 applications. Eng. Sci. Technol. Int. J. **36**, 101151 (2022)
17. Aivaliotis, S., et al.: An augmented reality software suite enabling seamless human robot interaction. Int. J. Comput. Integr. Manuf. **00**(00), 1–27 (2022)
18. Omerali, M., Kaya, T.: Augmented reality application selection framework using spherical fuzzy COPRAS multi criteria decision making. Cogent Eng. **9**(1), 1–38 (2022)
19. Tortorella, G.L., Prashar, A., Saurin, T.A., Fogliatto, F.S., Antony, J., Junior, G.C.: Impact of Industry 4.0 adoption on workload demands in contact centers. Hum. Factors Ergon. Manuf. **32**, 406–418 (2022)
20. Nasir, A., Zakaria, N., Yusoff, R.Z.: Cogent business & management the influence of transformational leadership on organizational sustainability in the context of Industry 4.0: mediating role of innovative performance the influence of transformational leadership on organizational sustainab. Cogent Bus. Manag. **9**(1), 0–31 (2022)
21. Grabowska, S., Saniuk, S., Gajdzik, B.: Industry 5.0: improving humanization and sustainability of Industry 4.0. Scientometrics **127**(6), 3117–3144 (2022)
22. Masinde, M., Phoobane, P., Brown, J.: Mkulima platform: an inclusive business platform ecosystem that integrates African Small-Scale Farmers into Agricultural Value Chain'. In: Sheikh, Y.H., Rai, I.A., Bakar, A.D. (eds.) e-Infrastructure and e-Services for Developing Countries. AFRICOMM 2021. Lect. Notes Inst. Comput. Sci. Soc. Telecommun. Eng. LNICST, vol. 443 LNICST, pp. 397–419 (2022) https://doi.org/10.1007/978-3-031-06374-9_26

23. Xie, X., Han, Y., Anderson, A., Ribeiro-Navarrete, S.: Digital platforms and SMEs' business model innovation: exploring the mediating mechanisms of capability reconfiguration. Int. J. Inf. Manage. **65**, 102513 (2022)

24. Rodrigues Dias, V.M., Jugend, D., de Camargo Fiorini, P., do A. Razzino, C., Paula Pinheiro, M.A.: Possibilities for applying the circular economy in the aerospace industry: Practices, opportunities and challenges. J. Air Transp. Manage. **102**, 102227 (2022)

25. Cheah, C.G., Chia, W.Y., Lai, S.F., Chew, K.W., Chia, S.R., Show, P.L.: Innovation designs of Industry 4.0 based solid waste management: machinery and digital circular economy. Environ. Res. **213**, 113619 (2022)

26. Pauna, V.H., Picone, F., Le Guyader, G., Buonocore, E., Franzese, P.P.: The scientific research on ecosystem services: a bibliometric analysis. Ecol. Quest. **29**(3), 53–62 (2018)

27. Phoobane, P., Masinde, M., Mabhaudhi, T.: Predicting infectious diseases: a bibliometric review on Africa. Int. J. Environ. Res. Public Health **19**(3), 1893 (2022)

28. Shuttleworth, L., Schmitz, S., Beier, G.: Impacts of Industry 4.0 on industrial employment in Germany: a comparison of industrial workers ' expectations and experiences from two surveys in 2014 and 2020. Prod. Manuf. Res. **10**(1), 583–605 (2022)

29. Tian, T., Fang, Z.: Attention-based autoencoder topic model for short texts. Procedia Comput. Sci. **151**, 1134–1139 (2019)

30. Aly, M., Khomh, F., Yacout, S.: What do practitioners discuss about IoT and Industry 4.0 related technologies? Characterization and identification of IoT and Industry 4.0 categories in stack overflow discussions. Internet of Things (Netherlands) **14**, 100364 (2021)

31. Dieng, A.B., Ruiz, F.J.R., Blei, D.M.: The Dynamic Embedded Topic Model, pp. 1–17 (2019)

32. Jelodar, H., et al.: Latent Dirichlet allocation (LDA) and topic modeling: models, applications, a survey. Multimedia Tools Appl. **78**(11), 15169–15211 (2018)

33. Chang, J., Blei, D.M.: Relational topic models for document networks. In: Proceedings of the 12th International Conference on Artificial Intelligence and Statistics (AISTATS) 2009, pp. 81–88 (2009)

34. Zhu, J., Ahmed, A., Xing, E.P.: MedLDA: maximum margin supervised topic models for regression and classification. In: Proceedings of the 26th International Conference on Machine Learning, pp. 1–8 (2009)

35. Zhu, J., Xing, E.P.: Maximum entropy discrimination Markov networks. J. Mach. Learn. Res. **10**, 2531–2569 (2009)

36. Lin, T., Lee, C.: Latent Dirichlet Allocation For Text And Image Topic Modeling, Na, pp. 1–6 (2013)

37. Goedecke, P.J.: Comparison of Methods for Choosing an Appropriate Number of Topics in an LDA Model, University of Memphis (2017)

38. Harandizadeh, B., Priniski, J.H. Morstatter, F.: Keyword assisted embedded topic model. In: WSDM 2022, pp. 372–380 (2021)

39. Hartung, A.F.: Computer Communications, Comput. (Long. Beach. Calif.) **6**(2), 13 (1973)

40. van Eck, N.J., Waltman, L.: Citation-based clustering of publications using CitNetExplorer and VOSviewer. Scientometrics **111**(2), 1053–1070 (2017). https://doi.org/10.1007/s11192-017-2300-7

41. van Eck, N.J., Waltman, L.: VOSviewer Manual. Univeristeit Leiden, Leiden (2013)

42. Thai, L., Trung, D., Van Le, H., Ngoc, G.: A bibliometric analysis of Research on Education 4.0 during the 2017–2021 period (2022)

A Conceptual Model for the Digital Inclusion of SMMEs in the Informal Sector in South Africa - The Use of Blockchain Technology to Access Loans

Lebogang Mosupye-Semenya[✉] [iD]

DSI/NRF/Newton Fund Trilateral Chair in Transformative Innovation, The 4IR and Sustainable Development, College of Business and Economics, Johannesburg Business School, 69 Kingsway Ave, Auckland Park, Johannesburg, South Africa
lsemenya@uj.ac.za

Abstract. Small, Medium, and Micro Enterprises (SMMEs) in the informal sector are faced with a myriad of challenges, including access to loans. Because of its immutability, blockchain technology is said to be the solution to these types of challenges. Through blockchain-enabled Mobile Applications, informal SMMEs can record their financials, and give permission to external viewers such as banks to view when applying for a loan. However, there exists a possibility that these informal SMMEs may be digitally excluded from the use and benefits of Blockchain technology due to issues such as affordability, informality, and lack of skills. For this reason, this study aims to develop a model for the digital inclusion of SMMEs in the informal sector in South Africa, using Blockchain technology to solve their challenge of access to loans. This was achieved through a combination of the Digital Inclusion Model and the Theory of Planned Behaviour. A literature review was conducted, from which propositions were derived to develop the model. Based on the literature, we found that lack of access to and affordability of smartphones and the internet, lack of digital skills, and poor internet connection may have a negative impact on digital inclusion. We conclude that pre-conditions such as digital infrastructure need to be in place for digital inclusion of SMMEs in the informal sector. Furthermore, SMMEs should be educated on Blockchain technology and its benefits. This has the potential to greatly impact their view of the technology, which will in turn improve adoption and therefore digital inclusion.

Keywords: Informal Sector · Blockchain · Small Medium and Micro Enterprises (SMMEs)

1 Introduction

There is a plethora of academic research and interest in the Fourth Industrial Revolution (4IR) and the technologies it brings to solve social and economic challenges in many countries. Despite the growing interest, it appears that these technologies are not directed

© ICST Institute for Computer Sciences, Social Informatics and Telecommunications Engineering 2023
Published by Springer Nature Switzerland AG 2023. All Rights Reserved
M. Masinde and A. Bagula (Eds.): AFRICATEK 2022, LNICST 503, pp. 95–110, 2023.
https://doi.org/10.1007/978-3-031-35883-8_7

towards the marginalized such as SMMEs in the informal sector in developing countries, who suffer from a myriad of socio-economic challenges that 4IR technologies have the potential to solve. This is perhaps due to the opinion of various researchers that suggests that the 4IR is incompatible with small businesses due to their underdeveloped capabilities, limitations of cost and personnel, business model, (Gumbi and Twinomurinzi 2020), technical skills and cognitive infrastructure (Adane 2018).

Nevertheless, this study aims to develop a model for the digital inclusion of SMMEs in the informal sector in South Africa, using Blockchain technology to solve their challenge of access to loans. Digital inclusion is about ensuring that everyone has access to and can benefit from digital technologies (Sharp 2022). In the context of this study, this means that for digital inclusion to take place, SMMEs must have access to Blockchain technology and its benefits. The benefits are various and include the opportunity to access loans, which various scholars have highlighted as the major challenge for SMMEs in the informal sector (Etim and Daramola 2020; Kelikume 2021; Tawodzera 2019; Wahome 2020; Aguera et al. 2020). Although used for various applications such as Bitcoin, Blockchain technology has the potential to solve the financial issues related to the lack of credit access in African countries (Mavilia and Pisani 2022), due to its immutability. With that said, there exists a possibility that these SMMEs may be excluded from the use and benefits of this technology due to issues such as affordability, informality and lack of skills.

In the literature, there exists a body of literature on Blockchain in SMEs, with a focus on various sectors such as ICT, manufacturing and agriculture (Molati et al. 2021; Mavilia and Pisani 2022; Saba 2021; Serumaga-Zake and van der Poll 2021), and transparency in the supply chain (Engström Roxendal and Westlund 2019). Furthermore, ICT-related innovations are said to be taking place in the informal sector, as highlighted by Kaplinsky and Kraemer-Mbula (2022), however, 4IR technologies such as Blockchain are receiving less attention, specifically in the context of the informal sector in South Africa.

To close this gap in the literature, this paper looks at how informal SMMEs can be included in the use and benefits of Blockchain technology. This is achieved by exploring the supply side as well as the Demand side (the SMMEs) of the technology through the Digital Inclusion Model and the Theory of Planned Behaviour. The aim of the study is to develop a model for the digital inclusion of informal SMMEs in South Africa, by determining the external factors that encourage or discourage SMMEs in the informal sector from using Blockchain Technology Apps/Platform as well as by examining the perception of Blockchain technology by SMMEs in the informal sector.

2   Literature Review

The Literature Review first gives a brief overview of the Informal Sector in South Africa, then discusses the sector's challenges (including access to loans) and then offers Blockchain as a solution.

2.1   A Brief Overview of the Informal Sector in South Africa

The informal sector is described by various scholars as the shadow economy or grey economy (Etim and Daramola 2020), where firms do not comply with business or labour regulations (Nguimkeu and Okou 2021). It consists of economic activities that are legal, but are not formalized, registered or even regulated and therefore not taxed by the Government (Etim and Daramola 2020; Nguimkeu and Okou 2021). These activities include retail trade (such as street vendors), construction, community & personal services (such as hairdressing), manufacturing, financial services and transport (Etim and Daramola 2020, Stats SA, 2022).

The importance of the informal sector cannot be over-emphasized. The sector contributes to employment and economic growth (Tawodzera 2019). It absorbs those retrenched from the formal sector (SEDA 2021) and provides an alternative form of employment to the unemployed (Mathibe et al. 2021). In most low-income countries, more than half of the population earns their living in the informal sector, even outside of Agriculture (Kaplinsky and Kraemer-Mbula 2022). In South Africa, statistics show that two-thirds of SMMEs (67%) operate in the informal sector, providing 13% of employment (SEDA 2021).

2.2   Challenges in the Informal Sector: Lack of Credit Access

There are countless challenges that small businesses face in the informal sector. These are operating challenges (such as lack of infrastructure to run the business, storage problems and lack of training), social challenges (such as crime/theft and confiscation of goods by police, lack of social protection) and economic challenges (such as lack of credit access and competition from large stores/supermarkets) (Etim and Daramola 2020; Tawodzera 2019).

As many as the challenges are, this study will focus on the lack of credit access. A number of scholars have listed the lack of credit access as a challenge for businesses in the informal sector (Etim and Daramola 2020; Kelikume 2021; Tawodzera 2019; Wahome 2020; Aguera et al. 2020). Tawodzera (2019) found that for food street vendors in Cape Town, only 2% were able to access capital from government schemes, denoting a challenge of access to finance from the government.

Similarly, access to loans is a challenge. Aguera et al. (2020) pointed out that the poor performance of smallholder farmers compared to large-holder farmers is primarily driven by their lack of credit access. Tawodzera (2019) explained that informal businesses find it difficult to access capital because banks rarely lend money to such businesses, mainly due to the disproportionately higher transaction costs of managing small amounts of money (Kelikume 2021), as well as risk considerations. Other scholars suggest that these SMMEs rarely meet the criteria set by financial institutions to access loans, such as collateral and information asymmetry (Mavilia and Pisani 2022; Vries 2019).

Information asymmetry in terms of credit stems from the fact that the borrower (SMME) usually knows more about their own creditworthiness than the lender (Bank) does (Ortlepp 2019). Therefore, the bank requires documents such as audited financial records to bridge the creditworthiness information gap. These financial records are expensive to produce and costly to maintain as alluded to by Kilekume (2021). However, without these, the bank is unable to assess the creditworthiness of the business, creating difficulties in accessing loans.

The lack of financial records in the informal sector was further explored by Jonck and Nwosu (2022). Jonck and Nwosu (2022) defined financial record keeping as documenting all financial transactions in a logical and systematic manner over a period of time. They found that the majority of small businesses in the informal sector do not practice record keeping, even though it is an effective financial tool that can assist with access to credit from financial institutions. Jonck and Nwosu (2022) cited a lack of knowledge and skills, focus on operations neglecting the administrative part of the business, and the avoidance of costs associated with financial record keeping as reasons why small businesses do not practice record keeping.

Based on the above, it is clear that a lack of recordkeeping leads to challenges in credit access for these small businesses. Access to credit is important in that it facilitates the entry of new companies into the market thereby increasing economic activity and reducing poverty (Kelikume 2021; Mavilia and Pisani 2022), which is one of South Africa's triple scourge.

The Fourth Industrial Revolution brings a myriad of choice technologies capable of solving most of South Africa's socio-economic challenges. These include AI, 3D printing, Blockchain, the Internet of things, machine learning and others. The challenge of recordkeeping could be possibly solved by two 4IR technologies namely Explainable AI and Blockchain. Explainable Artificial Intelligence (XAI) is put forth by recordkeeping professionals and scholars such as Bunn (2020), because of its characteristics of transparency which Bunn (2020) emphasizes is important in the context of recordkeeping. She exposes, however, the issue of trustworthiness, which in recordkeeping means the "accuracy" or "authenticity" of the record (pg. 149) while in AI the term means "respect for human autonomy" and "prevention of harm"(pg.149). Therefore, it would appear that using XAI as a solution for recordkeeping increases transparency but lacks in the area of the authenticity of the record. The authenticity of a record is important in the context of a loan application. Blockchain, on the other hand, is well known for its immutability. In other words, it solves the issue of the authenticity of a record in that once a transaction is added to a block, it cannot be changed. Therefore, for authentic financial records of SMMEs for the purpose of loan applications, Blockchain is put forth as a solution in this paper.

In the next section, Blockchain technology as a plausible solution to the challenge of record keeping and therefore to that of access to loans is further discussed in more detail. As a solution, Blockchain is in the R&D phase in South Africa, with the availability of Apps such as CreditRegster (Ortlepp 2019) and Block Records (Saba 2021) that run on Blockchain technology to solve credit records issues for the unbanked and for rural farmers. In Kenya, the Blockchain run Twigga Foods App is commercialized and is being utilised to keep track of transactions made by clients and uses these to determine their ability to access loans (Nalubega and Uwizeyimana 2019).

2.3 Blockchain Technology

Although used for various applications such as Bitcoin, Blockchain technology has the potential to solve a myriad of challenges which include:

a) financial issues related to lack of credit access in African countries: Mavilia and Pisani (2022) explain that because of Blockchain-based smart contracts, financial institutions such as Everex, are able to collect transaction data in real-time and thereby avail loans to borrowers in the agricultural sector in emerging economies.

b) elimination of intermediaries, such as auditors (Mavilia and Pisani 2022; Monrat et al. 2019). Auditing is meant to verify financial statements and render them true. Blockchain-based transactions or records do not need to be audited because of the immutability and decentralization associated with the technology.

Based on the above, Blockchain technology is explored as a solution to the credit access challenge of SMMEs in the informal sector in South Africa.

Blockchain is described as a distributed ledger that facilitates the process of recording transactions. It facilitates the reconciliation process of ledgers (Mavilia and Pisani 2022) and keeps a ledger of all transactions that occur in a particular Blockchain network for the purposes of traceability, thereby producing authentic transaction records (Saba 2021).

In its simplified form, Blockchain Technology is illustrated in Fig. 1.

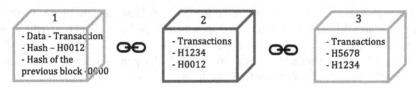

Fig. 1. Blockchain technology (Illustrated by the author from multiple online sources, hash numbers are made up for illustrative purposes)

As the name suggests, Blockchain is a chain of blocks, where each block represents a batch of transaction data using a ledger (Monrat et al. 2019). Each Block contains Data, a Hash and the Hash of the previous block. The data in the block is the details of the transactions, as you would record them in a ledger (such as the sender, receiver and transaction amount). The hash is the identification of the block and all its contents, similar to a fingerprint. In other words, it is the unique fingerprint of the block and it is calculated by an algorithm. In Fig. 1, Block 2's hash is H1234. The block also contains the hash of the previous block in the chain. As shown in Fig. 1, Block 3 contains the hash of the previous block (Block 2), which is H1234.

The most significant characteristic of Blockchain is its immutability. If one block in the chain is tampered with (in an effort to change the details of the transaction for example), the hash of the block and that of the previous block (and every other block in the chain) would be recalculated and changed. However, measures have been put in place such as consensus between the peers in the network, and proof of work (which this paper will not address in detail) to make it impossible to change the transaction data in the blocks. In this way, the transaction data in Blockchain is immutable and therefore reliable, resulting in authentic transaction records. Monrat et al. (2019) further explain that the immutability of Blockchain eliminates the need for intermediaries (such as auditors) to validate and verify the data.

The elimination of intermediaries such as auditors should make the production and maintenance of financial records significantly cheaper. In the informal sector, this means that SMMEs could use Blockchain to create financial records, which do not necessarily need to be audited, thereby reducing the costs significantly. As previously mentioned, there are a few Apps in the conceptual stage that have been created in South Africa.

One example is CreditRegister designed by Ortlep (2019) specifically for the financially excluded such as the unbanked and those living in informal settlements, basically those who do not necessarily have payment history records. The App runs on Blockchain technology, and it allows the loading of transactions by small businesses thereby creating a transaction history, which they give permission to external viewers such as banks to view their profile when they apply for a loan (Ortlepp 2019). Another Blockchain run application called Block Records was developed by Saba (2021). This Blockchain Mobile App enables the unbanked rural farmers in Qunu, Eastern Cape in South Africa, to have databases of their transaction records and make them publicly accessible to funders for financial assistance in their farming activities. In other words, there is a possibility that small businesses, even in the informal sector, can create a financial or credit history report, which should be sufficient as a financial record to access a loan because of its authenticity.

Although these Applications are in the Research & Development phase, there are more companies that have commercialized apps that run on Blockchain for credit access purposes. These include MyBank in South Africa, which uses Blockchain and AI to determine the creditworthiness of customers, while Twigga Foods in Kenya utilises Blockchain to keep track of transactions made my clients and uses these to determine their ability to access loans (Nalubega and Uwizeyimana 2019).

Therefore, it appears that the use of Blockchain to solve the financial record keeping issues in SMMEs in the informal sector is a plausible solution.

3 Theoretical Framework

In this section, the theoretical framework for this study is developed from two theories, which are then discussed in detail in the next sub-sections. The Digital Inclusion Model and the Theory of Planned Behaviour will be used. The proposed Conceptual Theoretical Framework is shown in Fig. 2:

The Digital Inclusion Model is illustrated in Fig. 2 (in blue). Although related to the internet and ICT technology, the Digital Inclusion Model was developed by Sharp (2022) after surveying digital inclusion literature. He found that the existing literature strongly focused on access to the technology exclusively, ignoring other factors that cause exclusion such as digital skills and affordability, especially in developing Sub-Saharan countries (Sharp 2022). He then developed the Digital inclusion model, in an attempt to create a multifaceted framework. The importance and relevance of this theory is that it separates the supply challenges from the demand side challenges of digital inclusion. It is suggested in the Gillwald et al. (2018) report that interventions that are only focused on the supply side, which fail to address the demand side challenges, will only perpetuate the existing digital inequalities. On that basis, it is of utmost importance in this study to holistically explore digital inclusion from both the supply and demand side, which is why this model is relevant.

In the Digital inclusion model, two key dimensions are put forth to consider on the demand side namely digital skills and affordability. In other words, this model states that a person is digitally excluded because they can't use technology and/or they can't afford it. Therein lies the limitation of this model. It is the author's opinion that there are more

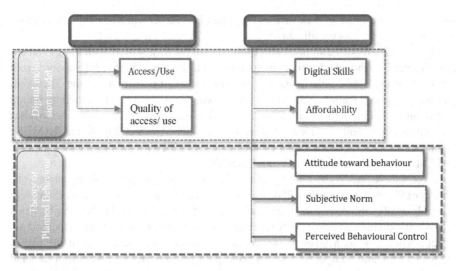

Fig. 2. Conceptual Theoretical Framework (Adapted from Sharp (2022) and Ajzen (1991))

dimensions to explore on the demand side, especially in the context of South Africa. Sharp (2022) admits that "of course, there are many other possible dimensions of digital inclusion" (pg. 6) in developing countries such as "lack of electricity, online safety/trust and content relevance"(pg. 6). In "The State of ICT in South Africa" conducted by Research ICT Africa (Gillwald et al. 2018), it is pointed out that South Africans are digitally excluded because of various issues such as locational inequalities, income levels and education levels. What is interesting about the report is that in studying the demand side, Gillwald et al. (2018) first identify those aspects that generally affect the population, and then move to those that affect the individual. The author borrows this perspective in this paper. In other words, she looks at the demand side from two lenses: 1. The general population aspects of exclusion (skills and affordability) and 2. Aspects on an individual level. For this reason, it is envisaged that a behavioural model such as the Theory of Planned Behavior (TBP) is suitable to complement the above Digital Inclusion model. TBP has a specific focus on the individual, on their participation in and perception of behaviour, which Sharp's (2022) model lacks. It is therefore proposed that Sharp's (2022) model be complemented by the Theory of Planned Behaviour.

There are various other behavioural theories, especially in technology (which is the focus of this study) that can explain the demand side. These are generally referred to as Technology Accepted models. Li (2010) conducted a critical review of Technology Acceptances literature. She found that there is a wide variety and number of these models such as the Technology Acceptance Model (TAM) (Davis 1989), TAM2 (Venkatesh and Davis 2000), the Unified Theory of Acceptance and Use of Technology (UTAUT) (Venkatesh et al. 2003) and the Motivational Model (Davis and Warshaw 1992). However, a critical review showed that these models have consistently failed to predict as they purported to in many empirical studies, delivering inconsistent results (Li 2010). For example, concerning the construct Social/ Subjective Norm, she found that some studies such as Karahanna et al. (1999) reported empirical evidence to prove the construct to be significant, while other studies such as Chau and Hu (2002) reported evidence to prove the construct to be non-significant.

Ajzen (2020) reported similar in his evaluation of the widely used Technology Acceptance Model. The model borrows constructs from the Theory of Planned Behavior. Ajzen (2020) adds that TAM fails to include certain important constructs of the Theory of Planned Behaviour namely Attitude and Perceived Behavioural Control, thereby failing to take into account factors that holistically predict behaviour. He explains that this has resulted in subsequent extended versions of the model (Ajzen 2020) such as TAM2 by Venkatesh and Davis (2000). In her critical review, Li (2020) found the extended models of TAM to be inadequate in predicting behavior as well.

It is for these reasons that the original theory these models are based on, namely The Theory of Planned Behaviour, will be used for this study to understand (comprehensively and holistically) the response to and behaviour of informal SMMEs in South Africa towards Blockchain technology. It is important to understand the SMMEs' perception of the technology, as a positive perception can ensure their inclusion in the use of the technology and a negative one can point policymakers in the direction of demand stimulation.

The proposed conceptual framework in Fig. 2 will be used to understand the supply side and demand side of digital inclusion as discussed next.

3.1 Supply Side of Digital Inclusion

3.1.1 Access/use

Sharp (2022) explained that this construct determines whether a person has access to or uses a technology. Lack of access to Blockchain technology can exclude informal SMME from its use and benefits. However, it must be stated here that for a business to access a Blockchain Application such as CreditRegister or Block Report, they must first have access to the internet, through a smart device such as a smartphone.

Gillwald et al. (2018) showed that 53% of South Africans have access to the internet. This suggests that access to the internet is only accessible to half the country. However, even with these challenges, some scholars found that lack of access to the internet is not necessarily a hindrance to using technology. Mabulele (2020) indicated that although there are barriers to gaining access to technology, such as infrastructure and internet connection, there is generally a positive attitude from SMME owners about access to technology. In other words, although access and connection to the internet may be a challenge, SMME owners have indicated that they have access to the technology tools they need to run their businesses. On the contrary, other scholars found a positive relationship between the internet and technology. In their study of e-commerce adoption by SMEs, Twi-Brempong et al. (2019) explained that the positive relationship is because, by definition, commercial activities are carried out online. The internet is necessary to download Blockchain Applications such as MyBank and to load receipts onto CreditRegister. The use of Blockchain-enabled Apps will in turn improve record keeping and therefore increased chances of accessing a loan. Thus, we state the following proposition:

P1a: Access to the internet increases the digital inclusion of SMMEs in the informal sector, resulting in increased chances of access to a loan.

Sharp (2022) further cited that access to a device is the reason why many in Africa do not use the technology. It appears from the literature that cellphones are important to SMMEs in running their businesses. Thabela et al. (2019) showed that most SMME owners in rural areas use cellphones as their primary ICT to access information. For a tailor, using WhatsApp enables them to get measurements from their client (Thabela et al. 2019). For a farmer, checking the prices of products similar to theirs helps them with a pricing strategy for their own products (Bhattacharya 2019). However, advanced digital technologies such as Blockchain App require a smartphone. Aguera et al. (2020) pointed out that although 85% of South Africans own cellphones, only 47% own smartphones. Therefore, it is possible that in the South African context, SMME owners do not necessarily have access to smartphones for various reasons including cost. Thus, we state the following proposition:

P1b: Access to a smartphone increases the digital inclusion of SMMEs in the informal sector, resulting in increased chances of access to a loan.

3.1.2 Quality of Access/Use

In his model, Sharp (2022) explains that the technical quality of the connection to the technology will determine potential use. He found that in developing countries, 2G mobile network is still in use even though it only offers limited speeds of less than 256 kbps (0.2 Mbps). It must be noted that although this is the case in other developing countries, it is not so in South Africa. In South Africa, the average speed is 4.36 Mbps, even though the country ranks 80th out of 189 in terms of download speeds in the world with an average download speed of 10 Mbps (Gillwald et al. 2018).

In using high digital technologies such as Blockchain, good quality access to the internet is important and may encourage the use thereof. The literature reports that poor internet connectivity acts as a barrier to technology adoption by SMMEs (Fortuin 2021). Twi-Brempong et al. (2019) also found that there was discouragement among Ghanaian SMEs to adopting e-commerce because of the poor quality and slow speed of available internet. Therefore, it appears that the poor quality of available internet discourages the use of technology amongst SMEs. In that regard, we state the following proposition:

P2: Poor internet connection decreases the digital inclusion of SMMEs in the informal sector, resulting in decreased chances of access to a loan.

3.2 Demand Side of Digital Inclusion

To ensure the participation of SMMEs in the use of Blockchain Technology, it is imperative that they have a positive perception of the technology. According to Ajzen (2020), understanding the responses of people toward emerging technologies will lead to the implementation of effective interventions to facilitate behavioural change. In other words, understanding the perception and response of SMMEs to Blockchain technology will lead to relevant and effective interventions to facilitate the use of Blockchain in the informal sector.

This section will address this through different constructs from the Digital Inclusion Model (skill and affordability) and the Theory of Planned Behaviour (Attitude, Social Norm and Perceived Behavioural Control).

3.2.1 Digital Skill

Skill is defined as the competency to use a technology (Farjona et al., 2019). One of the obstacles to using technology is skills (Bhattacharya 2019). Vrontis et al. (2022) also reported skills deficiency as a barrier to technology adoption. According to Thabela et al. (2019), digital skills lack among SMME owners in the Western Cape. Thabela et al. (2019) discovered that SME owners do not acquire the digital skills needed for their business because making money takes precedence. On the contrary, Fortuin (2021) found that SMMEs in the informal sector in Cape Town have the digital skills necessary to operate mobile cloud financial accounting tools, with only 14% reporting their lack of digital skills as an impediment to using the technology. Nevertheless, she recommends more digital skills training for these SMMEs. For an SMME owner to use a Blockchain Technology App or Platform, it is necessary that they have the necessary skills for such. A closer look at the user flow diagram of the CreditRegister App reveals that a business owner would need to be able to upload documents such as receipts and invoices onto the App, and that they would need to have the skills necessary to allow "viewing" of their profile and credit history by a bank for example (Ortlepp 2019). Although the App is simplified and user-friendly, it appears that some digital skills are necessary. Therefore, we state the following proposition:

P3: Lack of digital skills decreases the digital inclusion of SMMEs in the informal sector, resulting in decreased chances of access to a loan.

3.2.2 Affordability

Affordability could act as a factor of exclusion to the use of technology. One of the obstacles cited by Bhattacharya (2019) to the use of technology in SMMEs in the informal economy is the lack of capital. Thabela et al. (2019) found that SMMEs in rural areas were not keen on using technology because of its cost. The SMME owners explained that Yoco for example (a point-of-sale card machine) was still too expensive for them, as it costs R3000 with activation fees of R600 (Thabela et al. 2019). Therefore, this discourages and excludes SMMEs from using the technology.

Nevertheless, Ortlepp (2019) described the cost of the Blockchain App CreditRegister as affordable, including the cost of adding documents and the costs of loading the information onto a Block in Blockchain. He warned that although it is cheap to do so, these expenses are incurred every time a transaction is loaded which could make the process expensive, although not prohibitively costly (Ortlepp 2019). However, since the platform is a prototype, cheaper Blockchain with less flexibility could be used to make the use of the platform cheaper. It is envisaged that if using the App is affordable to SMMEs, then they are more likely to use it.

In the literature, affordability is not only perceived from the point of view of the technology itself. The cost of devices to access technology is also shown to be a barrier to digital inclusion. Gillwald et al. (2018) revealed that 36% of South Africans cited the cost of smart devices as the primary reason they are not online. Statistics further show that 15% of South Africans reported the internet to be too expensive while 47% said data limited their use of technology (Gillwald et al. 2018). This clearly indicates that the lack of affordability of devices, internet and data are causing digital exclusion. Therefore, we state the following proposition:

P4: Lack of affordability of technology (smartphone and internet) decreases the digital inclusion of SMMEs in the informal sector, resulting in decreased chances of access to a loan.

3.2.3 Attitude Towards the Use of Blockchain Technology

According to the Theory of Planned Behaviour, attitude refers to the degree to which a person has a favourable or unfavourable evaluation of a behaviour (Ajzen 1991). The more favourable the attitude, the stronger the intention to perform a behaviour (Ajzen 1991). In this study, this means that the more favourable the attitude toward the use of Blockchain technology, the stronger the intention to use it.

Vrontis et al. (2022) explain attitude with regard to entrepreneurship as an important factor that influences desirability which in turn influence intention. They found that the entrepreneurs' start-up attitude significantly and positively affects their intentions. In other studies, Farjona et al. (2019) found that teachers who had a positive attitude toward teaching technology were more likely to implement it in the classroom. For Blockchain technology, it is envisaged that a favourable attitude to the technology will increase the chances of its use. Therefore, according to the Theory of Planned Behaviour, we state the following proposition:

P5a: A favourable attitude toward Blockchain technology increases the digital inclusion of SMMEs in the informal sector, resulting in increased chances of access to a loan.

Furthermore, Ajzen (2020) adds that the attitude toward a behaviour is a function of a belief towards the behaviour's consequences. In other words, it is a belief that performing the behaviour will lead to a certain outcome or experience. In the literature, Bhattacharya (2019) points out that the issue with using technology is not only in its adoption but also in the purpose of adoption. In other words, what will the adoption of the technology help with, in the business? Based on the above, the SMME owner must perceive the usefulness or purpose of the technology in his business. Fortuin (2021) reported that 28% of the informal SMMEs in her sample indicated that they do not use financial accounting mobile cloud technologies because they do not find it relevant to their business. Some based the irrelevance on the point that the book (black journal) system satisfies their needs and others, to the point that their businesses were illegal, and they do not want to record their activities (Fortuin 2021). Nevertheless, for SMMEs who would like to access loans by proving accurate and reliable credit history and transactions, Blockchain seems viable. In this study, if the SMME believes that using Blockchain Technology will lead to access to loans, then they are more likely to use it. Therefore, according to the Theory of Planned Behaviour, we state the following proposition:

P5b: A positive perception of the purpose of Blockchain technology increases the digital inclusion of SMMEs in the informal sector, resulting in increased chances of access to a loan.

3.2.4 Subjective (Social) Norm

According to the Theory of Planned Behavior, Subjective Norm refers to the perceived social pressure to perform or not to perform the behavior in question (Ajzen 1991). It is the belief that a given referent group of people approve or disapprove of performing the behavior as well as the belief that the group itself performs or does not perform the behavior (Ajzen 2020). Put differently, it assesses an individual's behaviour in response to opinions or support from peers (Vrontis et al. 2022). The theory states that the more favourable the subjective norm with respect to the behaviour, the stronger should be an individual's intention to perform the behaviour under consideration (Ajzen 1991). In this study, this means that SMME owner's use of Blockchain technology Apps or Platform depends on the social pressure from their peers. The owner is more likely to use the technology if he perceives that other SMMEs at large approve of the technology and even use it themselves. Consistent with the Theory of Planned behaviour, Vrontis et al. (2022) found that subjective norms positively and significantly impacted on the entrepreneur's start-up intentions. The findings of other scholars are also in line with the Theory of Planned behaviour and suggest that subjective norms have a positive impact on technology adoption (Saeedi et al. 2020; Fauzi et al. 2021). Therefore, we state the following proposition:

P6: A positive social norm increases the digital inclusion of SMMEs in the informal sector, resulting in increased chances of access to a loan.

3.2.5 Perceived Behavioural Control

In the Theory of Planned Behaviour, perceived behavioural control refers to the perceived ease or difficulty of performing a behaviour (Ajzen 1991). This construct is based on the belief that facilitating or impeding factors are present such as skill, knowledge, money, time and so on (Ajzen 2020). The theory states that the greater the perceived behavioural control, the stronger the individual's intention to perform the behaviour under consideration (Ajzen 1991). In this study, this means that for an SMME to use Blockchain technology, the owner must perceive that it will be easy to do to so and that facilitating factors such as skill, money and time are available. Digital skills and Affordability are covered in this paper in Sects. 3.2.1 and 3.2.2 respectively. Therefore, in this subsection, only available time will be considered.

According to Muteti et al. (2018) and Jonck and Nwosu (2022), one of the main justifications for not keeping financial records is time management. Muteti et al. (2018) explained that SMEs in the informal sector lack time to do financial record keeping as the business goal of selling products takes precedence. However, there are SMMEs that keep a record using traditional methods such as writing in a book, but these also take time. Fortuin's (2021) findings reveal that 43% of her sample of SMMEs in the informal sector in Cape Town recorded their transactions in a book, while 33% said they kept a mental note. These methods are not accurate or reliable for the purpose of accessing a loan from a bank. She recommended the use of mobile cloud accounting tools, because 50% of her respondents who use it, pointed out that "it saves time that would have been incurred if traditional methods of recording financial transactions were used" (Fortuin 2021).

In that regard, Ortlepp (2019) stated that on his Blockchain-enabled prototype, CreditRegister, transactions take a few seconds to be added onto a block in Blockchain. However, the point is not to process the transaction but to keep a record of it after it has happened, as the business will collect the payment in cash most of the time, then upload the necessary documents (invoice or receipt) onto the Credit Register Platform. This is believed to be a fair amount of time necessary to record transactions and would be more accurate and reliable than recording in a book or keeping a mental note.

Therefore, it is envisaged that if the SMME owner perceives that using Blockchain technology will not take time from his business goals of selling products, then he is more likely to use the technology. On that basis, we state the following proposition:

P7:A positive perceived behavioural control increases the digital inclusion of SMMEs in the informal sector, resulting in increased chances of access to a loan.

4   Conceptual Model

With the input from the preceding sections, the conceptual model in Fig. 3 is proposed.

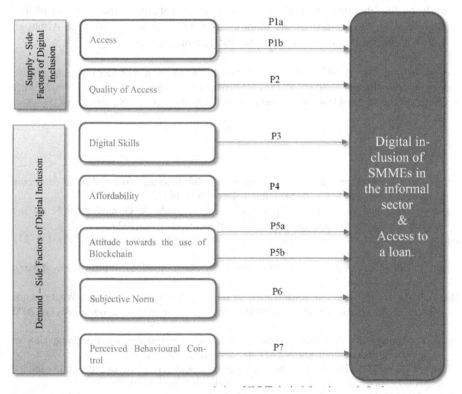

Fig. 3. Conceptual Model of The Digital Inclusion of SMMEs in the informal sector in South Africa

5 Conclusion, Limitations and Contribution of Study

It is evident from the framework that there are factors that may have a possible negative impact on the digital inclusion of informal SMMEs. These factors are access and affordability of smartphones and the internet, digital skills and poor internet connection. These are largely on the supply side of Blockchain technology. It is therefore the conclusion of this study that there are preconditions that exist in South Africa, that need to be in place for digital inclusion to take place, for example, the digital infrastructure that can improve internet access and speed, specifically 5G connectivity infrastructure. This appears to be well underway in South Africa, as the Independent Communications Authority of South Africa (ICASA) completed the radio frequency auction in March 2022, which will assist many South African individuals and businesses to access the internet, faster. We believe this will improve the digital inclusion of informal SMMEs.

Digital skills and attitudes toward technology are largely demand-side based. In this regard, it is the conclusion of this study that SMMEs should be educated on Blockchain technology and its benefits. This has the potential to greatly impact their view of the technology, which will in turn improve adoption and therefore digital inclusion.

As with all research, there are limitations to this study. The propositions were based entirely on the literature. Nevertheless, our study contributes to the narrative of 4IR technologies, in the context of the marginalized informal sector SMMEs. Although based on the literature, it paves the way for future empirical testing.

Acknowledgements. Thanks to the DSI/NRF/Newton Fund Trilateral Chair in Transformative Innovation, the 4IR and Sustainable Development for its support - this work has been fully supported by the National Research Foundation of South Africa (Grant Number: 118873).

References

Adane, M.: Cloud computing adoption: Strategies for Sub-Saharan Africa SMEs for enhancing competitiveness. Afr. J. Sci. Technol. Innov. Dev. **10**(2), 197–207 (2018)

Aguera, P., Berglund, N., Chinembiri, T., Comninos, A., Gillwald, A., Govan-Vassen, N.: Paving the way towards digitalising agriculture in South Africa, pp.1–42 (2020)

Ajzen, I.: The theory of planned behavior. Organ. Behav. Hum. Decis. Process. **50**(2), 179–211 (1991)

Ajzen, I.: The theory of planned behavior: frequently asked questions. Human Behav. Emerg. Technol. **2**(4), 314–324 (2020)

Bhattacharya, R.: ICT solutions for the informal sector in developing economies: What can one expect? The Electronic Journal of Information Systems in Developing Countries **85**(3), 12075 (2019)

Bunn, J.: Working in contexts for which transparency is important: a recordkeeping view of explainable artificial intelligence (XAI). Rec. Manag. J. **30**(2), 143–153 (2020)

Chau, P.Y.K., Hu, P.J.: investigating healthcare professionals' decisions to accept telemedicine technology: an empirical test of competing theories. Inf. Manag. **39**, 297–311 (2002)

Davis, F.D.: Perceived usefulness, perceived ease of use, and user acceptance of information technology. MIS Q. **13**(3), 319–339 (1989)

Davis, F.D., Warshaw, P.R.: Extrinsic and Intrinsic Motivation to Use Computers in the Workplace. J. Appl. Soc. Psychol. **22**(14), 1111–1132 (1992)

Engström Roxendal, P., Westlund, S.: Increasing transparency in the supply chain with blockchain technology: acase study of small and medium sized South African wine producers. Industrial Engineering and Management Master's Thesis. Karlstad Business School (2019)

Etim, E., Daramola, O.: The informal sector and economic growth of South Africa and Nigeria: a comparative systematic review. J, Open Innov. Technol. Mark. Complex. 6(4), 134 (2020)

Fauzi, R.U.A., Juliana, J., Djakasaputra, A., Pramono, R., Antonio, F., Purwanto, A.: The role of attitude, subjective norms and usefullnes on e-commerce intention and behavior. Acad. J. Digit. Economics and Stabil. 11, 55–72 (2021)

Fortuin, A.: The effects of mobile cloud accounting on the operations of small, medium and micro-enterprises in selected Cape Town markets. Doctoral dissertation Cape Peninsula University of Technology (2021)

Gillwald, A., Mothobi, O., Rademan, B.: The state of ICT in South Africa. Policy Paper no. 5, Series 5: After Access State of ICT in South Africa. (2018). https://researchictafrica.net/after-access-south-africa-stateof-ict-2017-south-africa-report_04. Accessed 21 May 2022

Gumbi, L., Twinomurinzi, H.: SMME readiness for smart manufacturing (4IR) adoption: a systematic review. In: Hattingh, M., Matthee, M., Smuts, H., Pappas, I., Dwivedi, Y.K., Mäntymäki, M. (eds.) Responsible Design, Implementation and Use of Information and Communication Technology. LNCS, vol. 12066, pp. 41–54. Springer, Cham (2020). https://doi.org/10.1007/978-3-030-44999-5_4

Jonck, P., Nwosu, L.: The influence of demographic variables on financial record-keeping in small- and medium-sized enterprises in the South African informal sector. J. Econ. Financ. Sci. 15(1), 9 (2022)

Kaplinsky, R., KraemerMbula, E.: Innovation and uneven development: the challenge for low-and middle-income economies. Res. Policy 51(2), 104394 (2022)

Karahanna, E., Straub, D.W., Chervany, N.L.: Information technology adoption across time: a cross-sectional comparison of pre-adoption and post-adoption beliefs. MIS Q. 23(2), 183–213 (1999)

Kelikume, I.: Digital financial inclusion, informal economy and poverty reduction in Africa. J. Enterp. Commun. People Places Global Econ. 15(4), 626–640 (2021)

Li, L.: A critical review of technology acceptance literature. Referred Research Paper, 4 (2010)

Mabulele, R.: Assessing technological challenges in black-owned SMMEs in selected provinces in South Africa. Doctoral dissertation, North-West University South Africa (2020)

Mathibe, M., Mochenje, T., Masonta, M.T.: assessing the effectiveness of 4ir strategy on South African township economy: smart township perspective. In: MBALI Conference 2021, p. 103 (2021)

Mavilia, R., Pisani, R.: Blockchain for agricultural sector: the case of South Africa. Afr. J. Sci. Technol. Innov. Dev. 14(3), 845–851 (2022)

Molati, K., Ilorah, A.I., Moeti, M.N.: Determinant Factors Influencing the Adoption of Blockchain Across SMEs in South Africa. In: 15th International Conference on Advanced Technologies, Systems and Services in Telecommunications, Telsiks, pp. 265–269. IEEE (2021)

Monrat, A.A., Schelén, O., Andersson, K.: A survey of blockchain from the perspectives of applications, challenges, and opportunities. IEEE Access 7, 117134–117151 (2019)

Muteti, N., Namusonge, M., Nzomo, D.: Accounting systems for records keeping practices for small enterprise development in Makueni county. Kenya. Open J. Account. 7, 181–190 (2018)

Nalubega, T., Uwizeyimana, D.E.: Public sector monitoring and evaluation in the Fourth industrial revolution: implications for Africa. Africa's Publ. Serv. Deliv. Perform. Rev. 7(1), 1–12 (2019)

Nguimkeu, P., Okou, C.: Leveraging digital technologies to boost productivity in the informal sector in Sub-Saharan Africa. Rev. Policy Res. 38(6), 707–731 (2021)

Ortlepp, B.: A Feasibility Study on Using the Blockchain to Build a Credit Register for Individuals Who Do Not Have Access to Traditional Credit Scores. Master's thesis, Faculty of Commerce (2019)

Saba, M.: A Mobile Blockchain-based Application for Record-Keeping in Branchless Banking Services for Farmers in Qunu. Rhodes University, Bachelor of Science (Honours) (2021)

Saeedi, S.A.W., Sharifuddin, J., Seng, K.W.K.: Intention on Adoption of Industry 4.0 Technology Among small and medium enterprises. Int. J. Sci. Technol. Res. **9**(2) (2020)

SerumagaZake, J.M., van der Poll, J.A.: Addressing the impact of fourth industrial revolution on South African manufacturing small and medium enterprises (SMEs). Sustainability **13**(21), 11703 (2021)

Sharp, M.: Revisiting digital inclusion: a survey of theory, measurement and recent research, https://doi.org/10.35489/BSG-DP-WP_2022/04. Accessed 01 June 2022

Small Enterprise Development Agency.: SMME Quarterly Update 1st Quarter (2021), www.seda.org.za. Last accessed 2022/06/13

StatsSA, www.statssa.co.za (2022), last accessed 2022/06/13

Tawodzera, G.: Food vending and the urban informal sector in Cape Town, South Africa. Waterloo, Ontario. Hungry Cities Partnership Discussion Paper (23). (2019)

Thabela, T., Kabanda, S., Chigona, W., Villo, Z.: Challenges of using ICTs for SMMEs in rural areas. In: Digital Innovation and Transformation Conference: Digital Skills 2019, p. 1 (2019)

TwiBrempong, C., et al.: The impact of access to electricity on e-commerce adoption in Ghanaian SMEs, an empirical analysis. Open J. Bus. Manage. **8**(01), 245 (2019)

Venkatesh, V., Davis, F.D.: A theoretical extension of the technology acceptance model: four longitudinal field studies. Manage. Sci. **46**(2), 186–204 (2000)

Venkatesh, V., Morris, M., Davis, G.B., Davis, F.D.: User acceptance of information technology: toward a unified view. MIS Q. **27**(3), 425–478 (2003)

Vries, M.: Crowdfunding for Start-up Financing in Kenya, South Africa and Uganda. Bachelor thesis, University of Twente, Netherlands (2019)

Vrontis, D., Chaudhuri, R., Chatterjee, S.: Adoption of digital technologies by SMEs for sustainability and value creation: moderating role of entrepreneurial orientation. Sustainability **14**(13), 7949 (2022)

Wahome, E.: Use of block Chain in the Informal distributed manufacturing industry in Kenya. Doctoral dissertation, University of Nairobi (2020)

Key 4IR Baseline Architectures

Multiple Mobile Robotic Formation Control Based on Differential Flatness

Lintle Tsiu$^{(\boxtimes)}$ and Elisha Didam Markus

Central University of Technology, Freestate, South Africa
lintletsiu@gmail.com, emarkus@cut.ac.za

Abstract. There are numerous applications whereby multi-robot cooperative systems are more useful than using a single robot. However, for a cooperative system to implement tasks accurately, an effective formation controller is essential. This paper presents a formation control method that is based on Differential Flatness theory to improve coordination control of a model-based cooperative multiple mobile robotic system. The Differential Flatness characterisation of the team robots allows for the linearization of the system to a stable linear equivalent. Also, the Flatness theory has the advantage of simplifying the trajectory planning task because nonlinear differential equations can be converted to algebraic equation, hence there is no need to integrate robot model differential equations. Each robot is represented by a reduced number of variables which greatly reduces the computational cost especially when dealing with multiple robots that can otherwise entail solving large robotic model differential equations. Simulations using a formation of three differentially driven mobile robots in a leader-follower formation, is used to validate the cooperative formation controller proposed in this paper.

Keywords: Formation control · cooperative control · Differential flatness · consensus control · synchronization control · differentially driven mobile robot

1 Introduction

Research on multiple robot formations has recently garnered a great deal of attention among robotics researchers [1–17]. This is because this type of system is more flexible, adaptable to unfamiliar environments, and robust than a single robot. Formation control applications include various cooperative tasks such as exploration [3], mining support [4], agriculture [5], to name a few. Several approaches to mobile robot formation control have been proposed in literature. These control approaches can be conceptually categorized into four categories, namely: cooperation, consensus synchronization, and coordination control.

In cooperative control, robots share information so that a common objective can be achieved. Potential application areas of this formation control include search and rescue, surveillance, and explorations. In a cooperative group, individual robots might have limited sensing, processing, and communication capabilities. It is for this reason that the study in [6] used a probabilistic localization and control method that considers the

© ICST Institute for Computer Sciences, Social Informatics and Telecommunications Engineering 2023
Published by Springer Nature Switzerland AG 2023. All Rights Reserved
M. Masinde and A. Bagula (Eds.): AFRICATEK 2022, LNICST 503, pp. 113–128, 2023.
https://doi.org/10.1007/978-3-031-35883-8_8

motion and sensing capabilities of individual robots. The method allowed for robots to alter their sensing topologies when needed. Additionally, to avoid communication break-down between robots, the author in [7, 8] minimizes the frequency of the cooperative robots' communication and use minimal vision-based data. This enables the multi-robot formations to navigate safely in cluttered environments.

Consensus control, on the other hand, involves robots constantly altering their data so that they all come to the same decision. The possibility of consensus never being reached is high, however, when there are time delays, miscommunications, and noise. The study by [9] applied frequency domain analysis to convert the characteristic system equations into quadratic polynomials with pure imaginary eigenvalues. This helped the system to gain the maximum stability state during time delays and noise disturbances. Similarly, [10] Converged the individual information of a robot with the information of its neighbours despite communication delays. Also, the authors in [11, 12] used Lyapunov-based controller while [13] used a knowledge-oriented task and motion planning method. These enabled the robotic system to create a feasible obstacle free path.

Alternatively, synchronization control is used in several studies. In this approach each robot follows a desired trajectory while keeping a synchronized formation two of its neighbouring. Synchronous formation control is generally decentralized. The author in [14] developed a nonlinear synchronization controller for nonholonomic unicycle robots that allowed for directed and undirected information flow between the robots. Thus, robustness is achieved despite disturbances. Alternatively, in [15], geometric path following was developed with Lyapunov theory, backstepping, and helmsman behaviours applied to each controlled path. Unlike other approaches synchronous formation control has a simpler control structure with elevated motion coordination and robustness.

Finally, coordination control entails maintenance of certain kinematic relationship between team robots. It is usually centralized. The authors in [16, 17] increased the coordination of the multi-AUV. This was achieved by designed an integrated algorithm which merges the homodromous degree, district-difference degree, and the dispersion degree into the potential field function of the surface-water environment. In this approach, no pre-learning procedure was required and the multi-AUV coordination was increased, thereby decreasing the computational cost.

This paper aims to improve coordination control of cooperative multiple mobile robotic system using differential flatness theory. The robotic formation is made up of three differentially driven mobile robots with similar dynamics. One robot is designated as a leader and the other two are followers. Using the kinematic models of the robots, the robot differential flatness characterization is executed to exploit flatness properties in order to design a flatness-based control algorithm for trajectories generation and tracking.

Moreover, literature indicates that there are several problems associated with con-trolling multi-robotic systems, including high energy consumption [16, 17], uncertainty in observing robot workspaces [9], and resolution of communication protocols [6–8]. Also, the larger the system the more the dynamics of the coupled robotic network, thus its control entail solving large robotic model differential equations which are almost intractable to solve. Therefore, the main contribution of this paper is to significantly reduce the computational cost involved in dealing with multiple robotic systems by representing the cooperative system with flat outputs and their derivatives up to a certain order instead of its system state variables. Also, to simplify the trajectory generation problem by using simple polynomials instead of integrating robot model differential equations. As a result, the proposed method therefore greatly simplifies the cooperative formation control.

This paper is sectioned as follows: Sect. 2 represent the mathematical of the cooperative multi-robotic system and the robots that make up the cooperative system. The concept of differential flatness is introduced, and a flatness analysis of a differential drive robot is presented in Sect. 3. Section 4 presents differential flatness-based trajectory generation and design of a flatness controller for trajectory tracking and for formation control. Also, the simulation tests results on effectiveness of the formation controllers designed in the previous section is presented in Sect. 5. Finally, Sect. 6 give some concluding remarks.

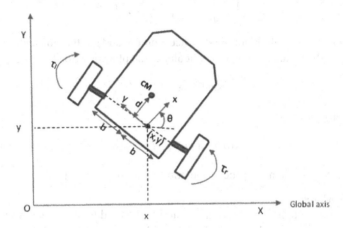

Fig. 1. Differentially driven wheeled mobile robot (DDWMR).

2   System Description

The cooperative multi-robotic system is homogeneous. That is, it is made up of a group of differentially driven wheeled mobile robots of similar physical characteristics. The differentially driven wheeled mobile robot shown in Fig. 1 is made up of two drive wheels attached on one axis, and each wheel is able to be independently driven forward or backward. Also, the robot is non-holonomic, which basically means it has constraints that cause a reduction in the local mobility of the robot.

The robot configuration is represented by the generalised coordinates $q \, [x \, y \, \theta]^T$ where (x, y) is the position and θ is the heading orientation expressed in cartesian coordinate system of inertial frame. The wheels with radii r are each positioned at a distance b from the centre of the robot chassis. The Cartesian coordinates $(x \, y)$ are located at a distance d from and the centre of mass (CM). In the kinematic model the system inputs are the wheel velocities $\dot{\theta}_r$ and $\dot{\theta}_l$, while in the dynamic model they are the driving motor torques τ_r and τ_l. The subscript r and l represent quantities of right and left wheels respectively.

A. Kinematic Model

The kinematics of the WMR including the nonholonomic constraints is described in [18] as:

$$\dot{q} = \begin{bmatrix} \dot{x} \\ \dot{y} \\ \dot{\theta} \end{bmatrix} = \begin{bmatrix} \cos\theta & 0 \\ \sin\theta & 0 \\ 0 & 1 \end{bmatrix} \begin{bmatrix} v \\ \omega \end{bmatrix} = S(q)\bar{v}(t) \tag{1}$$

Where v is the forward (linear) velocity and ω is the angular velocity. Furthermore, the equivalent wheel inputs are then given by:

$$\begin{bmatrix} \dot{\theta}_r \\ \dot{\theta}_l \end{bmatrix} = \frac{1}{r}\begin{bmatrix} 1 & b \\ 1 & -b \end{bmatrix}\begin{bmatrix} v \\ \omega \end{bmatrix} \tag{2}$$

Because robot is nonholonomic, its wheels do not slide to the sides, that is velocity component for the contact point perpendicular to the plane is zero. This is expressed as:

$$\dot{x}\sin\theta - \dot{y}\cos\theta = 0$$

Or in matrix form:

$$A(q) = [\sin\theta, -\cos\theta, 0] \tag{3}$$

Note that $S(q)$ is the null space of the non-holonomic constraint A(q).

B. Dynamic Model

Euler-Lagrange dynamic equations of motion are used to obtain the dynamic equations of the mobile robot However, friction and viscous forces will be ignored. The dynamic model is therefore given as:

$$M(q)\ddot{q} + V(q,\dot{q})\dot{q} = E(q)\tau - A^T(q)\lambda \tag{4}$$

Or can also be written as:

$$\begin{bmatrix} m_0 & 0 & -dm_0\sin\theta \\ 0 & m_0 & dm_0\cos\theta \\ -dm_0\sin\theta & dm_0\cos\theta & d^2m_0 + I_0 \end{bmatrix}\begin{bmatrix} \ddot{x} \\ \ddot{y} \\ \ddot{\theta} \end{bmatrix}$$

$$+ \begin{bmatrix} 0 & 0 & -dm_0\dot{\theta}\cos\theta \\ 0 & 0 & -dm_0\dot{\theta}\sin\theta \\ 0 & 0 & 0 \end{bmatrix} + \begin{bmatrix} 0 & 0 & -dm_0\dot{\theta}\cos\theta \\ 0 & 0 & -dm_0\dot{\theta}\sin\theta \\ 0 & 0 & 0 \end{bmatrix}\begin{bmatrix} \dot{x} \\ \dot{y} \\ \dot{\theta} \end{bmatrix}$$

$$= \frac{1}{r}\begin{bmatrix} \cos\theta & \cos\theta \\ \sin\theta & \sin\theta \\ b & -b \end{bmatrix}\begin{bmatrix} \tau_r \\ \tau_l \end{bmatrix} - \begin{bmatrix} \sin\theta \\ -\cos\theta \\ 0 \end{bmatrix}^T\begin{bmatrix} \lambda_1 \\ \lambda_2 \\ \lambda_3 \end{bmatrix}$$

For a mobile robot with n degree-of-freedom (DOF) that is subjected to m constraints and has p inputs the generalized coordinates are $q(t) \in \mathbb{R}^{n \times 1}$ and $M(q) \in \mathbb{R}^{n \times n}$ is the symmetric positive-definite inertia matrix. $V(q, \dot{q}) \in \mathbb{R}^{n \times n}$ is the centripetal and Coriolis force matrix, $E(q) \in \mathbb{R}^{n \times p}$ is the actuation matrix, $\tau \in \mathbb{R}^{p \times 1}$ is the input vector, $A^T(q) \in \mathbb{R}^{m \times n}$ is the kinematic constraint matrix associated with the nonholonomic constraint equation, and $\lambda \in \mathbb{R}^{m \times 1}$ is the vector of constraint forces. m_o is the robot mass while I_o is the total equivalent moment of inertia. The input driving motor torques τ_r and τ_l provide the robot motion hence the position of the robot (output) changes.

The unconstrained form Eq. (4) is attained by eliminating λ by multiplying $S(q)^T$ on both sides of the equation and taking $\bar{v}(t) = [v, \omega]^T$ as the minimal projected coordinate. Recall from the kinematic model, S(q) is the null space of the nonholonomic constraint $A(q)$. That is, $A(q).S(q) = 0$. Thus, the dynamic model is then written in the state space form as:

$$\dot{x} = f(x) + g(x)u \tag{5}$$

By choosing the state variables as: $x_2 = y, x_3 = \theta$,
$x_4 = v$ and $x_5 = \omega$, the first order differentiation of equations is given as:

$$\dot{x}_1 = \dot{x} = v \cos \theta = x_4 \cos x_3$$
$$\dot{x}_2 = \dot{y} = v \sin \theta = x_4 \sin x_3$$
$$\dot{x}_3 = \dot{\theta} = \omega = x_5$$
$$\dot{x}_4 = \dot{v} = d\dot{\theta}^2 - \frac{1}{Rm_0}(\tau_r + \tau_l) = dx_5^2 - \frac{1}{Rm_0}(u_1 + u_2) \tag{6}$$
$$\dot{x}_5 = \dot{\omega} = \frac{1}{d^2 m_o + I_o}\left[-dm_o v\dot{\theta} - \frac{b}{R}(\tau_r - \tau_l) \right]$$
$$= \frac{1}{d^2 m_o + I_o}\left[-dm_o x_4 x_5 - \frac{b}{R}(u_1 - u_2) \right]$$

Finally, the dynamics of the differential drive robot in State space is given as:

$$\dot{x} = \begin{bmatrix} \dot{x}_1 \\ \dot{x}_2 \\ \dot{x}_3 \\ \dot{x}_4 \\ \dot{x}_5 \end{bmatrix} = \begin{bmatrix} 0 & 0 & 0 & \cos x_3 & 0 \\ 0 & 0 & 0 & \sin x_3 & 0 \\ 0 & 0 & 0 & 0 & 1 \\ 0 & 0 & 0 & 0 & dx_5 \\ 0 & 0 & 0 & \frac{-dm_o x_5}{d^2 m_o + I_o} & 0 \end{bmatrix} \begin{bmatrix} x_1 \\ x_2 \\ x_3 \\ x_4 \\ x_5 \end{bmatrix} + \frac{1}{R} \begin{bmatrix} 0 & 0 \\ 0 & 0 \\ 0 & 0 \\ -\frac{1}{m_0} & -\frac{1}{m_0} \\ \frac{-b}{d^2 m_o + I_o} & \frac{b}{d^2 m_o + I_o} \end{bmatrix} \begin{bmatrix} u_1 \\ u_2 \end{bmatrix} \tag{7}$$

C. Modelling the Cooperative System

The cooperative robotic system is homogeneous, that is, all the robots have similar physical parameters and dynamics. In this study, leader-follower formation approach is applied. This means, the system is designed such that a leader robot moves along a desired trajectory and the two followers maintain a desired distance and orientation in relation to the leader robot. Note that leader robot is the only one with information about the desired trajectories to be tracked and the followers use information from the leader to coordinate their motion.

Let the leader and a follower robot be denoted as R_j and R_i, respectively. In this study, the subscript "j" and "i" denotes leader and follower, respectively. Also, q_j and

q_i are the generalized coordinates of the leader robot and follower robot respectively. Thus, the states and the inputs of the leader and a follower can now be denoted as:

$$\dot{q}_j = \begin{bmatrix} \dot{x}_j \\ \dot{y}_j \\ \dot{\theta}_j \end{bmatrix} = \begin{bmatrix} \cos\theta_j & 0 \\ \sin\theta_j & 0 \\ 0 & 1 \end{bmatrix} \begin{bmatrix} v_j \\ \omega_j \end{bmatrix}$$

$$\dot{q}_i = \begin{bmatrix} \dot{x}_i \\ \dot{y}_i \\ \dot{\theta}_i \end{bmatrix} = \begin{bmatrix} \cos\theta_i & 0 \\ \sin\theta_i & 0 \\ 0 & 1 \end{bmatrix} \begin{bmatrix} v_i \\ \omega_i \end{bmatrix} \tag{8}$$

Moreover, the constant relative distance between the leader and the follower robot is denoted as l^{ref} and the separation bearing angle is ϕ^{ref}. These are defined as:

$$d^{ref} = \sqrt{(x_j - x_i)^2 + (y_j - y_i)^2}$$
$$\phi^{ref} = \pi - \arctan2(y_i - y_j, x_i - x_j) - \theta_j \tag{9}$$

In order to maintain the desired l^{ref} and ϕ^{ref} a reference robot for the follower should exist and it is given by:

$$q_{ref} = \begin{bmatrix} x_{ref} \\ y_{ref} \\ \theta_{ref} \end{bmatrix} = \begin{bmatrix} x_j - l^{ref}\cos(\phi^{ref} + \theta_i) \\ y_j - l^{ref}\sin(\phi^{ref} + \theta_i) \\ \theta_i \end{bmatrix} \tag{10}$$

The velocity equation of the reference robot is given by:

$$\dot{q}_{ref} = \begin{bmatrix} \dot{x}_{ref} \\ \dot{y}_{ref} \\ \dot{\theta}_{ref} \end{bmatrix} = \begin{bmatrix} \dot{x}_j + l^{ref}\sin(\phi^{ref} + \theta_i)\dot{\theta}_i \\ \dot{y}_j - l^{ref}\cos(\phi^{ref} + \theta_i)\dot{\theta}_i \\ \dot{\theta}_i \end{bmatrix} \tag{11}$$

The acceleration equation of the reference robot is given by:

$$\ddot{q}_{ref} = \begin{bmatrix} \ddot{x}_{ref} \\ \ddot{y}_{ref} \\ \ddot{\theta}_{ref} \end{bmatrix} = \begin{bmatrix} \ddot{x}_j + l^{ref}[\ddot{\theta}_i\sin(\phi^{ref} + \theta_i) + \dot{\theta}_i^2\cos(\phi^{ref} + \theta_i)] \\ \ddot{y}_j - l^{ref}[\ddot{\theta}_i\cos(\phi^{ref} + \theta_i) - \dot{\theta}_i^2\sin(\phi^{ref} + \theta_i)] \\ \ddot{\theta}_i \end{bmatrix} \tag{12}$$

For a non-linear system

$$\dot{x} = f(x, u) \tag{13}$$

Where x is the state vector, ($x \in R^n$), and u is the control input vector ($u \in R^m$) where $m \leq n$.

The system is differently flat if there exists an output y of m dimensions, such that y is locally a function of x, u and a finite number of successive derivatives of the component of u. That is:

$$(y_1 \ldots \ldots \ldots y_m) = h(x, u, \dot{u}, \ddot{u} \ldots \ldots u^{(l)}) \tag{14}$$

Conversely, x and u should be able to be expressed as functions of y up to a finite number of its successive derivative, that is:

$$x = \alpha(y, \dot{y}, \ddot{y} \ldots \ldots y^{(q)}), \quad u = \beta(y, \dot{y}, \ddot{y} \ldots \ldots y^{(q+1)}) \tag{15}$$

If x and u are then substituted in the non-linear system equation, it gets identically satisfied:

$$\dot{\alpha} = f(\alpha, \beta) \tag{16}$$

Thus, y is a complete parametrization of the trajectories of the system, and hence y is called a *flat output*.

A. Robot's Differential Flatness Characterisation

The robots forming the cooperative system are differentially driven mobile robots and their flatness analysis is similar. The kinematic model has two control inputs. Therefore, the two flat outputs that have been selected are x and y. This is because the number of flat outputs is always equal to the number of control inputs [19]. Thus:

$$F = \begin{bmatrix} F_1 \\ F_2 \end{bmatrix} = \begin{bmatrix} x \\ y \end{bmatrix} \tag{17}$$

When (17) is differentiated with respect to time the following equation is obtained:

$$\dot{F} = \begin{bmatrix} \dot{F}_1 \\ \dot{F}_2 \end{bmatrix} = \begin{bmatrix} \dot{x} \\ \dot{y} \end{bmatrix} = \begin{bmatrix} \cos\theta & 0 \\ \sin\theta & 0 \end{bmatrix} \begin{bmatrix} v \\ \omega \end{bmatrix} \tag{18}$$

$$\dot{x} = v\cos\theta$$
$$\dot{y} = v\sin\theta$$
$$\dot{v} = \bar{u}$$
$$\dot{\theta} = \omega \tag{19}$$

Where the new input for the new extended system is $\bar{u}$. To linearize the system a second derivative of the system is given as:

$$\ddot{F} = \begin{bmatrix} \ddot{F}_1 \\ \ddot{F}_2 \end{bmatrix} = \begin{bmatrix} \ddot{x} \\ \ddot{y} \end{bmatrix} = \begin{bmatrix} \cos\theta & -v\sin\theta \\ \sin\theta & v\cos\theta \end{bmatrix} \begin{bmatrix} \bar{u} \\ \omega \end{bmatrix} \tag{20}$$

To create diffeomorphism between the original states and flat outputs and their derivatives, input prolongation is used.

Therefore, $\ddot{F}$ is linear with respect to the new input $\bar{u}$ and ω only if v not zero. For a flat system, all the state variables can be expressed in terms of the flat outputs and their derivatives as follows:

$$x = F_1$$
$$y = F_2$$
$$\theta = \tan^{-1} \frac{\dot{F}_1}{\dot{F}_2}$$
$$v = \sqrt{\dot{F}_1^{\,2} + \dot{F}_2^{\,2}}$$
$$\bar{u} = \dot{v} = \frac{\dot{F}_1 \ddot{F}_1 + \dot{F}_2 \ddot{F}_2}{\sqrt{\dot{F}_1^{\,2} + \dot{F}_2^{\,2}}}$$
$$\omega = \dot{\theta} = \frac{\dot{F}_1 \ddot{F}_2 - \dot{F}_2 \ddot{F}_1}{\dot{F}_1^{\,2} + \dot{F}_2^{\,2}}$$
$$(21)$$

Furthermore, the flat outputs and their derivatives can completely be expressed in terms of all the state variable and their derivatives:

$$F_1 = x$$
$$F_2 = y$$
$$\dot{F}_1 = \dot{x} = v \cos \theta$$
$$\dot{F}_2 = \dot{y} = v \sin \theta$$
$$\ddot{F}_1 = \bar{u} \cos \theta - v\omega \sin \theta$$
$$\ddot{F}_2 = \bar{u} \sin \theta - v\omega \cos \theta \qquad (22)$$

Moreover, this diffeomorphic relationship proves that there exists a one-to-one relationship between the state space and the flat output space. This makes it possible to obtain full state.

3   Motion Planning and Control

A. Trajectory Generation

Recall that leader robot is the only one with information about the desired trajectories to be tracked. Therefore, this section presents a polynomial-based trajectory planning that satisfies a specific set of terminal conditions for the leader robot.

Since there are six terminal conditions for the six states $x, y, \theta, v, \bar{u}$ and ω, a fifth-order polynomial is used:

$$F_1(t) = a_5 t^5 + a_4 t^4 + a_3 t^3 + a_2 t^2 + a_1 t + a_0$$
$$F_2(t) = b_5 t^5 + b_4 t^4 + b_3 t^3 + b_2 t^2 + b_1 t + b_0 \qquad (23)$$

With consideration of the limits of the robot, the terminal conditions are set and used to determine the coefficients a_k and b_k where $k = [1, ...,5]$.

With the terminal conditions shown in Table 1, a_k and b_k were obtained and the desired trajectories were derived. The destination should be reached in fifteen seconds, thus $t = 15$ s. The robot is driven from rest-to-rest positions.

As a result, the corresponding leader's desired trajectories are:

$$F_1^d(t) = 0.00001185t^5 - 0.0004444t^4 + 0.004444t^3$$
$$F_2^d(t) = 0.000003951t^5 - 0.0001481t^4 + 0.001481t^3 \tag{24}$$

The leader will then track these trajectories and the followers will follow the leader while maintaining a desired distance l^{ref} and orientation ϕ^{ref} in relation to the leader robot.

B. Flatness-Based Controller Design

Following the derivation of the desired trajectory, a tracking controller based on flatness is developed. Given that, $F_1(t)$ and $F_2(t)$ are the actual flat output trajectories, and $F_1^d(t)$ and $F_2^d(t)$ are the desired flat output trajectories, then error is defined as:

$$e_1 = F_1^d - F_1$$
$$e_2 = F_2^d - F_2 \tag{25}$$

Let

$$\begin{bmatrix} \ddot{F}_1 \\ \ddot{F}_2 \end{bmatrix} = \begin{vmatrix} \delta_1 \\ \delta_2 \end{vmatrix} \tag{26}$$

then the feedback *control laws* to the new inputs can then be defined as:

$$\delta_1 = \ddot{F}_1^d + \rho_1 \dot{e}_1 + \rho_0 e_1$$
$$\delta_2 = \ddot{F}_2^d + \tilde{\rho}_1 \dot{e}_2 + \tilde{\rho}_0 e_2 \tag{27}$$

Where $\tilde{\rho}_1, \tilde{\rho}_0, \rho_1, \rho_0$ are control the gains. Next the error dynamics of the system in flat output space is determined.

$$\ddot{F}_1^d - \delta_1 = \ddot{F}_1^d - \ddot{F}_1 = \ddot{e}_1$$
$$\ddot{F}_2^d - \delta_2 = \ddot{F}_2^d - \ddot{F}_2 = \ddot{e}_2 \tag{28}$$

Therefore, the closed-loop error dynamics is defined as:

$$0 = \ddot{e}_1 + \rho_1 \dot{e}_1 + \rho_0 e_1$$
$$0 = \ddot{e}_2 + \tilde{\rho}_1 \dot{e}_2 + \tilde{\rho}_0 e_2 \tag{29}$$

To guarantee exponential stability, the control gains were chosen such that all the roots of the equations in (29) lie in the left half-plane of the complex plane.

C. Flatness-based Formation Controller

Desired trajectories of the flat outputs of the followers can be constructed using the position output of the leader and predefined distance l^{ref} and orientation ϕ^{ref} with respect to the leader robot. For the first follower (follower1):

$$\begin{bmatrix} F_1^{f1}{}_{ref} \\ F_2^{f1}{}_{ref} \end{bmatrix} = \begin{bmatrix} F_1 - l^{ref1}\cos(\phi^{ref1} + \theta_{i1}) \\ F_2 - l^{ref1}\sin(\phi^{ref1} + \theta_{i1}) \end{bmatrix} \tag{30}$$

And for the second follower (follower2):

$$\begin{bmatrix} F_{1\,ref}^{f2} \\ F_{2\,ref}^{f2} \end{bmatrix} = \begin{bmatrix} F_1 - l^{ref2}cos(\phi^{ref2} + \theta_{i1}) \\ F_2 - l^{ref2}sin(\phi^{ref2} + \theta_{i1}) \end{bmatrix} \tag{31}$$

Having constructed the desire trajectories, the next step is to define the error.

$$\begin{aligned} e_1{}^{f1} &= F_{1\,ref}^{f1} - F_1^{f1} \\ e_2{}^{f1} &= F_{2\,ref}^{f1} - F_2^{f1} \\ e_1{}^{f2} &= F_{1\,ref}^{f2} - F_1^{f2} \\ e_1{}^{f2} &= F_{2\,ref}^{f2} - F_2^{f2} \end{aligned} \tag{32}$$

Let $\begin{bmatrix} \ddot{F}_1^{fs} \\ \ddot{F}_2^{fs} \end{bmatrix} = \begin{vmatrix} \delta_1{}^{fs} \\ \delta_2{}^{fs} \end{vmatrix}$ then the feedback control laws to the new inputs can then be defined as

$$\begin{aligned} \delta_1{}^{fs} &= \ddot{F}_{1\,ref}^{fs} + \rho_1{}^{fs}\dot{e}_1{}^{fs} + \rho_0{}^{fs}e_1{}^{fs} \\ \delta_2{}^{fs} &= \ddot{F}_{2\,ref}^{fs} + \tilde{\rho}_1{}^{fs}\dot{e}_2{}^{fs} + \tilde{\rho}_0{}^{fs}e_2{}^{fs} \end{aligned} \tag{33}$$

Where $\tilde{\rho}_1{}^{fs}, \tilde{\rho}_0{}^{fs}, \rho_1{}^{fs}, \rho_0{}^{fs}$ are control the gains and subscript s = [1, 2] specifies the robot. Next the error dynamics of the system in flat output space is determined.

$$\begin{aligned} \ddot{F}_{1\,ref}^{fs} - \delta_1{}^{fs} &= \ddot{F}_{1\,ref}^{fs} - \ddot{F}_1 = \ddot{e}_1{}^{fs} \\ \ddot{F}_{2\,ref}^{fs} - \delta_2{}^{fs} &= \ddot{F}_{2\,ref}^{fs} - \ddot{F}_2 = \ddot{e}_2{}^{fs} \end{aligned} \tag{34}$$

Therefore, the error dynamics is defined as:

$$\begin{aligned} 0 &= \ddot{e}_1^{fs} + \rho_1^{fs}\dot{e}_1^{fs} + \rho_0^{fs}e_1^{fs} \\ 0 &= \ddot{e}_2^{fs} + \tilde{\rho}_1^{fs}\dot{e}_2^{fs} + \tilde{\rho}_0^{fs}e_2^{fs} \end{aligned} \tag{35}$$

To track the reference trajectory with added disturbances or uncertainty, [1] defines a fd which represents the set of variables (x and u) of the actual follower robot that is set to converge to their reference $F_L^d(t)$. The control law and error e_s where $e_s = F_L^d - F_f$, are such that

$$\dot{e}_s(t) = f_d\left(e_s(t) + F_L^d(t), u\left(e_s(t) + F_L^d(t)\right)\right) - f\left(F_L^d(t), u(t)\right)$$

is asymptotically stable for all disturbances.

4   Simulation and Results

MATLAB/Simulink simulation software is used to demonstrate the effectiveness of the flatness controller. Two main cases are presented in this section. Firstly, the ability of leader to follow its predefined trajectories and secondly, the ability of the followers to maintain a desired distance and orientation in relation to the leader robot. As previously mentioned, the system is made up of three similar robots, one of the robots is a leader and the other two are followers.

A. Effect of a Flatness Controller on the Leader Robot

Using fifth-degree polynomial together with terminal conditions shown in Table 1 below, the desired trajectories have been derived (Eq. 24). The robot should reach its desired destination in fifteen seconds, thus $t = 15$ s. The robot is driven from rest-to-rest positions.

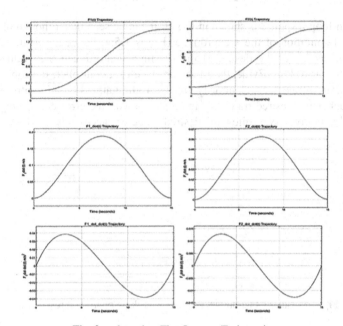

Fig. 2. ader robot Flat Outputs Trajectories.

Figure 2 therefore shows the desired trajectories of flat outputs F_1 and F_2, together with their desired velocities and accelerations (Table 1).

Table 1. Leader's Desired Terminal Conditions.

State	Initial condition	Final condition
x(m)	0.0	1.5
y(m)	0.0	0.5
θ(rad)	0.0	0.0
v(m/s)	0.0	0.0
ω(rad/s)	0.0	0.0
$\bar{u}$(m/s²)	0.0	0.0

Furthermore, the effectiveness of this controller was tested. A comparison was made between WMR's open-loop response, which is the response of WMR without a controller, and its response with a flatness-based controller. The flatness controller gains were chosen to be:

$$\rho_{0x} = 2, \rho_{1x} = 1, \tilde{\rho}_{1y} = 6, \tilde{\rho}_{0y} = 9$$

The open-loop response is shown in Fig. 3. It can be seen that although the desired final terminal condition of the x-coordinate (F1) is 1.5m, the actual value reached is 0.78m. Also, instead of the desired 0.5m, the final y-coordinate (F2) value reached by the WMR was 1.25m. Evidently, in the absence of a controller, the robots fails to follow the desired trajectory. Contrarily, in Fig. 4, the flatness-based control performs well and reaches the desired trajectory in about 0 s with the error converging to zero. Consequently, the robot can follow the desired trajectory accurately.

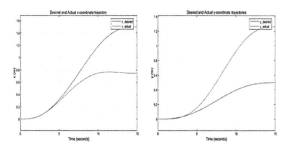

Fig. 3. Leader's Flat output Trajectory tracking open-loop response.

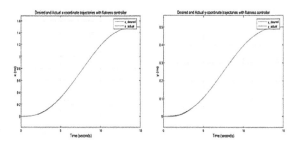

Fig. 4. Leader's Flat output Trajectory tracking response with flatness-based controller.

B. Effect of a Flatness based Controller on the Robotic Formation

To maintain formation, the followers track the leader, while maintaining a constant bearing ϕ^{ref} and distance d^{ref} to the leader. Using the trajectory of the leader and the desired bearing and distance from the leader, terminal conditions and desired trajectories of the followers can be constructed. Table 2 shows these terminal conditions, together with the desired distance and orientation of follower to the leader. Figure 5 then presents the reference trajectories of the followers such that formation is maintained and the desired terminal conditions in Table 2 are met. The flatness property of each robot is established, and flatness controllers are used on each robot to track these trajectories. Here again a comparison between WMR's open-loop response and a flatness-based controller response is made. Figure 6 shows the F_1 and F_2 open-loop response of follower1 and follower2. From this figure compares the F_1 and F_2 desired and actual trajectories. The two robots fail to track the desired trajectories, therefore there is a need for a controller.

Recall that the desired trajectories are calculated such that they ensure maintenance of a constant distance and orientation relative to the leader. Therefore, failure for the follower robots in tracking these trajectories means failure in the maintenance of the predefined formation. This is evident of the errors in the separation distance and bearing from the leader as seen in Fig. 7 and Fig. 8. It can be seen from the two figures that the distance and orientation errors do not converge to zero. This is a clear indication that the three robots are out of formation.

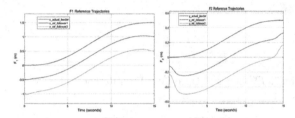

Fig. 5. F_1 and F_2 Formation Reference Trajectories for Formation Maintenance.

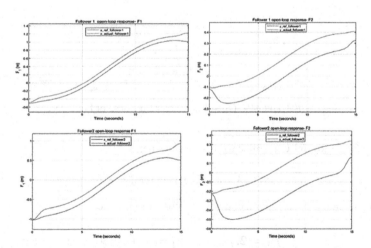

Fig. 6. followers' open loop response: F_1 and F_2 trajectory tracking.

The distance and bearing errors are significant, as a result formation is not achieved. It is therefore evident that there is a need for a controller in order to compensate for the open-loop insufficiency. As a result, a flatness controller was designed for each follower.

Table 2. Desired Terminal Conditions for followers.

Robot	Initial (F1)m	Final (F1) m	Initial (F2) m	Final (F2) m	Distance (d^{ref})m	Bearing (ϕ^{ref}) rad
Leader	0	1.5	0	0.5	–	–
Follower 1	−0.49	1	−0.11	0.33	0.52	0.2276
Follower2	−1.03	0.17	−0.22	0.5	1.054	0.2109

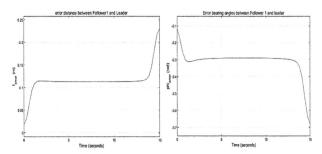

Fig. 7. l^{ref} and φ^{ref} Open-Loop Error Response of Follower1.

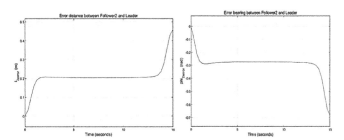

Fig. 8. l^{ref} and φ^{ref} Open-Loop Error Response of Follower2.

The gains for follower1 controller were chosen to be:

$$\rho_0 = 3, \rho_1 = 2, \tilde{\rho}_1 = 5, \tilde{\rho}_0 = 8$$

Also, the gains for follower2 controller were chosen to be:

$$\rho'_0 = 2, \rho'_1 = 1, \tilde{\rho}'_1 = 6, \tilde{\rho}'_0 = 9$$

Figure 9 shows the tracking response of the follower robots when flatness-based controllers are used. Furthermore, in this case, it is evident the tracking ability of the robot has improved; the robots successfully track the desired trajectories. Thus, the distance and bearing errors converge to zero and thus a constant distance and bearing is maintained (Fig. 10). Both robots can maintain the desired distance and bearing relative to the leader, thus formation was successfully maintained.

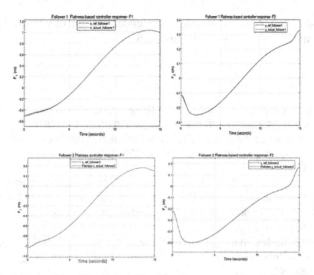

Fig. 9. Flatness-Based Trajectory Tracking Response of the Follower Robots.

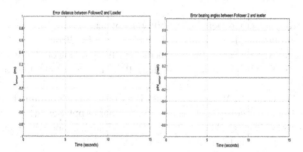

Fig. 10. Separation Distance l^{ref} and Separation Bearing φ^{ref} Error Response for the Followers with Flatness-Based controller.

5   Conclusion

This paper presented coordination control of a leader-follower cooperative multiple mobile robotic system using differential flatness theory. Simulations are presented to demonstrate the effectiveness of the approach. The formation is made up of three differentially driven mobile robots with similar dynamics. One robot is a leader, while the other two are followers. Using their kinematic models, the robots' flatness properties were exploited to design a flatness-based control algorithm for motion planning. Moreso, trajectories were generated and tracked such that the follower robots maintained a constant desired relative distance and orientation with reference to the leader. Based on the results obtained, differential flatness characterisation enabled the linearization of the system to a stable linear equivalent system and significantly reduced the computational cost especially when dealing with multiple robots that can otherwise entail solving large robotic model differential equations. For further study, the effects of flatness trajectory planning would be tested for the mobile robots under friction, or with modelling errors, unreliable estimates, and additional perturbation.

References

1. Markus, E.D., Yskander, H., Agee, J.T., Jimoh, A.A.: Coordination control of robot manipulators using flat outputs. Robot. Auton. Syst. **83**, 169–176 (2016)
2. Tsiu, Lintle, Markus, Elisha Didam: a survey of formation control for multiple mobile robotic systems. Int. J. Mech. Eng. Robot. Res. 1515–1520 (2020). https://doi.org/10.18178/ijmerr. 9.11.1515-1520
3. Petrovsky, A., Kalinov, I., Karpyshev, P., Tsetserukou, D., Ivanov, A., Golkar, A.: The two-wheeled robotic swarm concept for Mars exploration. Acta Astronaut. **194**, 1–8 (2022)
4. Li, Y., et al.: Development and applications of rescue robots for explosion accidents in coal mines. J. Field Robot. **37**(3), 466–489 (2020)
5. Lei, G., Zheng, Y.: Research on cooperative trajectory planning algorithm based on Tractor-Trailer Wheeled Robot. IEEE Access **10**, 64209–64221 (2022). https://doi.org/10.1109/ACC ESS.2021.3062392
6. Hausman, K., Müller, J., Hariharan, A., Ayanian, N., Sukhatme, G.S.: Cooperative multi-robot control for target tracking with onboard sensing. Int. J. Robot. Res. **34**(13), 1660–1677 (2015)
7. Panagou, D., Kumar, V.: Cooperative visibility maintenance for leader–follower formations in obstacle environments. IEEE Trans. Rob. **30**(4), 831–844 (2014)
8. Jain, R.P., Aguiar, A.P., de Sousa, J.B.: Cooperative path following of robotic vehicles using an event-based control and communication strategy. IEEE Robot. Autom. Lett. **3**(3), 1941–1948 (2018)
9. Wei, H., Lv, Q., Duo, N., Wang, G., Liang, B.: Consensus algorithms based multi-robot formation control under noise and time delay conditions. Appl. Sci. **9**(5), 1004 (2019)
10. Wang, G., Wang, C., Du, Q., Li, L., Dong, W.: Distributed cooperative control of multiple nonholonomic mobile robots. J. Intell. Rob. Syst. **83**(3), 525–541 (2016)
11. Liu, L., Yu, J., Ji, J., Miao, Z., Zhou, J.: Cooperative adaptive consensus tracking for multiple nonholonomic mobile robots. Int. J. Syst. Sci. **50**(8), 1556–1567 (2019)
12. Du, H., Wen, G., Cheng, Y., He, Y., Jia, R.: Distributed finite-time cooperative control of multiple high-order nonholonomic mobile robots. IEEE Trans. Neural Networks Learn. Syst. **28**(12), 2998–3006 (2016)
13. Akbari, A., Muhayyuddin, Rosell, J.: Knowledge-oriented task and motion planning for multiple mobile robots. J. Experim. Theoret. Artific. Intell. **31**(1), 137–162 (2019)
14. Gutiérrez, H., Morales, A., Nijmeijer, H.: Synchronization control for a swarm of unicycle robots: analysis of different controller topologies. Asian J. Control **19**(5), 1822–1833 (2017)
15. Xiang, X., Liu, C., Lapierre, L., Jouvencel, B.: Synchronized path following control of multiple homogenous underactuated AUVs. J. Syst. Sci. Complexity **25**(1), 71–89 (2012)
16. Ge, H., Chen, G., Xu, G.: Multi-AUV cooperative target hunting based on improved potential field in a surface-water environment. Appl. Sci. **8**(6), 973 (2018)
17. Zhao, R., Xiang, X., Yu, C., Jiang, Z.: Coordinated formation control of autonomous underwater vehicles based on leader-follower strategy. In: OCEANS 2016 MTS/IEEE Monterey, pp. 1–5. IEEE (2016)
18. Tang, C.P.: Differential flatness-based kinematic and dynamic control of a differentially driven wheeled mobile robot. In: 2009 IEEE International Conference on Robotics and Biomimetics (ROBIO), pp. 2267–2272. IEEE (2009)
19. Sira-Ramirez, H., Agrawal, S.K.: Differentially Flat Systems. Crc Press (2018)

A Comparison of Publish-Subscribe and Client-Server Models for Streaming IoT Telemetry Data

Olasupo Ajayi$^{(\boxtimes)}$ ⓘ, Antoine Bagula ⓘ, Joshua Bode, and Moegammad Damon

Department of Computer Science, University of the Western Cape, Cape Town, South Africa
ooajayi@uwc.ac.za

Abstract. In recent years, the Internet of Things (IoT) has become a household name both in research and commercial domains. There are numerous practical applications of IoT, ranging from sophisticated solutions in big factories to simple smart homes devices, such as temperature monitors. Common to these solutions is the need to transmit data from a sensing source to a different location where the data is read, processed, analyzed, or simply stored. Numerous models and protocols have been developed to ferry IoT data, including queueing, client-server, and publish-subscribe models, all with their merits and demerits. In this paper, a comparison of two models for transmitting live/streaming IoT telemetry data is done. The Message Queue Telemetry Transport (MQTT), a publish-subscribe model, is compared with WebSocket, a client-server model, in terms of throughput, round trip time and system utilization. Obtained results reveal that MQTT is more suited for transmitting live IoT data than WebSocket, as it had better throughput, utilized less system resource, however it was slightly slower than WebSocket.

Keywords: Client-Server · Internet of Things · MQTT · Publish-Subscribe · Round Trip Time · WebSocket

1 Introduction

Advances in technology has enabled easy communication between humans and machines (Human to machine or H2M), machines and machines (M2M), and machines and humans (M2H). The Internet of Things (IoT) is one of the primary enablers of this communication [1]. By fitting everyday objects or "things" with sensing, actuating, and communication abilities, IoT has created a new technology domain which we refer to as the "smart ecosystem". This ecosystem ranges from simple devices, such as temperature sensors, that measure and communicate ambient temperature readings, to more advanced and complex solutions capable of sensing, acting, and mimicking human decision making through artificial intelligence. Regardless of the use case, IoT devices generally collect data about/from a source and transmit same to a different (remote) destination. There are several protocols used in transferring telemetry data, including Advanced

© ICST Institute for Computer Sciences, Social Informatics and Telecommunications Engineering 2023
Published by Springer Nature Switzerland AG 2023. All Rights Reserved
M. Masinde and A. Bagula (Eds.): AFRICATEK 2022, LNICST 503, pp. 129–139, 2023.
https://doi.org/10.1007/978-3-031-35883-8_9

Message Queuing Protocol (AMQP)/RabbitMQ, Message Queuing Telemetry Transport (MQTT), Constrained Application Protocol (CoAP), HyperText Transfer Protocols (HTTP), most of which have been reviewed in [2]. These protocols can broadly be categorized into Client-Server or Publish-Subscribe architecture.

The Client-Server architecture is one in which one or more clients connect to central server. In this architecture, clients request for services or information from the server, which in turn actively waits for requests from clients and response to them. Common roles of the server include web hosting, database server, and application server. Figure 1a gives a high-level depiction of a Client-Server architecture. The Publish-Subscribe architecture on the other hand is an architecture made up of three primary components – the publisher(s), the subscriber(s), and the broker, as shown in Fig. 1b. Unlike the Client-Server where clients send request directly to the server, in publish-subscribe model the senders (publishers) are usually unaware of the type or number of receivers (subscribers), hence, does not send messages directly to them. Instead, messages from the publishers are categorized into "topics" and sent to an intermediary broker. Similarly, the subscribers are often also unaware of the publishers and simply subscribe to topics of interest on the broker. Thus, the broker serves as an intermediary between the publisher and the subscribers, handling tasks such as filtration, storage, message forwarding, and message delivery management.

In this work, the authors seek to compare the performance of the classic client-server architecture with the publish-subscribe architecture in streaming IoT telemetry data from source to destination. For the client-server architecture, the WebSocket is considered as a use case, while MQTT is considered for the publish-subscribe architecture. These protocols are briefly described in the following subsections.

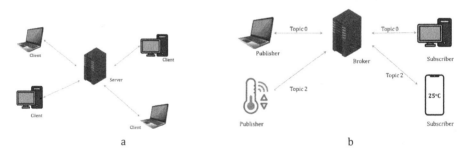

a   b

Fig. 1. a: Client-Server Architecture, b: Publish-Subscribe Architecture

1.1 WebSocket

WebSocket is a Transmission Control Protocol (TCP) based client-server model, that offers full duplex communication between clients and server [3]. Like HTTP, WebSocket is based on TCP, hence, the basic processes of creating a secure communication channel between the client and server are also observed with WebSocket. These include link establishment/handshaking, the server actively waiting for requests, clients initiating requests, server responding, and the final acknowledgment sent by the client. However, unlike in HTTP, WebSocket connections are usually persistent, thus, avoiding the need to re-establish connections for each client's request. This significantly improves the performance of WebSockets compared to non-persistent HTTP [4]. A major disadvantage of the WebSocket is that the client and server must remain tightly coupled to each other. In essence, both the client and server must be available at the same time for information exchange to occur.

1.2 MQTT

Message Queuing Telemetry Transport (MQTT) is a lightweight messaging protocol that employs the publish-subscribe model. Since it is based on the publish-subscribe architecture, the sender and receiver are decoupled from each other and can operate independent of the other. The broker serves as a "binding" or intermediary component via which communication takes place. The broker is synonymous to a message notice board onto which publishers "write" messages under specific topics, and subscribers "read" messages under topics that interest them. Moreover, the decoupled nature of the various components of MQTT improves its scalability. Being decoupled and independent of each other there is a high risk of message loss in most publish-subscribe based protocols. These protocols define 3 levels of QoS, viz., Level 0 (which provides no guarantee of message delivery), Level 1 (which guarantees that messages sent will be received at least once during a transmission process), and Level 2 (which ensures that messages are delivered and decoded by the subscribers) [5].

2 Related Works

MQTT is a protocol that has been well used in numerous IoT related projects. In [6], the author carried out a comparative evaluation of several publicly and locally deployed MQTT brokers. For the public brokers, they considered Mosquitto, HiveMQ, and Bevywise, while ActiveMQ, Bevywise MQTT, Mosquitto, and RabbitMQ were deployed locally. Obtained results show that for the public brokers, Mosquitto performed best for Quality of Service (QoS) levels 0 and 2 in terms of message throughput and delivery times. For the local brokers, HiveMQ and Mosquitto were the top performers in terms of message delivery time. In [7], the authors compared the performance of two telemetry protocols – MQTT and CoAP, both of which are based on different architectures. MQTT which runs on Transmission Control Protocol (TCP) and utilizes the publish-subscribe architecture, while CoAP runs on User Datagram Protocol (UDP) and utilizes a Request-Response model (like a scaled down HTTP). CoAP also uses URI (Universal Resource Identifiers) rather than Topics as used in MQTT. A common gateway, compatible with both protocols, was developed by the authors and used to compare them, in terms of packet loss and delays, message throughput, and message size. The performance of both protocols was network dependent as both outperformed each other at different conditions. Ref. [8] compared MQTT to classic HTTP based on three criteria, i.) Message consumption, for which MQTT performed 25 times faster than HTTP. ii.) Data throughput, wherein MQTT was shown to be significantly faster and more frugal on traffic utilization. iii.) Energy consumption, which was tested using a Raspberry pi, and showed that MQTT utilized 22% less energy than HTTP for the same task. In [9], AMQP was compared with MQTT in a dynamic environment using message loss, delay, jitter, and saturation boundaries as metrics. Experimental results showed that i.) AMQP delivered messages in a last in first out order, while MQTT used the first in first out order. ii.) There were no message losses across both protocols except when the publisher was overloaded. iii.) AMQP was more secure, while MQTT was more scalable. Ref. [10] compared three distributed MQTT brokers (EMQX, HiveMQ, VerneMQ) on multiple criteria including throughput, scalability, and resilience. They concluded that EMQX had the highest message throughput, while HiveMQ was the most resilient and extensible. In [11], several IoT protocols were compared including AMQP, CoAP, MQTT, REST, XMPP (Extensible Messaging and Presence Protocol), and WebSocket, based on various criteria, including security and quality of service (QoS). In term of architectures, CoAP and REST are based on Request/Response architecture, MQTT, AMQP are Publish/Subscribe, XMPP employs both Request/Response and Publish/Subscribe, while WebSocket is based on a Client/Server architecture. All protocols provide some form of QoS, except XMPP, REST, and WebSocket. The authors also reported that all protocols supported TLS (Transport Layer Security), except CoAP and REST which use Datagram Transport Layer Security (DTLS) and HTTPS respectively. Using the ESP8266, Oliveria *et al.* [12] compared the performance of MQTT and WebSocket protocols based on round-trip time (RTT). They concluded that WebSocket was better than MQTT for applications that required low RTT, while MQTT utilized lower memory space.

3   Methodology

This section presents the methodology and experimental setup used in this work for both WebSocket and MQTT. Though Fig. 1 show a depiction of generic client-server and publish-subscribe architectures, for this work, we only used subsets of these architecture as shown in Figs. 2 and 3. Our network set up consisted of only one client (or publisher) and one server (or subscriber) because we wanted to reduce the impact of uncontrollable factors, such as network delays, bandwidth congestion, and bottlenecks (network and server), which might emanate from using multiple nodes, active devices, and service providers. We believe our chosen set up allows us to compare both protocols in a "relatively controlled" environment.

For the client (or publisher), we used a Raspberry Pi version 4 B, with 4 GB RAM and 4 CPU cores running at 1.5 GHz [13]. This was chosen because of its GPIO ports (to connect sensors) and its stripped-down Linux operating system, which helps minimize the impact of complex operating system overheads. For the server (subscriber), a computer with an 8 core Intel Core i7 generation 10 CPU, 16 GB of RAM and running Windows 11 was used. This system was more than capable to act as a server for a single client.

Figure 2 shows the deployment setup for WebSocket. A Raspberry Pi was used to collect readings from the sensors, which in our use case were temperature and humidity collected from the Sensor Hat emu. Telemetry data were then sent to the WebSocket server running on the Windows PC. The PC also ran the SQLite server, onto

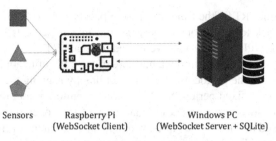

Fig. 2. WebSocket architecture

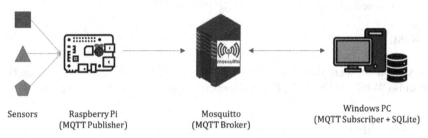

Fig. 3. MQTT architecture

which the received telemetry data were saved. Two Python scripts were written, the first "WebSocket_client.py" ran on the Raspberry Pi (WebSocket client) to capture and send telemetry data to the Windows PC (WebSocket server), while the second "Web-Socket_Server.py" ran on the Windows PC, to receive data from the client and save same on the SQLite database.

Figure 3 shows the MQTT architecture used in this work and comprises of a Raspberry Pi (to collect sensor readings), a broker (Mosquitto), and a Windows PC acting as the MQTT subscriber and SQLite host. Like with the WebSocket, two Python scripts "mqtt_publisher.py" and "mqtt_subscriber.py" were ran on the Raspberry Pi and Windows PC respectively.

For each deployment scenario, the same Raspberry Pi and Windows PC were used to ensure consistent results, only the Python script being run for each experiment was changed. The Raspberry Pi was set to a local IP address of 10.0.2.15, while the Windows PC was set to 192.168.2.112. For the WebSocket, port 54786 and 12000 were opened on the client (Raspberry Pi) and server (Windows PC) respectively; while for MQTT, ports 47143 and 1883 were used for the publisher (Raspberry Pi) and subscriber (Windows PC) respectively.

In the experimental setup used to test the performance of WebSocket and MQTT for IoT data streaming, the following metrics were considered:

- Throughput, which is the rate at which data are transferred between the sender and the receiver. It is measured in bits/second. We used Wireshark statistics to calculate throughput for both models.

- Round Trip Time (RTT), the time taken for a packet to travel from a sender to the receiver and back to the sender. It is measured in milliseconds (ms). The Packet Internet Gropper (PING) messages were used to obtain RTT.
- System performance, this is simply a measure of the CPU utilization (in percentage) while using any of the protocols. We obtained this by running the System Activity Report (SAR) for a fixed period. SAR is used to monitor system resources, such as CPU usage, memory, and network utilization in a Linux operating system. For this study we focused on the "%idle" time, which is the percentage of time the CPU was idle, and "%IOwait", which is the percentage of time the CPU was idle because it was waiting for one or more IO requests to be completed and there were no other tasks to schedule.

4 Results

This section presents the obtained results of the experiments carried out. For both protocols (WebSocket and MQTT), a Raspberry Pi and a Windows PC were used.

4.1 Throughput

Data required to determine the throughput were obtained from Wireshark's conversations statistics [14]. This shows the packet count, packet size, packet direction, start and end times, and average data size transmitted across two end points. We obtained throughput by dividing the total number message size (in bits) by total time. Graphical depictions of the obtained results are shown in Figs. 4 and 5.

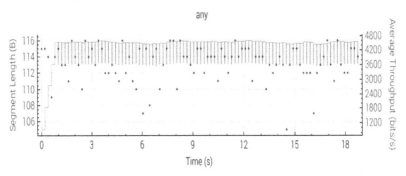

Fig. 4. Average Throughput for WebSocket

When comparing both graphs, Fig. 5 shows that MQTT had a higher throughput (5100 bits/s on the average) compared to WebSocket's average of 4500 bits/s. This implies that about 13% more packets were processed per unit time when MQTT was used versus when WebSocket was used.

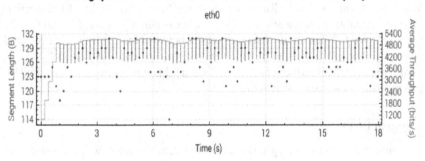

Fig. 5. Average Throughput for MQTT

4.2 Round Trip Time (RTT)

For both protocols, we measured the time it took to send messages from the Raspberry Pi to the Windows PC. We used ICMP Echo and Echo Reply messages (PING) to calculate RTT. For accuracy, we ran PING several times, with each run lasting 20 s. We then plotted the average RTT for both protocols as depicted in Figs. 6 and 7.

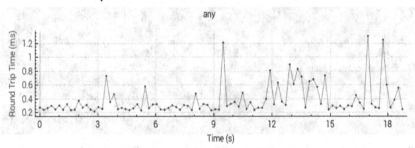

Fig. 6. RTT for WebSocket

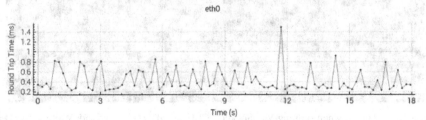

Fig. 7. RTT for MQTT

Figures 6 and 7 show the time it takes for packets to travel from the Raspberry Pi to the Windows PC and back to the Raspberry Pi, using WebSocket and MQTT respectively. The figures reveal that on the average, WebSocket is slightly faster than MQTT. This is expected as MQTT has an intermediary broker between the publisher (Raspberry Pi) and the subscriber (Windows PC), which though transparent, still runs a "stored and forward" process for all arriving messages. Despite this intermediary broker, MQTT is only marginally slower than WebSocket.

4.3 System Load

To determine the impact of both protocols on the system resources, we performed system utilization tests while running the respective protocols. Since the Raspberry Pi runs a Linux operating system, we used SAR (System Activity Report) to obtain this report. SAR (System Activity Report) is used in Linux to monitor system resource such as CPU, Memory, Disk usage, I/O activities, etc. Two metrics were of utmost importance, namely the average CPU load (%idle) and the IO wait time (%IOwait). To achieve obtained this we ran the "*sar -u 2 600*" command, which gave system reports every 2 s for 20 min and took the average values reported.

Figures 8, 9 and 10 show snapshots of the CPU load of the Raspberry Pi. The last column (in red text) represents the average load of all the Raspberry Pi's 4 CPUs, i.e., %idle, while the third to the last represents the %IOwait times.

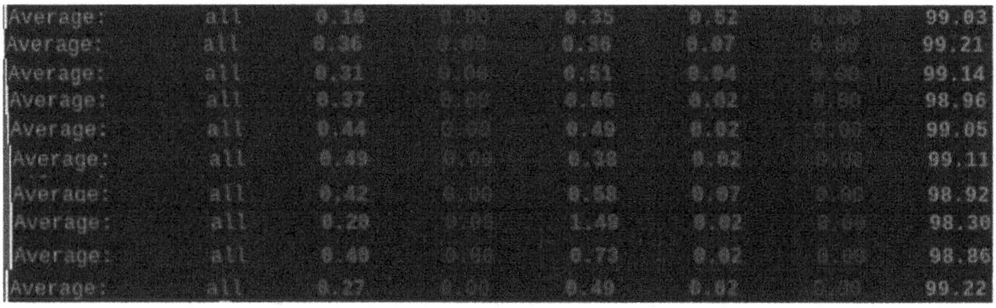

Average:	all	0.10	0.00	0.35	0.52	0.00	99.03
Average:	all	0.36	0.00	0.30	0.07	0.00	99.21
Average:	all	0.31	0.00	0.51	0.04	0.00	99.14
Average:	all	0.37	0.00	0.66	0.02	0.00	98.96
Average:	all	0.44	0.00	0.49	0.02	0.00	99.05
Average:	all	0.49	0.00	0.38	0.02	0.00	99.11
Average:	all	0.42	0.00	0.58	0.07	0.00	98.92
Average:	all	0.20	0.00	1.48	0.02	0.00	98.30
Average:	all	0.40	0.00	0.73	0.02	0.00	98.86
Average:	all	0.27	0.00	0.49	0.02	0.00	99.22

Fig. 8. System load at idle state – CPU = 1.02% average load, Waiting for IO = 0.08% average

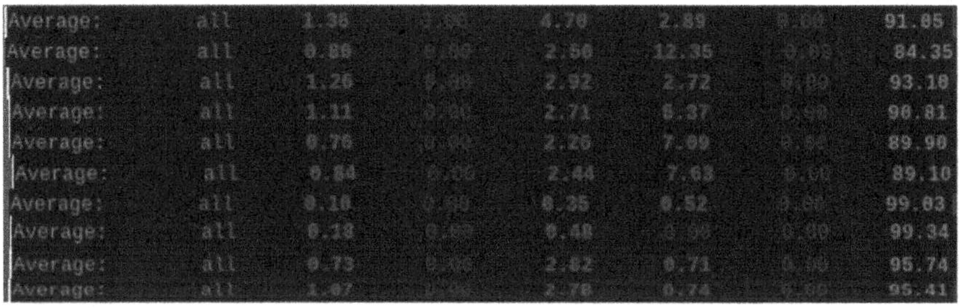

Average:	all	1.36	0.00	4.70	2.89	0.00	91.05
Average:	all	0.80	0.00	2.50	12.35	0.00	84.35
Average:	all	1.20	0.00	2.92	2.72	0.00	93.10
Average:	all	1.11	0.00	2.71	6.37	0.00	90.81
Average:	all	0.76	0.00	2.26	7.09	0.00	89.90
Average:	all	0.84	0.00	2.44	7.63	0.00	89.10
Average:	all	0.10	0.00	0.35	0.52	0.00	99.03
Average:	all	0.18	0.00	0.48	0.00	0.00	99.34
Average:	all	0.73	0.00	2.82	0.71	0.00	95.74
Average:	all	1.07	0.00	2.78	0.74	0.00	95.41

Fig. 9. System load when running WebSocket – CPU = 7.02% average load, Waiting for IO = 4% average

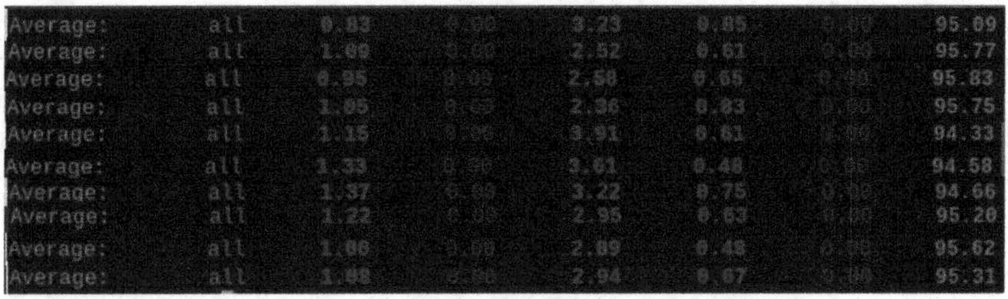

Average:	all	0.83	0.00	3.23	0.85	0.00	95.09
Average:	all	1.09	0.00	2.52	0.61	0.00	95.77
Average:	all	0.95	0.00	2.58	0.65	0.00	95.83
Average:	all	1.85	0.00	2.36	0.83	0.00	95.75
Average:	all	1.15	0.00	3.91	0.61	0.00	94.33
Average:	all	1.33	0.00	3.61	0.48	0.00	94.58
Average:	all	1.37	0.00	3.22	0.75	0.00	94.66
Average:	all	1.22	0.00	2.95	0.63	0.00	95.20
Average:	all	1.86	0.00	2.89	0.48	0.00	95.62
Average:	all	1.48	0.00	2.94	0.67	0.00	95.31

Fig. 10. System load while running MQTT – CPU = 4.78% average load, Waiting for IO = 0.66% average

The figures show that when running only the MQTT publisher script, the CPUs were less loaded at 4.78% compared to the WebSocket script's load of 7.02%. When the IO wait times were considered, MQTT is significantly better than WebSocket, as the CPUs were only idle 0.66% of the time waiting for IO request to finish, compared to 4% of the time when WebSocket was used. This is most likely because WebSocket keeps a persistent connection open with the server and must wait for responses from the server. MQTT does not have this issue as the components are decoupled as described in the Sect. 1.2. Though "%IOwait" might not only be because of the CPU waiting for packets to arrive, in our use case we tried to ensure that no other processes that might cause IO interrupt were running on the Raspberry Pi when the measurements were taken.

From the three results shown, we can conclude that MQTT is a better choice for streaming IoT telemetry data than WebSocket. This is because MQTT can transmit more data per unit time (higher throughput), uses less CPU resources, and is only marginally slower than WebSocket. Beyond this, the decoupled architecture of MQTT is much suited for IoT applications, where the sensors might be installed in a human body (e.g., heart monitors), or remote locations, such as underground or offshore in water bodies, while the broker and subscribers are in globally dispersed locations. Waiting for the client or server to be available before transmitting, as done with the WebSocket, would be detrimental.

5   Conclusion and Further Work

The objective of this paper was to compare the performance and suitability of Client-Server and Publish-Subscribe architectures for streaming IoT telemetry data. Two protocols were considered for the comparison, namely WebSocket, a client server protocol, and MQTT, a publish-subscribe protocol. The two protocols were tested using live data from sensors connected to a Raspberry Pi, using throughput, round trip time (RTT) and system load as metrics. A combination of Python scripts, Wireshark and Linux scripts were used to carry out the tests and obtained results show that MQTT performed better than WebSocket in all but RTT. The delay in RTT was very marginal and attributed to the intermediary broker.

This paper is a work-in-progress report and represents only a subset of bigger project. In future, the authors seek to expand the testing to include multiple clients, publishers, and subscribers. The performance of single versus multiple brokers in multi-publisher-multi-subscriber scenarios is also a planned work. Moreover, real world testing in scenarios such as those described in [15, 16], using additional metrics and other protocols, such as Data Distribution Service (which is tailored for M2M communication [17]), might also be opportunities that the authors might consider exploring in future works.

References

1. Want, R., Schilit, B.N., Jenson, S.: Enabling the internet of things. Computer **48**(1), 28–35 (2015)
2. Machaka, P., Ajayi, O., Maluleke, H., Kahenga, F., Bagula, A., Kyamakya, K.: Modelling DDoS Attacks in IoT Networks Using Machine Learning (2021). arXiv preprint arXiv:2112. 05477
3. Fette, I., Melnikov, A.: The WebSocket protocol (No. rfc6455) (2011)
4. Kurose J., Ross, K.: Computer Networking: A Top-Down Approach, Pearson (2016)
5. Stansberry, J.: MQTT and CoAP: Underlying Protocols for the IoT. Electron. Des, pp. 1–8 (2015)
6. Mishra, B.: Performance evaluation of MQTT broker servers. In: Gervasi, O., et al. (eds.) ICCSA 2018. LNCS, vol. 10963, pp. 599–609. Springer, Cham (2018). https://doi.org/10. 1007/978-3-319-95171-3_47
7. Thangavel, D., Ma, X., Valera, A., Tan H., Tan, C.: Performance evaluation of MQTT and CoAP via a common middleware. In: IEEE 9th International Conference on Intelligent Sensors, Sensor Networks and Information Processing (ISSNIP), pp. 1–6 (2014). https://doi.org/ 10.1109/ISSNIP.2014.6827678
8. Bartnitsky, J.: HTTP vs MQTT performance tests (2018). https://flespi.com/blog/http-vs-mqtt-performance-tests. Accessed 25July 2022
9. Luzuriaga, J., Perez, M., Boronat, P., Cano, J., Calafate, C., Manzoni, P.: A comparative evaluation of AMQP and MQTT protocols over unstable and mobile networks. In: 12th IEEE Consumer Communications and Networking Conf. (CCNC2015), pp. 931–936 (2015).https://doi.org/10.1109/CCNC.2015.7158101
10. Koziolek, H., Grüner, S., Rückert, J.: A comparison of mqtt brokers for distributed iot edge computing. In: Jansen, A., Malavolta, I., Muccini, H., Ozkaya, I., Zimmermann, O. (eds.) Software Architecture: 14th European Conference, ECSA 2020, L'Aquila, Italy, September 14–18, 2020, Proceedings, pp. 352–368. Springer International Publishing, Cham (2020). https://doi.org/10.1007/978-3-030-58923-3_23
11. El Ouadghiri, M., Aghoutane, B., El Farissi, N.: Communication model in the Internet of Things. Procedia Comput. Sci. **1**(177), 72–77 (2020)
12. Oliveira, G., Costa, D., Cavalcanti, R., Oliveira, J., et al.: Comparison between MQTT and WebSocket protocols for Iot applications using ESP8266. In: 2018 Workshop on Metrology for Industry 4.0 and IoT 2018 Apr 16, pp. 236–241. IEEE (2018)
13. Raspberry Pi.com. Raspberry Pi 4 Tech Specs. https://www.raspberrypi.com/products/raspbe rry-pi-4-model-b/specifications/. Accessed 13 Nov 2022
14. Lamping, U., Warnicke, E.: Wireshark user's guide. Interface **4**(6), 1 (2004). https://www.wir eshark.org/docs/wsug_html_chunked/ Accessed 13/11/2022

15. Ajayi, O.O., Bagula, A.B., Maluleke, H.C., Gaffoor, Z., Jovanovic, N., Pietersen, K.C.: Water-Net: a network for monitoring and assessing water quality for drinking and irrigation purposes. IEEE Access **10**, 48318–48337 (2022)
16. Mandava, T., Chen, S., Isafiade, O., Bagula, A.: An iot middleware for air pollution monitoring in smart cities: a situation recognition model. In: Proceedings of the IST Africa 2018 Conference, Gabarone, Botswana, pp. 9–11 (2018)
17. Kang, W., Kapitanova, K., Son, S.H.: RDDS: a real-time data distribution service for cyber-physical systems. IEEE Trans. Industr. Inf. **8**(2), 393–405 (2012)

Fourth Industrial Revolution Research Outputs in Africa: A Bibliometric Review

Paulina Phoobane[(✉)]

The Independent Institute of Education, IIE MSA, Roodepoort, South Africa
mpmakoetlane@gmail.com

Abstract. The world is currently transitioning through the fourth industrial revolution (4IR) era. 4IR research outputs are growing exponentially. Although African governments have been promoting fourth industrial revolution research and making initiatives to leverage it, these research outputs have not been analyzed. There is a dearth of publications that provide an up-to-date overview and a knowledge mapping analysis of 4IR literature in Africa. For this study, a bibliometric analysis of 912 scholarly papers published in Web of Science (WoS) core collection was conducted to reflect the research trends, 4IR themes, and gaps in 4IR publications in Africa. VOSviewer software was used to analyze the data. The results indicate that there has been a gradual growth in 4IR publications in Africa with a peak of 227 publications in 2021 according to the WoS database. South Africa is the most contributing and collaborative country, with most publications produced by the University of Johannesburg. The results suggest limited collaborations among African institutions and authors in this field. The 4IR research hotspots as revealed by keywords co-occurrences in Africa include machine learning, cloud computing, remote sensing, big data, and internet of things mainly for predictions and classification. The areas that may have received the least research focus include smart cities, block-chain, ecosystem service, policy, health care, and precision agriculture. By highlighting the research trends and gaps in 4IR literature in Africa, this study suggests possible directions for future 4IR research.

Keywords: Fourth industrial revolution · bibliometric analysis · research trends · 4IR trending technologies · Africa

1 Introduction

Fourth Industrial revolution, also known as industrial 4.0 or 4IR conceptualizes the 21st century's rapid transformation in technology, profound shift in production, business models and processes, transportation, and service delivery fostered by the blurring of the boundaries between the digital, physical, and biological domains [1, 2]. Industrial revolutions are the transformations in the systems and technology that surround humans and the way humans interact with these systems and technology, which in turn shape the ways of perceiving, acting, and being [1]. The first industrial revolution was a major innovation in the late 1700s and early 1800s [3]. It was a shift from handicraft economy

© ICST Institute for Computer Sciences, Social Informatics and Telecommunications Engineering 2023
Published by Springer Nature Switzerland AG 2023. All Rights Reserved
M. Masinde and A. Bagula (Eds.): AFRICATEK 2022, LNICST 503, pp. 140–160, 2023.
https://doi.org/10.1007/978-3-031-35883-8_10

to machine-powered economy characterized by using steam engines and mechanical manufacturing for production of goods and services [3]. The second industrial revolution or technological revolution made its debut in 19th centuries [4]. This revolution marked the shift from mechanical manufacturing and steam engine to electronic technology for mass production. The invention of assembly lines in the second revolution resulted in exponential growth in the industrial sector [2]. The second industrial revolution was followed by the third industrial revolution also known as digital revolution, in 20th century. This revolution was punctuated by a transition from the analogue electronic technology to the digital electronics [2, 5]. In third industrial revolution Information Technology and electronics were used to automate the production processes [6]. This phase of industrial revolution marked the era of information age, information systems-based economy [5]. The fourth industrial revolution emerged in the 21st century. The hallmark of the fourth industrial revolution is the remarkable upsurge in technological breakthroughs, their unlimited scope of application, and their tremendous impact in reshaping the way of living [7]. One of the prominent features of 4IR is the capability of the new technology to fuse the physical, biological, and digital world [8]. Some of the eminent and powerful technologies that have made a great mark in 4IR include artificial intelligence, machine learning, Internet of Things (IoT), quantum computing, robotics, 3-D printing, cloud computing, big data, and augmented reality [2, 7–9]. Even though each industrial revolution may be seen as individual entity, each industrial revolution is rather an advancement of the previous one.

The inexorable changes brought by fourth industrial revolution on nearly the entire gamut of human's life has attracted attention of several researchers globally [1, 3, 7, 8, 10–15], resulting in rich literature around 4IR. Literature on 4IR range from the application and use of 4IR in different sectors such as education, health, industries, agriculture, governance etc., to review papers. For instance, [16] explored the use of machine learning in agriculture, while [15, [17–23] used artificial intelligence and machine learning in health. On the other hand, [24] used IoT in in agriculture, [25] used IoT in the optimization of the state management of economy, while [13, 26–37] conducted systematic review studies in 4IR in different disciplines.

In Africa, governments and institutions have been promoting fourth industrial revolution research and making initiatives to leverage it [38]. Consequently, there are several research studies on 4IR conducted in Africa to tackle some of the prominent challenges that Africa face such as drought, diseases, and food security [39–41]. For instance, [42] used machine learning to optimize cropping farming by small scale farmers, [15] utilized machine learning to predict malaria, and [40, 43] used artificial neural networks to predict drought. There are also studies in Africa that focus on the challenges and opportunities of 4IR in Africa [10, 12]. However, previous studies reported low contribution of Africa in the research output [44, 45]. Limited research output in Africa is in part impacted by poor infrastructure [46], brain drain of African expertise [47], insufficient funds for research studies [46, 48, 49], African researchers having high teaching loads and receiving little incentives [48], and inadequate research collaboration networks [50]. Faced with these opportunities and challenges in 4IR Africa, there is a little known about the development in the 4IR research output in Africa.

To provide a comprehensive analysis of the 4IR literature in Africa, some authors proposed review studies [51–53]. However, most of these review papers are systematic reviews focusing mainly on the comprehensive analysis of the content of the publications and a few focus on the bibliometric analysis. A bibliometric analysis provides an overview and a knowledge mapping of the literature in a specific research area [54]. There have been several bibliometric analyses in other geographical areas outside Africa or on isolated 4IR technologies. For example,[55] focused on the bibliometric review of Machine learning on COVID-19, while [11, 56, 57] focused on bibliometric review of 4IR on supply chain, knowledge management, and agriculture 4.0, respectively. Bibliometric analysis to review 4IR has not been fully exploited, especially in African context. Therefore, this research study focuses on bibliometric analysis on fourth industrial revolution publications to explore research developments in this field in Africa. Bibliometric analysis on fourth industrial revolution can unpack the status of fourth industrial revolution literature in Africa: research and technological trends, hot spots areas as well as the gaps.

Given the above research gap, this paper aims at answering the following research question:

What is the current state of the fourth industrial revolution literature in Africa?

To answer the above questions the following research objectives were demarcated:

1. To characterize the current state of the fourth industrial revolution research in Africa.
2. To identify trends in fourth industrial revolution research related to Africa.
3. To identify the technological trends in fourth industrial revolution research in Africa
4. To identify the research gaps and opportunities in fourth industrial revolution in Africa.

This paper proceeds as follows: Sect. 2 outlines research methodology, and Sect. 3 evaluates publication trends and identifies emerging themes in fourth industrial revolution. The fourth section focuses on the assessment of gaps and possible research opportunities in the fourth industrial revolution in Africa. Lastly, Sect. 5, concludes the paper by detailing the study's main contribution.

2   Material and Methods

The dataset used in this research study was extracted from WoS. Web of Science is one of the most widely used standard indexes in the computer science and engineering community [58]. The search was conducted with all time span (All years (1996 – 07/08/2022)). Though there were no restrictions on language or document type, the geographic scope of publication was restricted to Africa. The search was done at the topic level which searches for the match in the paper title, abstract and keywords. The following search string was used to get the dataset:

TS = ("Industry 4.0*" OR '4IR' OR "Fourth industrial revolution" OR "machine learning" OR "artificial intelligence" OR "big data" OR "Internet of Things" OR 'IoT' OR "quantum computing" OR 'robotics' OR "3D printing" OR "cloud computing" OR "augmented reality" OR "Block chain") AND TS = ("Africa").

The search resulted in 1 663 papers from Web of Science. The dataset comprised of the following bibliographic meta data of the retrieved papers and their cited papers:

information about authors, document, content, citation, and funding. To improve the data quality. The documents were further screened manually at the tittle, abstract and where required at the full paper level. Papers that did not meet the inclusion criteria were removed. The inclusion criteria were that the paper should be on any technology in fourth industrial revolution (artificial intelligence, IoT, machine learning, cloud computing, etc.,) and conducted in Africa. Nine duplicates were also removed. After this manual screening, there were 924 papers that met the inclusion criteria. Figure 1 below shows the search process of identifying papers for inclusion.

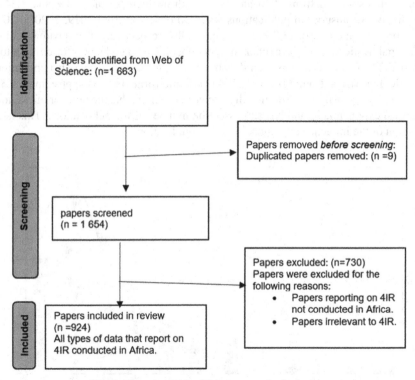

Fig. 1. Process of identifying papers for inclusion.

The dataset was then analyzed using VOSviewer version 1.6.18 to create visualization maps. Visualization maps play a critical role in describing the structure and evolution of a certain research field. VOSviewer is a widely used efficacious tool for bibliometric analysis. For example, [59] used VOSviewer to provide a knowledge mapping analysis of the prediction of infectious diseases literature. On the other hand, [60] used VOSviewer to explore methods and tools used to monitor and predict drought in Africa, while [61] and [62] deployed VOSviewer to quantify the research output on Ebola virus and COVID-19, respectively. In this study, VOSviewer was used to determine the research trends, gaps, and future research opportunities in the field of fourth industrial revolution in the context of Africa, and the following maps were created: co-citation, keywords co-occurrence, and co-authorship maps.

3 Results

3.1 The Fourth Industrial Revolution Research Trends in Africa

Evolutionary Trajectories of Publications in Fourth Industrial Revolution in Africa
Figure 2 depicts the number of publications in fourth industrial revolution in Africa from 2011 to 2022. The year with the highest publications is 2021 while 2011 is the year with the lowest publications It can be observed that from 2011 to 2014, the literature on fourth industrial revolution was very sparse. The significant increase in the number of publications started from 2016 and 2017 with an increase of 4.93% and 7.34%, respectively. An upsurge in publications was also observed from 2019, 2020 to 2021 with publication increase of 13.9%, 18.2% and 24.8%, respectively. The apparent decline in 2022 publications could be explained by the fact the data collection for only up to 8 August 2022. Overall, there has been slow but notable increase in the yearly publications in this field in Africa, from 2011 to 2022, this is demonstrated by the approximate 2.3% annual average growth rate. Additionally, it can be observed that the number of citations has grown exponentially and has surpassed the number of the publications. This is an indication of the influence and impact of these publications.

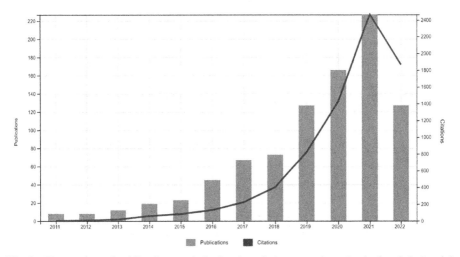

Fig. 2. The number of publications and citations' evolutionary trajectories in fourth industrial revolution in Africa from 2011 to 2022.

Document Types of Fourth Industrial Revolution Publications in Africa
Table 1 illustrates different types of documents that were considered for further analysis after the manual screening. It can be noted that the dataset consists mainly of articles, and conference papers followed by review articles. Books, news items and letters were the least presented papers in the dataset.

Table 1. Document types of the fourth industrial revolution publications in Africa.

Document Types	Record Count	Percentage of 912
Article	620	67.98
Proceeding Paper	236	25.88
Review Article	42	4.61
Early Access	29	3.18
Book Chapters	18	1.97
Editorial Material	18	1.97
Meeting Abstract	6	0.66
Data Paper	3	0.33
Letter	3	0.33
Book	1	0.11
News Item	1	0.11

Web of Science Categories

The 4IR publications in Africa as per the dataset come from different disciplines such as Economics and Infectious Diseases. Figure 3 shows different WoS categories or disciplines in the development of fourth industrial revolution research in Africa. The WoS categories that had a minimum of 20 research outputs were considered in the graph. It can be observed that documents in fourth industrial revolution in Africa were from the environmental science, followed by Remote Sensing, Computer Science Theory Methods, Image Science Photographic Technology, Telecommunications and Multidisciplinary Science. The results (not depicted in the graph) show that there are 25 WoS disciplines that may be under-represented in 4IR literature as they each only have one publication in 4IR. These disciplines include Sport Sciences, Nuclear Science Technology, History, Criminology Penology, Family Studies, and Pharmacology Pharmacy.

Top Ten Most Productive Countries in Fourth Industrial Revolution Literature in Africa

Several countries have contributed to 4IR publications in Africa, and Fig. 4 shows the top leading countries. Countries were ranked based on the first author's country of affiliation, and only the top 10 countries were considered.

South Africa is the leading country in publications on fourth industrial revolution in Africa, accounting for 49.9% of the publications. South Africa is followed by the United States of America (USA), England, Germany, and Kenya. Europe is the mostly represented continent in the top 10 and it is represented by four countries. The top ten list has got three African countries (South Africa, Kenya, and Nigeria) and two American countries (USA and Canada). The continent that is least represented is Asia while other continents such as Oceanica are not represented at all.

The Most Productive Authors

There are several authors who have contributed to the 4IR literature in Africa. Figure 5

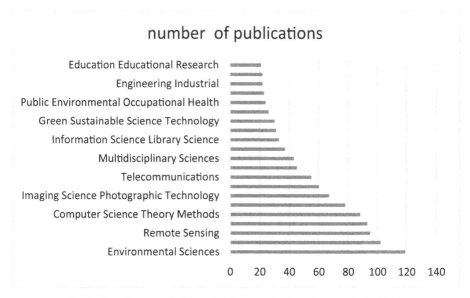

Fig. 3. Top 10 most publishing WoS categories in 4IR research in Africa.

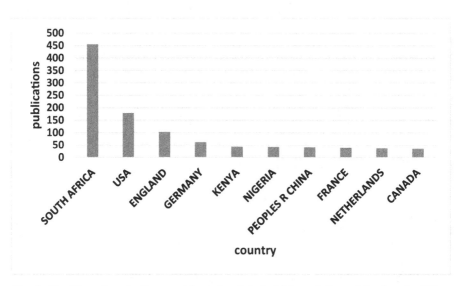

Fig. 4. Top 10 most productive countries in fourth industrial revolution publications in Africa.

illustrates the top 10 most contributing authors in this field. At the top is Bag. S, followed by Muntanga. O, Adam. E, Dube. T, Hasan. AN., and Stopforth, R. All the authors in the top 10 have at least seven papers published in this field.

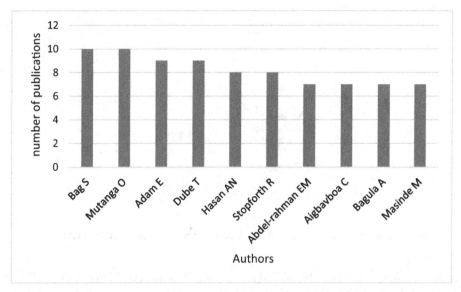

Fig. 5. Top 10 most contributing authors in fourth industrial revolution publications in Africa.

3.2 VOSviewer Visualization Maps

A VOSviewer map consists of nodes which are also called circles or items, and edges that connect the nodes. A node represents the item of interest in the map while the edge indicates the relationship between two nodes that it connects [63]. For instance, in the authors co-authorship map, the items of interest will the authors and an edge connecting two authors would indicate collaboration between those authors. The items with strong relatedness are grouped in one cluster and are given the same color [63].

Country Collaboration Map
Country co-authorship map illustrates the number of co-authored documents between countries and, therefore, reflects the strength or extend of collaborations among the countries [63]. Figure 6 below depicts the VOSviwer visualization map of country collaboration.

The map groups countries with high collaboration in the same cluster. The countries denoted with bigger circles indicate dominating countries in the fourth industrial revolution literature in Africa. These countries include South africa, the USA and England. These countries also appeared in Fig. 4 as top 10 leading countries in number of research outputs. It can be noted that these countries also tended to be more collaborative. South Africa is the most collaborative country in 4IR publications with the total collaboration strength of 289. South Africa is followed by the USA, England, Germnany and France. South Africa collaborates with both countries abround and in Africa. The other countries with a strong collaborative strength in Africa include Kenya, Tanzania, Ghana, Ethopia, and Nigeria, each with a collaboration total strength of 105, 79, 66, 63 and 62, respectively. Non African countries that show strong collaborations include India, People Republic of China and Neverlands. On the other hand, the least collaborating countries

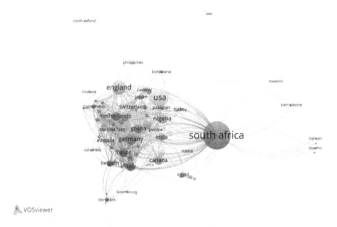

Fig. 6. Country collaboration in fourth industrial revolution publications in Africa.

include Lesotho, Mauritius, Tunisa and Zwaziland. These countries have mostly collaborate with South Africa. They are also the least contributing countries in this field; this is denoted by the small circles that represent these countries in the visualization map.

In this map, there are 14 clusters. The biggest cluster with the most countries is the red cluster consisting of 14 countries that include France, Mali, Guinea Bissau, Morocco and Ukraine. Even though South Africa is clustered with countries like Lesotho, Sierra Leon and Mariatius, it also shows a very strong collaboration with countries such as the USA, England and Ghana. The cluster with the smallest number of the countries is the purple clustered consisting of Peru, England and Northern Ireland.

Institution Collaboration Map

There are 1331 institutions that contributed to 4IR literature in Africa according to the WoS database. Figure 7 shows the institution collaboration map which indicates the co-authorship among the institutions on 4IR literature in Africa. The relatedness of the items (institutions) is based on the number of papers co-authored [63]. Only institutions meeting the default threshold of five co-authored documents per an institution were considered, and consequently, 62 institutions were included in the map.

Institutions with the strong collaboration among themselves are clustered together and there are 10 clusters in this map. The red cluster is the biggest cluster and comprised of institutions such as the University of Ghana, the University of Maryland and NASA. The dark blue cluster shows the collaboration among South African institutions only. The purple cluster also depicts collaboration mainly between the South African institutions, with the University of Nairobi as well as the University of Antwerp. Similar observations can be made on the light blue cluster (containing the University of Johannesburg) and the orange cluster (showing the University of KwaZulu Natal), South African institutions dominate the clusters and are the most collaborative institutions among themselves and with other institutions. Table 2 illustrates the top 10 most contributing institutions in 4IR in Africa.

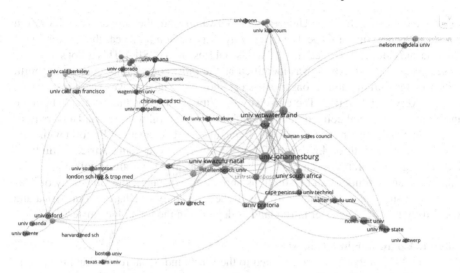

Fig. 7. Institutions collaboration in fourth industrial revolution publications in Africa.

Table 2. Top ten most productive institutions in the research of 4IR in Africa.

Rank	Institutions	Publications	citations	Total strength of collaboration	Country
1	University of Johannesburg	87	816	19	South Africa
2	University of Witwatersrand	52	370	46	South Africa
3	University of KwaZulu Natal	48	359	43	South Africa
4	University of Cape Town	47	327	39	South Africa
5	University of South Africa	31	25	11	South Africa
6	University of Pretoria	30	117	22	South Africa
7	CSIR	30	292	20	South Africa
8	University of Western Cape	27	176	17	South Africa
9	Stellenbosch University	21	154	12	South Africa
10	North -West University	19	72	5	South Africa

The institution with the highest number of publications is the University of Johannesburg. Though the University of Johannesburg is the leading institution in 4IR in Africa, it is not relatively collaborative. The top 11 most contributing institutions are from South

Africa, and these include the University of Witwatersrand, the University of KwaZulu Natal, the University of Cape Town, the university of South Africa, the University of Pretoria and Council for Scientific and Industrial Research (CSIR). This is not surprising to see because South Africa was identified as the most contributing country in fourth industrial revolution publications in Africa as shown in Fig. 4 above. These institutions are also very collaborative. The university of Witwatersrand is the most collaborative institution with a total collaboration strength of 46. It is followed by the University of KwaZulu Natal, the University of Cape Town, and the University of Pretoria with total collaboration strength of 43, 39 and 22, respectively. These South Africa institutions have strong collaboration among themselves, and they also have strong collaborate with other African institutions and institutions abroad. For instance, the University of Witwatersrand shows strong collaboration with the University of Khartoum in Africa and the University of Manchester in England as depicted in the light blue cluster.

Authors Co-authorship Analysis

There are 3337 authors who contributed to the fourth industrial revolution literature in Africa according to WoS. To create the authors co-authorship visualization map only authors with minimum of three papers were considered and 63 authors met the threshold. In the co-authorship map, the relatedness of authors is based on the number of papers co-authored [63]. The authors with a strong co-authorship are clustered together. Figure 8 below illustrates the author co-authorship map.

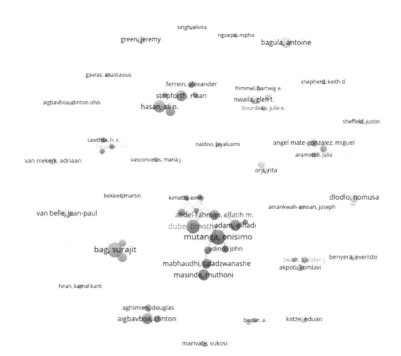

Fig. 8. Authors co-authorship in fourth industrial revolution publications in Africa.

Based on the outcome of co-authorship analysis as illustrated in Fig. 8 above, there are 30 clusters. Fifteen of these clusters consist of one author per cluster, indicating that the author has not collaborated with other authors. The high number of clusters and small number of authors in the clusters indicate limited collaboration among the authors in 4IR publications in Africa. For instance, authors such as Kotze Eduan, Ngoepe Mpho, and Van Niekerk Adriaan have contributed significantly to 4IR literature, but they are the least collaborative authors in this literature. The red cluster has the highest number of authors, and these include Masinde Muthoni, Madhaudhi Tafadwanashe, Adam Elhadi and Mutanga Onisimo. These are also the most contributing authors in the field of 4IR in Africa as indicated by the bigger circle in the map. Another cluster containing many authors is the blue cluster with six authors that include Dube Timothy and Mudereri Bester Tawona. The author with the strongest collaboration is Mutanga Onisimo collaborating with six authors with a total collaboration strength of 17. The results suggest that generally the most contributing authors are also very collaborative.

Authors Co-citation Analysis

In the author co-citation map, the relatedness of the authors is determined by the number of times the authors are cited together [63]. Authors' co-citation determines the knowledge structure or different subfields in specific research field and identifies the most influential researchers and their interrelationships [64, 65]. Authors meeting the threshold of 10 times minimum of citations were considered, and 182 authors met the criteria. Figure 9 depicts the author' co-citation map with eight clusters. The most influential authors in 4IR research in Africa include the World Health Organization (WHO), The world bank, Breiman, I., Schwab, K., Bag, S., Kuhn, M., and Mutanga, O.

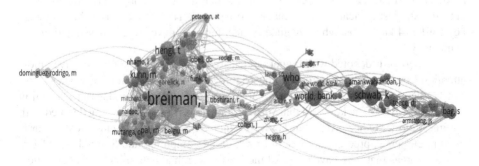

Fig. 9. Authors co-citation visualization map on 4IR publications in Africa.

Key Words Co-occurrence Analysis

Keywords co-occurrence was used in this research study to reveal the 4IR technological trends, hot spots, and gaps in fourth industrial revolution. In a key words co-occurrence map, the relatedness of the keywords is based on number of times the keywords appear together in a paper[63]. Figure 10 shows the keywords co-occurrence map.

The keywords with high frequency of appearance in the literature are represented with bigger circles to show dominance. The keywords that appear together are placed in

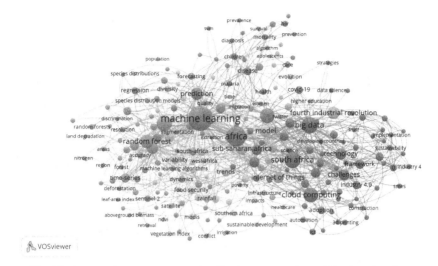

Fig. 10. Key words co-occurrence visualization map on 4IR publications in Africa

one cluster. There were 4346 keywords in fourth industrial revolution in Africa as per WoS, and only keywords that appeared four times or more in the WoS database were considered. Consequently, only 306 were included in the keywords co-occurrence analysis. The keywords were grouped into seven clusters. The biggest cluster (red cluster) consisted of 81 keywords which include industrial 4.0, South Africa, COVID-19, Robotics, internet of things, sustainability, smart cities, and block chain. The green cluster is the second largest cluster with 75 keywords such as classification, image classification, random forest, west Africa, satellite image and patterns. The orange cluster has the least keywords, 14 keywords, which include Africa, farmers, poverty, text classification and democracy.

The keywords denoted with bigger circles are the keywords that have received most attention from researchers in fourth industrial revolution research in Africa. These keywords, therefore, indicate possible research hot spots in fourth industrial revolution research in Africa. The keyword that appeared most was machine learning denoted with a biggest circle. Other prominent keywords include South Africa, classification, artificial intelligence, prediction, random forest, cloud computing and Sub Sahara Africa. Research areas that may have received the least research attention include smart cities, text classifications, block chain, ecosystem service, k-means clustering, energy consumption, policy, health care, sustainable development goals, and precision agriculture. These words are represented with small circles to denote the low frequency of occurrence.

To further understand Fig. 10 above, the top 20 keywords in the literature of fourth industrial revolution in Africa as per WoS are shown in Table 3.

These keywords suggest fourth industrial revolution themes and areas of applications that have been significantly researched in Africa. The keyword with the highest frequency is Machine Learning, followed by Africa, Big data, and South Africa. According to Table 3, the fourth industrial revolution themes or technologies that are most explored include Machine learning, Africa artificial intelligence, big data, remote sensing, cloud

Table 3. Top 20 keywords in fourth industrial revolution literature in Africa.

Rank	Keywords	Frequency	Rank	Keywords	Frequency
1	Machine learning	151	11	Fourth Industrial Revolution	38
2	Africa	98	12	model	37
3	Big data	66	13	Remote sensing	35
4	South Africa	66	14	challenges	29
5	Classification	62	15	Internet of Things	29
6	Artificial intelligence	54	16	performance	27
7	Cloud computing	54	17	Climate-change	27
8	Random forest	46	18	impact	26
9	prediction	39	19	management	24
10	Sub-Sahara Africa	38	20	Deep learning	24

computing, Random Forest (machine learning) and Internet of Things. The keywords in Table 3 suggest the use of fourth industrial revolution in Africa to be mainly for prediction and classification. It is interesting to note that keywords such as climate change have been widely researched in the fourth industrial revolution in Africa. On the other hand, it is not surprising to see South Africa as the top four leading keyword in Fourth Industrial Revolution in Africa. The previous analyses such as in Figs. 4, 6 and 7, and Table 2, have already pointed out South Africa as a dominating country in fourth industrial revolution research in Africa.

4 Discussion

4.1 State of Fourth Industrial Revolution Research in Africa

The results indicate a gradual growth in fourth industrial revolution publications between 2011 and 2022 in Africa, with a peak of 227 publications in 2021. The significant growth in the publications intensified between 2016 and 2017. The upsurge in the number of publications in 2016 and 2017 may be in part attributed to the contribution made by Schawb Klause in this field in 2017 with his book titled "The fourth Industrial Revolution" [2]that popularized the term fourth industrial revolution and possibly triggered more interest in research in this field. Most of the publications in 4IR in Africa are mostly journal articles and proceeding papers from environmental science, remote sensing, computer science, telecommunications, and multi-disciplinary science. The disciplines such as Sport Sciences, Nuclear Science Technology, History, Criminology Penology, Family Studies, and Pharmacology Pharmacy are under-represented in fourth industrial revolution literature. This calls for more research in fourth industrial revolution in these disciplines.

South Africa is the major contributing country in 4IR publications with almost half of African publications (49.9%) originating from its institutions. South African institutions are the most productive and collaborative, with most publications coming from the University of Johannesburg and the University of Witwatersrand. These findings concur with results from bibliometric studies conducted previously [60, 66, 67]. This, therefore, marks a remarkable growth by South Africa in the research studies conducted in Africa. Even though South Africa faces challenges in 4IR[10], it has shown some advancement in infrastructure and investments in research which can explain its high research output especially in 4IR. For example, South Africa has an ample number of higher education institutions and independent research institutes undertaking research in different disciplines [68]. Sutherland [10], and Ayentimi and Burgess [12] emphasize that there is a dire need in Africa to ensure proper infrastructure, and a sufficient supply of skills to boost 4IR. Countries like Lesotho represented with a small circle in Fig. 6, have one publication in 4IR as per data from Wos. On the other hand, countries such as Swaziland are not presented at all. Countries like Lesotho have limited resources, poor infrastructure which can impede their 4IR developments and research outputs [69]. Moreover, Lesotho collaborates only with South Africa in 4IR research as seen in Fig. 6. The literature has highlighted the poor infrastructure, unavailability of resources and low collaboration network as major hindrance in research output.

Even though South Africa is the most productive country in 4IR research in Africa, most of the countries in the top 10 leading countries in 4IR in Africa are from Europe and North America. [70], explains underrepresentation of African in African studies as partly due to imbalance distribution of global research funds. For example, from USD 1.51 trillion research grants from 521 organizations around the world, African institutions receive only 14.5% for climate research while European and North American institutions receive 78% funding for climate research on Africa [70].

The most contributing authors in the 4IR publications include Bags, S., Mutanga, O., and Amad, E, while the most influential authors include WHO, WHO), The world bank, Breiman, I., Schwab, K., and Bag, S. The findings also indicate low collaboration among the countries, institutions, and authors in this field. Mbaye *et al.*, [45]and, Yang *et al.*, [71]emphasize the importance of collaboration in research especially on multi-disciplinary areas such as 4IR. Literature pointed out inadequate research collaboration networks as one of the factors that Africa contributes less than 1–1.5% to the global research output [50].

4.2 4IR Trending Technologies and Research Trends in Africa

From the bibliometric analysis the following fourth industrial revolution themes stood out in the fourth industrial revolution literature in Africa: Machine learning (deep learning, random forest), artificial intelligence, Internet of things, big data, remote sensing, cloud computing. Additionally, the keywords co-occurrence analysis also highlighted the following words as the trending research keywords in fourth industrial revolution research in Africa: South Africa, classification, prediction, climate change, challenges, and Sub Sahara Africa. These findings suggest Machine learning, artificial intelligence, internet of things, big data, remote sensing, cloud computing to be the fourth industrial revolution technology trends in Africa. Moreover, the findings highlight that the application of fourth industrial revolution technologies in Africa to be mostly for predictions and classification purposes and to tackle climate change challenges. For instance, the study by [60] pointed machine learning as a tool used for drought prediction in Africa. On the other hand, South Africa appearing among the trending keywords highlights again the dominance of South Africa in fourth industrial revolution research output in Africa. Moreover, there are also several research studies that built prediction machine learning models to address some of the prominent challenges in Africa such as infectious diseases [39]. This can explain the trending of 4IR technologies such as artificial intelligence and machine learning.

4.3 Research Gaps and Future Research Directions

- Future studies should explore 4IR technologies such as robotics, block-chain, quantum computing, virtual reality, 3-D printing as they are under-researched in Africa. Even though these technologies were included in the search strings for paper retrieval as depicted in Sect. 2, they appeared less than eight times in the retrieved data while some keywords such as quantum computing had zero appearance.
- The fourth industrial revolution technologies should also be extended in areas such as ecosystem service, energy consumption, health care, sustainable development goals, and precision agriculture. Unlike prediction and classifications, these words have not been explored significantly in 4IR research in Africa. The keyword, policy also appeared under-researched in 4IR in Africa. Naidoo[72], Sutherland [10], and Ayentimi and Burgess [12] emphasize that there is a need in Africa to ensure proper policy in 4IR to promote 4IR in Africa.
- Disciplines such as Sport Sciences, Nuclear Science Technology, Criminology Penology, Family Studies, and Pharmacology Pharmacy are under-research disciplines in 4IR in Africa as reported in Sect. 3.1. Future studies need to explore 4IR technologies in these disciplines.
- Future studies should be collaborative work. There is a limited research collaboration among the African institutions and authors in 4IR research as pointed in Sect. 4.1. Fourth industrial revolution can be viewed as transdisciplinary that requires knowledge from different disciplines. This therefore calls for, among many, collaboration between scholars in various disciplines and experts from the industries to bring in different expertise necessary to boost the research output in fourth industrial revolution in Africa.

5 Conclusion

There has been a gradual growth in research publications on 4IR in Africa between 2011 and 2022. South African institutions dominate the 4IR publishing space, contributing almost half (49%) of all research outputs. The results also suggest limited collaborations among African researchers in 4IR research which calls for research capacity building. Most research themes in 4IR research in Africa revolve around artificial intelligence, machine learning, big data, internet of things for predictions and classification purposes.

Research trends in 4IR in Africa include South Africa, classification, prediction, climate change, challenges, and Sub Sahara Africa. The findings from this study suggests that there are limited research efforts in areas such as robotics, quantum computer, virtual reality, and disciplines such Sport Sciences, Criminology Penology, Family Studies in 4IR in Africa.

Future studies may also incorporate other dataset from databases such as Scopus and Google Scholar for a more comprehensive review. Results from this research study can be a valuable resource to researchers, practitioners, policy makers and research funding agencies interested in 4IR research in Africa. This research study provides knowledge and grasp the research characteristic of 4IR research studies in Africa.

References

1. Petrillo, A., De Felice, F., Cioffi, R., Zomparelli, F.: Fourth industrial revolution: current practices, challenges, and opportunities. In: Petrillo, A., Cioffi, R., De Felice, F. (eds.) Digital Transformation in Smart Manufacturing. InTech (2018). https://doi.org/10.5772/intechopen.72304
2. Schwab, K.: The Fourth Industrial Revolution, 1st edn. Crown business, New York (2017)
3. Xu, M., David, J.M., Kim, S.H.: The fourth industrial revolution: opportunities and challenges. Int. J. Finan. Res. **9**(2), 90–95 (2018). https://doi.org/10.5430/ijfr.v9n2p90
4. Assistant Professor, H., Kumar Mohajan, H.: The Second Industrial Revolution has Brought Modern Social and Economic Developments (2020)
5. Martin, Janicke, J.K.: A Third Industrial Revolution. Long-Term Governance For Social-Ecological Change. Routledge, New York (2013)
6. Brettel, M., Friederichsen, N., Keller, M., Rosenberg, M.: How virtualization, decentralization and network building change the manufacturing landscape: an Industry 4.0 perspective. Int. J. Inform. Commun. Eng. **8**(1), 37–44 (2017)
7. Philbeck, T.: The fourth industrial revolution. J. Int. Aff. **72**(1), 17–22 (2018)
8. Dimitrieska, S., Stankovska, A., Efremova, T.: The fourth industrial revolution-advantages and challenges. Econ. Manage. **XV**(2), 182–187 (2018)
9. Ghobakhloo, M., Fathi, M., Iranmanesh, M., Maroufkhani, P., Morales, M.E.: Industry 4.0 ten years on: A bibliometric and systematic review of concepts, sustainability value drivers, and success determinants. J. Clean. Product. **302**, 127052 (2021). https://doi.org/10.1016/j.jclepro.2021.127052
10. Sutherland, E.: The Fourth industrial revolution-the case of South Africa. Politikon **47**(2), 233–252 (2020). https://doi.org/10.1080/02589346.2019.1696003
11. Barata, J.: The fourth industrial revolution of supply chains: a tertiary study. J. Eng. Tech. Manage. **60**, 101624 (2021). https://doi.org/10.1016/J.JENGTECMAN.2021.101624
12. Ayentimi, D.T., Burgess, J.: Is the fourth industrial revolution relevant to sub-Sahara Africa? Technol. Anal. Strateg. Manag. **31**(6), 641–652 (2019). https://doi.org/10.1080/09537325.2018.1542129
13. McCoy, J.T., Auret, L.: Machine learning applications in minerals processing: a review. Miner Eng **132**, 95–109 (2019). https://doi.org/10.1016/J.MINENG.2018.12.004
14. Theocharides, S., Makrides, G., Georghiou, G.E., Kyprianou, A.: Machine learning algorithms for photovoltaic system power output prediction. In: 2018 IEEE International Energy Conference, Energycon 2018, no. October, pp. 1–6 (2018). https://doi.org/10.1109/ENERGYCON.2018.8398737

15. Nkiruka, O., Prasad, R., Clement, O.: Prediction of malaria incidence using climate variability and machine learning. Inform. Med. Unlocked **22**, 100508 (2021). https://doi.org/10.1016/j. imu.2020.100508
16. Almadani, B., Mostafa, S.M.: IIoT based multimodal communication model for agriculture and agro-industries. IEEE Access **9**, 10070–10088 (2021). https://doi.org/10.1109/ACCESS. 2021.3050391
17. Hu, Z., Ge, Q., Li, S., Xiong, M.: Artificial intelligence forecasting of Covid-19 in China. Int. J. Educ. Excell. **6**(1), 71–94 (2020). https://doi.org/10.18562/ijee.054
18. Frandsen, A.J.: Machine Learning for Disease Prediction. Brigham Young University, ScholarsArchives, p. Paper 5975 (2016). https://scholarsarchive.byu.edu/etd/5975
19. Patel, A., Gandhi, S., Shetty, S., Tekwani, B.: Heart disease prediction using data mining. Int. Res. J. Eng. Technol. **4**(1), 4–6 (2017). https://irjet.net/archives/V4/i1/IRJET-V4I1339.pdf
20. Pradhan, N., Rani, G., Dhaka, V.S., Poonia, R.C.: Diabetes prediction using artificial neural network. Deep Learn. Techn. Biomed. Health Inform. **121**, 327–339 (2020). https://doi.org/ 10.1016/b978-0-12-819061-6.00014-8
21. Sadek, R.M., et al.: Parkinson's Disease Prediction Using Artificial Neural Network. vol. 3, no. 1, pp. 1–8 (2019). http://dstore.alazhar.edu.ps/xmlui/handle/123456789/302
22. Vaishya, R., Javaid, M., Khan, I.H., Haleem, A.: Artificial Intelligence (AI) applications for COVID-19 pandemic. Diabetes Metab. Syndr. **14**(4), 337–339 (2020). https://doi.org/10. 1016/j.dsx.2020.04.012
23. Yadav, M., Perumal, M., Srinivas, M.: Analysis on novel coronavirus (COVID-19) using machine learning methods. Chaos Solitons Fract. **139** (2020). https://doi.org/10.1016/j.chaos. 2020.110050
24. Zhang, L., Dabipi, I.K., Brown, W.L.: Internet of Things applications for agriculture. In: Qusay, H. (ed.): Internet of Things A to Z: Technologies andA, pp. 507–528 (2018)
25. Popkova, E.G., Egorova, E.N., Popova, E., Pozdnyakova, U.A.: The model of state management of economy on the basis of the internet of things. In: Popkova, E.G. (ed.) Ubiquitous Computing and the Internet of Things: Prerequisites for the Development of ICT. SCI, vol. 826, pp. 1137–1144. Springer, Cham (2019). https://doi.org/10.1007/978-3-030-13397-9_116
26. Graham, S., et al.: Artificial intelligence for mental health and mental illnesses: an overview. Curr. Psychiatry Rep. **21**(11), 1–18 (2019). https://doi.org/10.1007/s11920-019-1094-0
27. Iqbal, S., Altaf, W., Aslam, M., Mahmood, W., Khan, M.U.G.: Application of intelligent agents in health-care: review. Artif. Intell. Rev. **46**(1), 83–112 (2016). https://doi.org/10.1007/s10 462-016-9457-y
28. Khan, M., et al.: Applications of artificial intelligence in COVID-19 pandemic: a comprehensive review. Expert Syst. Appl. **185**, 115695 (2021). https://doi.org/10.1016/j.eswa.2021. 115695
29. Lalmuanawma, S., Hussain, J., Chhakchhuak, L.: Applications of machine learning and artificial intelligence for Covid-19 (SARS-CoV-2) pandemic: a review. Chaos, Solitons and Fractals, vol. 139. Elsevier Ltd, Oct. 01 (2020). https://doi.org/10.1016/j.chaos.2020.110059
30. Loh, E.: Medicine and the rise of the robots: a qualitative review of recent advances of artificial intelligence in health. BMJ Leader, vol. 2, no. 2. BMJ Publishing Group, pp. 59–63 (2018). https://doi.org/10.1136/leader-2018-000071
31. Schwendicke, F., Samek, W., Krois, J.: Artificial intelligence in dentistry: chances and challenges. J Dent Res **99**(7), 769–774 (2020). https://doi.org/10.1177/0022034520915714
32. Liakos, K., Busato, P., Moshou, D., Pearson, S., Bochtis, D.: Machine learning in agriculture: a review. Sensors **18**(8), 2674 (2018). https://doi.org/10.3390/s18082674
33. Sharma, A., Jain, A., Gupta, P., Chowdary, V.: Machine learning applications for precision agriculture: a comprehensive review. IEEE Access **9**, 4843–4873 (2021). https://doi.org/10. 1109/ACCESS.2020.3048415

34. González-Calatayud, V., Prendes-Espinosa, P., Roig-Vila, R., Carpanzano, E.: Applied sciences review artificial intelligence for student assessment: a systematic review. Appl. Sci **2021**, 5467 (2021). https://doi.org/10.3390/app

35. Upadhyay, A.K., Khandelwal, K.: Applying artificial intelligence: implications for recruitment. Strat. HR Rev. **17**(5), 255–258 (2018). https://doi.org/10.1108/SHR-07-2018-0051

36. Deiva Ganesh, A., Kalpana, P.: Future of artificial intelligence and its influence on supply chain risk management – a systematic review. Comput. Ind. Eng. **169**, 108206 (2022). https://doi.org/10.1016/J.CIE.2022.108206

37. Loureiro, S.M.C., Guerreiro, J., Tussyadiah, I.: Artificial intelligence in business: state of the art and future research agenda. J. Bus. Res. **129**, 911–926 (2021). https://doi.org/10.1016/J.JBUSRES.2020.11.001

38. Okoye, U.M., Ogbu, E.O., Ome, G.E.: The place of Africa in the fourth industrial revolution. Filosofia Theoretica **9**(3), 65–84 (2020). https://doi.org/10.4314/ft.v9i3.5

39. Masinde, M.: Africa's malaria epidemic predictor: application of machine learning on malaria incidence and climate data. In: Proceedings of the 2020 the 4th International Conference on Compute and Data Analysis, pp. 29–37 (2020)

40. Masinde, M., Mwagha, M., Tadesse, T.: Downscaling africa's drought forecasts through integration of indigenous and scientific drought forecasts using fuzzy cognitive maps. Geosciences (Switzerland) **8**(4) (2018). https://doi.org/10.3390/geosciences8040135

41. Pahar, M., Klopper, R., Warren, R., Niesler, T.: COVID-19 cough classification using machine learning and global smartphone recordings. Comput. Biol. Med. **135**(2021). https://doi.org/10.1016/j.compbiomed.2021.104572

42. Nyetanyane, J., Masinde, M.: Integration of indigenous knowledge, climate data, satellite imagery and machine learning to optimize cropping decisions by small-scale farmers. a case study of umgungundlovu district municipality, South Africa. In: Thorn, J.P.R., Gueye, A., Hejnowicz, A.P. (eds.) InterSol 2020. LNICSSITE, vol. 321, pp. 3–19. Springer, Cham (2020). https://doi.org/10.1007/978-3-030-51051-0_1

43. Adede, C., Oboko, R., Wagacha, P.W., Atzberger, C.: A mixed model approach to vegetation condition prediction using Artificial Neural Networks (ANN): case of Kenya's operational drought monitoring. Remote Sens. **11**(9), 1099 (2019). https://doi.org/10.3390/rs11091099

44. Naidoo, A.V., Hodkinson, P., King, L.L., Wallis, L.A.: African authorship on African papers during the COVID-19 pandemic. BMJ Global Health **6**(3), e004612 (2021). https://doi.org/10.1136/bmjgh-2020-004612

45. Mbaye, R., et al.: Who is telling the story? A systematic review of authorship for infectious disease research conducted in Africa, 1980–2016. BMJ Glob Health (2019). https://doi.org/10.1136/bmjgh-2019-001855

46. Kayembe, C., Nel, D.: Challenges and Opportunities for Education in the Fourth Industrial Revolution (2019)

47. Chand, M.: Brain drain, brain circulation, and the African diaspora in the United States. J. Afr. Bus. **20**(1), 6–19 (2019). https://doi.org/10.1080/15228916.2018.1440461

48. North, M.A., Hastie, W.W., Hoyer, L.: Out of Africa: the underrepresentation of African authors in high-impact geoscience literature. Earth-Sci. Rev. **208**, 103262 (2020). https://doi.org/10.1016/j.earscirev.2020.103262

49. Chu, K.M., Jayaraman, S., Kyamanywa, P., Ntakiyiruta, G.: Building research capacity in Africa: equity and global health collaborations. PLoS Med **11**(3), 1–4 (2014). https://doi.org/10.1371/journal.pmed.1001612

50. Fonkou, M.D.M., Bragazzi, N.L., Tsinda, E.K., Bouba, Y., Mmbando, G.S., Kong, J.D.: Covid-19 pandemic related research in Africa: bibliometric analysis of scholarly output, collaborations and scientific leadership. Int. J. Environ. Res. Public Health **18**(14), 7273 (2021). https://doi.org/10.3390/ijerph18147273

51. Alimi, O.A., Ouahada, K., Abu-Mahfouz, A.M.: A review of machine learning approaches to power system security and stability. IEEE Access **8**, 113512–113531 (2020). https://doi.org/10.1109/ACCESS.2020.3003568

52. Sinayobye, J.O., Kiwanuka, F., Kaawaase Kyanda, S.: A state-of-the-art review of machine learning techniques for fraud detection research. In: Proceedings - International Conference on Software Engineering, pp. 11–19 (2018). https://doi.org/10.1145/3195528.3195534

53. Iorliam, A., Bum, S.: Internet of Things for Smart Agriculture in Nigeria and Africa: A Review (2021). www.ijltemas.in

54. Osareh, F.: 10.1515_libr.1996.46.3.149 (1). Bibliometncs, Citation Analysis and Co-Citation Analysis: A Review of Literature, vol. 46, pp. 149–158 (1996)

55. Chiroma, H., Ezugwu, A.E., Jauro, F., Al-Garadi, M.A., Abdullahi, I.N., Shuib, L.: Early survey with bibliometric analysis on machine learning approaches in controlling COVID-19 outbreaks. PeerJ Comput. Sci. **6**, e313 (2020). https://doi.org/10.7717/peerj-cs.313

56. Manesh, M.F., Pellegrini, M.M., Marzi, G., Dabic, M.: Knowledge management in the fourth industrial revolution: mapping the literature and scoping future avenues. IEEE Trans. Eng. Manage. **68**(1), 289–300 (2021). https://doi.org/10.1109/TEM.2019.2963489

57. Singh, G., Sahu, R.: A bibliometric analysis on Agriculture 4.0. NOLEGEIN-J. Oper. Res. Manage. **2**(2), 6–13 (2019)

58. Singh, V.K., Singh, P., Karmakar, M., Leta, J., Mayr, P.: The journal coverage of Web of Science, Scopus and Dimensions: a comparative analysis. Scientometrics **126**(6), 5113–5142 (2021). https://doi.org/10.1007/s11192-021-03948-5

59. Yang, W., Zhang, J., Ma, R.: The prediction of infectious diseases: a bibliometric analysis. Int. J. Environ. Res. Public Health **17**(17), 6218 (2020). https://doi.org/10.3390/ijerph17176218

60. Adisa, O.M., Masinde, M., Botai, J.O., Botai, C.M.: Bibliometric analysis of methods and tools for drought monitoring and prediction in Africa. Sustainability **12**(16), 6516 (2020). https://doi.org/10.3390/su12166516

61. Kawuki, J., Xiaojin, Y., Musa, T.H.: Bibliometric analysis of ebola research indexed in Web of Science and Scopus (2010-2020). BioMed Res. Int. **2020**, 1–12 (2020). https://doi.org/10.1155/2020/5476567

62. Yu, Y., et al.: A bibliometric analysis using VOSviewer of publications on COVID-19. Ann. Transl. Med. **8**(13) (2020). https://doi.org/10.21037/atm-20-4235

63. van Eck, N.J., Waltman, L.: Citation-based clustering of publications using CitNetExplorer and VOSviewer. Scientometrics **111**(2), 1053–1070 (2017). https://doi.org/10.1007/s11192-017-2300-7

64. White, H.D., McCain, K.W.: Visualizing a discipline: an author co-citation analysis of information science, 1972–1995. J. Am. Soc. Inform. Sci. **49**(4), 327–355 (1998). https://doi.org/10.1002/(SICI)1097-4571(19980401)49:4%3c327::AID-ASI4%3e3.0.CO;2-W

65. Shiau, W.L., Chen, S.Y., Tsai, Y.C.: Management information systems issues: co-citation analysis of journal articles. Int. J. Electron. Commerce Stud. **6**(1), 145–162 (2015). https://doi.org/10.7903/ijecs.1393

66. Guleid, F.H., Oyando, R., Kabia, E., Mumbi, A., Akech, S., Barasa, E.: A bibliometric analysis of COVID-19 research in Africa. BMJ Global Health **6**(5), e005690 (2021). https://doi.org/10.1136/bmjgh-2021-005690

67. Igwaran, Edoamodu, C.E.: Bibliometric analysis on tuberculosis and tuberculosis-related research trends in Africa: a decade-long study. Antibiotics **10**(4), 423 (2021). https://doi.org/10.3390/antibiotics10040423

68. CommonWealth Network South Africa, Research Institutes in South Africa (2020). https://www.commonwealthofnations.org/sectors-south_africa/education/research_institutes/

69. Dunn, R.S.D., Dadischeck, M., Tsephe, R.: The Fourth Industrial Revolution: cyberpsychology-and-well-being. Global Foundation for Cyber Studies And Research (2021)

70. Overland, I., et al.: Funding flows for climate change research on Africa: where do they come from and where do they go? Clim. Dev (2021). https://doi.org/10.1080/17565529.2021.1976609

71. Yang, W., Zhang, J., Ma, R.: The prediction of infectious diseases: a bibliometric analysis. Int. J. Environ. Res. Public Health **17**(17), 1–19 (2020). https://doi.org/10.3390/ijerph17176218

72. Naudé, W.: Discussion PaPer series Entrepreneurship, Education and the Fourth Industrial Revolution in Africa (2017). www.iza.org

Modelling DDoS Attacks in IoT Networks Using Machine Learning

Pheeha Machaka[1,2]([✉]), Olasupo Ajayi[2], Ferdinand Kahenga[2], Antoine Bagula[2], and Kyandoghere Kyamakya[3]

[1] University of South Africa, Johannesburg 1709, South Africa
machap@unisa.ac.za
[2] University of Western Cape, Cape Town 7535, South Africa
[3] Alpen-Adria-Universität Klagenfurt, 9020 Klagenfurt, Austria

Abstract. The Internet-of-Things (IoT) relies on the TCP protocol to transport data from a source to a destination. Making it vulnerable to DDoS using the TCP SYN attack on Cyber-Physical Systems (CPS). Thus, with a potential propagation to the different servers located in both fog and the cloud infrastructures of the CPS. This study compares the effectiveness of supervised, unsupervised, semi-supervised machine learning algorithms, as well as statistical models for detecting DDoS attacks in CPS-IoT.

The models considered are broadly grouped into three: (i) ML-based detection - Logistic Regression, K-Means, and Artificial Neural Networks with two variants based on traffic slicing. We also investigated the effectiveness of semi-supervised hybrid learning models, which used unsupervised K-Means to label the data, then fed the output to a supervised learning model for attack detection. (ii) Statistic-based detection - Exponentially Weighted Moving Average and Linear Discriminant Analysis. (Iii) Prediction 'algorithms - LGR, Kernel Ridge Regression and Support Vector Regression. Results of simulations showed that the hybrid model was able to achieve 100% accuracy with near zero false positives for all the ML models, while traffic slicing traffic helped improved detection time; the statistical models performed comparatively poorly, while the prediction models were able to achieve over 94% attack prediction accuracy.

Keywords: Anomaly Detection · Distributed Denial of Service · Internet of Things · Machine Learning · Regression Analysis

1 Introduction

The Internet of Things (IoT) provides a platform that allows objects to connect and communicate with one another using devices that can sense, identify and locate "things" in their surroundings, in order to better comprehend happenings in their environment. IoT devices are used for autonomous and intelligent tasks in residences, retail outlets office buildings, transportation [1], agriculture, healthcare [2], and manufacturing plants, among other places. The IoT market is growing at an exponential rate and is estimated

© ICST Institute for Computer Sciences, Social Informatics and Telecommunications Engineering 2023
Published by Springer Nature Switzerland AG 2023. All Rights Reserved
M. Masinde and A. Bagula (Eds.): AFRICATEK 2022, LNICST 503, pp. 161–175, 2023.
https://doi.org/10.1007/978-3-031-35883-8_11

to have grown to over 41 billion devices by 2027. Recently, the IoT has also expanded its reach beyond terrestrial networks by using drones [3] to complement the services delivered by semi-static IoT networks located on the ground [4–6]. The security of the complex network infrastructure resulting from the combination of terrestrial and airborne nodes, which use devices designed to operate in settings with limited resources (computing power, storage capacity, battery), is a challenging issue that requires incorporating security principles into different layers of the IoT protocol stack. For example, attacks such as Denial of Service (DoS) or Distributed DoS (DDoS) can be launched at the network, transport or application layers of the Internet stack, to easily compromise IoT devices [7] when such devices run routing protocols that use these layers for the transport of sensor readings, as illustrated on Table 1.

Table 1. IoT Specific Protocols

Protocol	Underlying protocol	Architecture	DDoS prone	Ref.
AMQP (RabbitMQ)	TCP	Publish/Subscribe	Yes	[8]
CoAP	UDP	Publish/Subscribe	No *	[9]
DDS	TCP	Publish/Subscribe	Yes	[10]
MQTT	TCP	Publish/Subscribe	Yes	[11]
XMPP	TCP	Both	Yes	[12]

Table 1 shows some IoT, and/or message telemetry specific protocols, including Message Queuing Telemetry Transport (MQTT), Extensible Messaging and Presence Protocol (XMPP), Advanced Message Queuing Protocol (AMQP), and their corresponding underlying protocols. The table shows that protocols with publish/subscribe architecture rely on TCP protocol for data telemetry and are thus susceptible to DDoS based TCP SYN attacks. It is important to note that though Constrained Application Protocol (CoAP) does not run on TCP, it is still vulnerable to DDoS attacks such as UDP Flood.

Cyber Physical Systems IoT subsystem (CPS-IoT) [13], such as that shown in Fig. 1, rely on a mix of traditional IP networks and IoT specific protocols to move data from devices (physical and virtual sensors, actuators, edge devices and gateways) to / from the Cloud. An IoT specific protocol, such as MQTT or AMQP, is used for message telemetry between device(s) and the Fog infrastructure, as shown in Fig. 1; while an IP protocol, such as the Hypertext Transfer Protocol (HTTP), is used between the Fog and Cloud infrastructures. While both protocols (MQTT and HTTP) belong to different stacks, they are both guided by the TCP protocol in transporting data from source to destination. Hence, DDoS attacks such as the TCP SYN can be plausible tools that attackers use to mislead the operation of CPS and potentially cause critical damages.

Having shown through Fig. 1 and Table 1 that CPS-IoT data telemetry protocols mostly run on TCP/IP - HTTP (TCP port 80 or 8080) and MQTT (TCP port 1883 or 8883) [11] or AMQP (TCP port 5671 or 5672) [8] - we now focus on modelling DDoS attacks on the underlying TCP/IP network layer in the rest of this paper.

Due to the Internet's phenomenal development over the last few decades, attackers now have access to a growing number of vulnerable devices and often use the IoT subsystem of CPS (where these devices are located) to launch vicious attacks that can adversely affect the CPS as a whole. For instance, an attacker may use a large number of these susceptible devices to initiate an attack on a server located in a Fog close to the devices or in a Cloud infrastructure located far away. These attacks often have various modes of intensity, with attacks that are perpetrated with low intensities, often able to evade detection by current detection techniques.

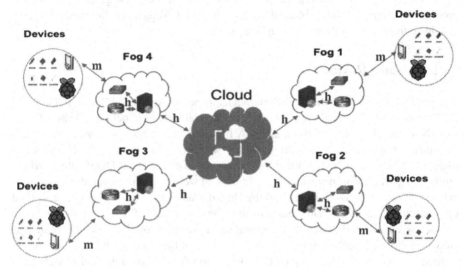

Fig. 1. A Generic CPS-IoT Subsystem

Through this research we explore the application of machine learning (ML) models, including classification and prediction, to model DDoS attacks, specifically SYN attacks in IP networks, such as those upon which CPS-IoT subsystems are built. A potential use case of our research is in sensor virtualization in CPS-IoT systems. In this use case, virtual sensors are in the Fog or Cloud infrastructure to enhance real sensors with the capability of differentiating and classifying incoming traffic into genuine or bogus traffic in real-time. This discerning ability is a key requirement for the efficient operation of next generation CPS, where security would be of paramount importance. The selection of the most efficient algorithms for the classification of the sensor data traffic and the prediction of future attacks on the CPS-IoT are other key requirements for ensuring the safe operation of CPS infrastructures. However, these processes are beyond the scope of this work.

The specific contributions of this work include:

- Comparison of the efficiency of supervised, unsupervised, semi-supervised ML models and statistical models in modelling DDoS attacks, in a bid to distinguish between safe and adversarial network traffic.

- The development of a semi-supervised learning model, capable of auto-labelling traffic and using the labelled traffic to accurately identify malicious traffic. This is achieved by hybridizing supervised and unsupervised machine learning models.
- Determining the impact, if any, of splitting network traffic into window sizes versus using the entire traffic stream in detecting malicious attacks.
- Exploring the effectiveness of regression models in predicting potential DDoS attacks, in a bid to move the safety of IP networks from reactive to proactive.

The rest of the paper is structured as follows, related literature is reviewed in Sect. 2, while our research methodology is presented in Sect. 3. Section 4 gives details of our implementation process and obtained results, while Sect. 5 concludes the paper and gives insights into potential future research directions.

2 Literature Review

The first DDoS assault on the public Internet happened in August 1999 [14]. In February 2000, a year after the initial event, several commercial websites, including Yahoo, CNN, and eBay, saw their first DDoS attacks. A high number of requests overloaded these websites, forcing their services to go offline which resulted in considerable financial losses. The July 4 2009 cyber-attacks are well-known examples of DDoS attack, where prominent government, news media, and financial websites were targeted in a series of cyber-attacks across South Korea and the United States [15]. Researchers have worked on techniques to combat DDoS attack even in the context of IoT, for example authors in [16] surveyed IoT related security challenges and potential solutions for attacks such as DoS. The three key technologies that form the basis of the majority of today's detection techniques are machine learning (ML), information theory, and statistical models [17]. Artificial Neural Networks (ANN), support vector machine (SVM), and other ML techniques in cybersecurity are helpful for decision making analysis [18]. The paragraphs that follow highlight some of the related work in application of ML to DDoS attack detection.

In order to detect DDoS attacks, the authors in [19] proposed combining feature selection with an ANN MLP (multilayer perceptron) model. This strategy was used to choose the best features during the training phase, and they created a feedback system to reconstruct the detector when significant detection faults were detected dynamically. With a 98% accuracy rate, the proposed methodology proved effective.

Chaudhary et al. [20] also suggested a ML technique for detecting DDoS assaults that involved filtering crucial network packet parameters such as packet size and interval size. SVM, Random Forest, Decision Tree, and Logistic Regression were used and Random Forest surpassed the other models with a DDoS attack detection accuracy of 99.17%. In [21], the authors used flow features of network traffic, such as packet size, packet interval, protocol, bandwidth, and destination IP, to construct a model to detect DDoS attacks. They used SVM, K-Nearest Neighbour (KNN), Random Forest, Decision Tree, and ANN in their models. The results of the experiment showed that Random Forest and ANN have 99% accuracy in detecting malicious traffic.

For detecting DDoS attacks in Software Defined Networks (SDN), [22] employed SVM, KNN, ANN, and Naive Bayes. Initially, the authors specified twelve features, but the algorithms chose a subset of these features based on threshold values. The algorithms analysed flow traffic data and detected DDoS with 98.3% accuracy.

The accurate and timely detection of DDoS attacks remains a priority for researchers in the field of cybersecurity, however, attackers keep modifying and developing new attacks in order to evade detection techniques. In this research study we distinguish between normal and DDoS attack network traffic and compare the performance of supervised, unsupervised, and semi-supervised machine learning techniques.

Additionally, the efficacy of two approaches for forecasting possible DDoS attacks was investigated. In the section that follows, we will provide a detailed account of the methodological approach followed in this study.

3   Methodology

Figure 2 gives an overview of the proposed system. The important components are data pre-processing, supervised learning, semi-supervised learning, unsupervised learning and prediction. Each of these components described as follows:

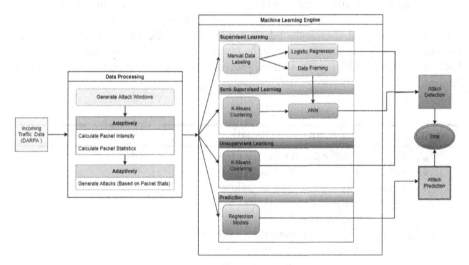

Fig. 2. Proposed System Architecture

3.1   Data Pre-processing and Labelling

For this work, we used the DAPRA IDS evaluation dataset [23], which was prepared by the MIT Lincoln Laboratory under DARPA and AFRL sponsorship. We used this dataset because we had earlier inferred that IoT systems have an underlying IP network upon which they run, hence still vulnerable to classic IP attacks such as DDoS. The tcpdump format was used, wherein all network activities, including the whole payload of each packet, were recorded and supplied for assessment.

We processed the raw dataset by writing a Python script to count the number of network packets that arrived at a given host per 10 s interval. We used this as each 10 s block as zero (0), corresponding to no DDoS attack [24]. We then introduced malicious attacks to the dataset by manually increasing the number of packets arriving in randomly selected intervals. We labelled these as one (1), implying DDoS attack.

3.2 Supervised Learning

This component is labelled "Supervised Learning" in Fig. 2 and it involved applying supervised ML on manually labelled data. Supervised learning is a class of machine learning (ML) wherein an ML model is trained using pre-labelled data, which serve as "examples" for the ML model. Once the model has been trained, it can then be exposed to new (test) data for classification or prediction. In our system, we considered Logistic Regression (LGR) and Artificial Neural Network (ANN) models.

Data Framing.
Data framing was done for ANN only and three variants were considered. In the first, data framing was not considered, and this served as the base line; while in the second, the dataset was split into "frames" of size 12, corresponding to 120 s of traffic flow (at 10 s interval). In the third, the standard deviation of values in the frame was calculated and appended to the frame, thus increasing the frame size to 13. The data frames were then fed to the ANN model. The data framing process is summarized with the pseudocode in Algorithm 1.

Algorithm 1: Data Framing Algorithm

- Divide the entire dataset into data blocks of 120 seconds.
- For each 120 second data block in the dataset:
1. Create a 3 by 4 data frame as follows:
   - Set t = 0
   - For row = 1 to 4
   a) *col1 = Packet □ Count(t); t+ = 10*
   b) *col2 = Packet □ Count(t); t+ = 10*
   c) *col3 = Packet □ Count(t); t+ = 10*
2. Calculate the stand deviation (σ) for the data block. //for option 1 only

---

For each data frame, the standard deviation (σ) is calculated. This standard deviation is used to further verify the probability that a malicious attack has occurred. Within a data frame, if the data points are far from the mean, then the deviation of values within the frame would be higher, which implies that an attack occurred in that data frame. The opposite holds true for data points that are closer as their deviation from the mean would be smaller. This can be interpreted as an absence of attack(s). Finally, in instances where all 12 entries in a data frame are high (full DDoS attacks), the standard deviation value from the mean would be small. To distinguish between this full attack situation and a safe situation, a threshold value is used. If the calculated σ is greater than this threshold value, then the frame is classified as being under attack.

Machine Learning Models.
As mentioned above, both LGR and ANN were considered in this work. For LGR, an 80:20 split was used for training and test data, using the One-over-rest (OvR) training scheme and linear memory BFGS (Broyden–Fletcher–Goldfarb–Shanno) algorithm. In this work, we used it to model DDoS attacks in IP networks and we considered a 3 layered ANN architecture. At the input layer we had 12 or 13 nodes (σ included), the hidden layer had 6 nodes, while the output layer had 1 node. The data frames obtained in the previous subsection were fed in, with the corresponding standard deviation value used as the 13th node. The ReLU (Rectified Learning Unit) activation was used for the input and hidden layers, while Sigmoid activation was used at the output layer. The processes involved in our ANN supervised learning component are depicted in Fig. 3.

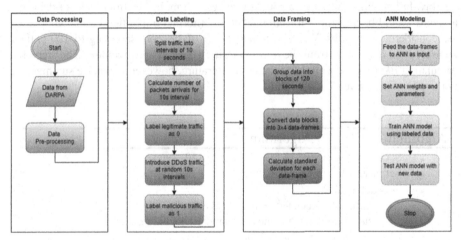

Fig. 3. ANN Supervised Learning Process

3.3 Unsupervised Learning

As an alternative to manually labelling the dataset, we considered the K-means clustering technique for automatic labelling. K-Means is a centroid based clustering algorithm that determines cluster membership based on the proximity of data points to a centre point (centroid) [25]. In IP networks security, millions of packets often traverse the network per unit time and need to be classified (labelled) as either legitimate or malicious traffic. Manually doing this would be slow and laborious in such cases, hence the use of an automatic classifier is desirable, in our case K-Means. In our work, traffic flow falls into one of two categories (legitimate or malicious), thus, k value is set to 2.

3.4 Semi-supervised Learning

Our semi-supervised learning component, which is labelled "Semi-Supervised Learning" in Fig. 2, is like the supervised learning described earlier. The major difference is that rather than using manually labelled data as input to the ML models, we fed the output of the unsupervised learning (K-Means clustering) into the models. In essence, K-Means is used to automatically label (classify) the data, which is then used to train the supervised model. Thus, creating a semi-supervised model. The output of this model is then compared to the two other models (supervised and unsupervised).

3.5 Statistical Models

For completeness, we performed data classification using a classic statistical model – the Exponentially Weighted Moving Average (EWMA) [26]. By placing more emphasis on recent data points than on older ones, EWMA can detect anomalies in observed data quickly. In applying EWMA, we sought to detect anomalies within blocks of data. An anomaly would be a disruption from the "norm" (normal traffic flow). Such anomalies are considered as attacks. We set a window size of 12, corresponding to 120 s, then measured the deviations from the average traffic count in each window. The steps for calculating EWMA are well documented in literature, however, a concise summary of our application is given in Algorithm 2.

Algorithm 2: EWMA Algorithm

- Set a window size of 12 (data blocks of 120   seconds).
- Set mean, std, thresholdUp, thresholdDw to 0
- For each window:
    1. mean += calculate the moving average.
    2. std += calculate the moving standard deviation.
    3. *thresholdUp = mean + std*
    4. *thresholdDw = mean - std*
    5. Slide the window by 1 (10 seconds)
- For each data point (d) in the dataset:
    1. If d > *thresholdUp* or d < *thresholdDw* : attack = True.
    2. Else attack = False.

Linear Discriminant Analysis (LDA) is a statistical model used for feature reduction and distinguishing between data entries in a dataset. In this work we are only concerned with its application in data classification abilities, specifically binary classification of data traffic into normal or attack. The steps of the 2-dimensional (binary) LDA classification are well documented in literature, having initially being proposed in the early 1930s by Fisher [26]. For brevity the steps are repeated in this work but refer interested readers to the work of Fisher for details.

3.6 Prediction

Having successfully classified and distinguished between legitimate and malicious attacks, the next logical step might be to predict the possible occurrence of such attacks. This would help the network administrator put preventive measures in place to mitigate them, essentially changing the defence strategy from reactive to proactive. This is highlighted in green in Fig. 2. Three regression models were considered in this work for prediction, the Logistic Regression (LGR), Kernel Ridge Regression (KRR) and Support Vector Regression (SVR).

4 Implementation

For this work, implementation was carried out on Google Colab, with a Python 3 Google Compute module, configured with 12 GB of RAM, 2.3 GHz 2 Core Intel Xeon CPU and GPU hardware accelerators. Keras and Sci-Kit learn were used for machine learning; Smote was used for data balancing; Pandas, NumPy were used for data manipulation, while matplotlib was used for data visualization. Finally, an 80:20 split was used for training and testing data for the supervised learning algorithms.

4.1 Metrics

Six metrics were used to compare the performance of the models considered, these are false positive, false negative, average execution time, accuracy, coefficient if determination (R^2), and Root Mean Square Error (RMSE). The first 4 are specific to classification models, while the last 3 (accuracy inclusive) are for the regression models.

4.2 Supervised Learning

Table 2 summarizes the results of the supervised learning models. From the table, the pure ANN model resulted in the highest accuracy, followed by ANN + Data framing + SD. Logistic Regression (LGR) also had high accuracy value but resulted in the highest number of false negatives, meaning that LGR wrongly classified more legitimate traffic as attacks. Conversely, data framing adversely affected the false positive rate, resulting in about 2% of bogus traffic (DDoS attacks) being misclassified as safe. Among the three ANN models considered, the variant without data framing only slightly edged out the variant with data framing and standard deviation (SD) at 99.414% vs. 99.405%. The impact of Data framing + SD is also evident here as the combination resulted in the lowest false negative of all the models compared.

W.r.t execution time, Fig. 4 shows that the pure ANN was the slowest of all four models, taking over 2 min to classify traffic flow. This would be unacceptable in real-time environments, where high-speed data analysis and classification are paramount. In contrast, the variants of ANN based on data framing were significantly faster than both LGR and the pure ANN at just 11s vs 51s and 130s respectively. This shows that breaking traffic into data frames or "windows" and processing them accordingly can be significantly beneficial with regards to processing time.

4.3   Unsupervised Learning

Running the K-Means classifier with K = 2, resulted in an accuracy of 96.76%, with zero false positives.

Table 2. Anomaly Detection Using Supervised Learning Models

Model	Accuracy	False positives	False negatives
LGR	99.192	0	1.6215
ANN	99.414	0	0.6695
ANN + Dataframing	98.842	2.1805	0.1295
ANN + Dataframing + SD	99.405	0.9565	0.0965

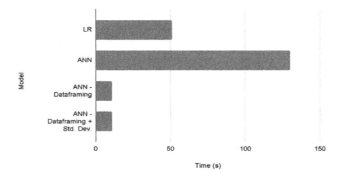

Fig. 4. Average Execution Time

4.4   Semi-supervised Learning

The labelled outputs from K-Means (unsupervised learning) were used as input to the supervised learning models, in essence creating a form of semi-supervised model. Table 3 shows the performance of this hybrid combination. From the table the incorporation of the K-Means classifier resulted in a significant boost in the performance of all the models. Both LGR and the pure ANN resulted in perfect accuracies, zero false positives and zero false negatives.

Similarly, the accuracies of both variants of ANN with data framing increased from 98.842% to 99.64% and 99.41 to 99.69% respectively. Of important note is the reduction in false positive and false negative values of ANN + Data framing and ANN + Data framing + SD. Respectively. For the former, the false positive dropped from about 2.18% to just 0.73%, while the false negative value dropped to 0.07. For ANN + Data framing + SD, the false positive value dropped to 0.67%. The overall improvements in the results on Table 2 compared to Table 3 shows the efficacy of our proposed hybrid (semi-supervised) model in detecting malicious attacks. However, the fact that both variants of ANN did not yield 100% accuracy cannot be ignored. A possible explanation for this is that the dataset was not split into data frames of equal sizes, hence some data frames (especially those at the tail end of the traffic flow) contained less data i.e., less than the window size (12 data points).

Table 3. Anomaly Detection Using Semi-Supervised Models

Model	Accuracy	False positive	False negative
K-Means + LGR	100	0	0
K-Means + ANN	100	0	0
K-Means + ANN + Data framing	99.64	0.73	0.07
K-Means + ANN + Data framing + SD	99.69	0.67	0.01

4.5 Statistical Models

Table 4 summaries the results of the statistical methods used for detecting malicious (abnormal / attack) traffic. For comparison purposes, we also included the result of the pure Logistic Regression model (LGR).

Table 4. Anomaly Detection Using Statistical Models

Model	Accuracy	False positives	False negatives
EWMA	71.299	12.102	57.268
LDA	99.837	7.797	37.870
LGR	99.192	0	1.6215

Compared to LGR, both EWMA and LDA performed poorly w.r.t False Negatives and False Positives. The false positive and negative values in EWMA are understandably high because the model uses simple moving standard deviation and mean of observed samples to determine differentiate attacks. This means that for every subsequent traffic window (120 s interval), EWMA would compare the mean and standard deviation of that window with its preceding window. If the difference is much, EWMA flags that window as being attacked. To elaborate, if we assume that little or no data traffic arrive during the first 120 s, EWMA establishes a base line with this first window size using the mean and standard deviation (SD). If during the next few seconds, significant number of legitimate traffic arrive, EWMA calculates the mean and SD of this new block. It then compares the new mean and SD with the base line. The new values would be higher than the base line and EWMA would flag this new window as malicious because of the higher traffic count. The reverse is the case with the false negatives.

Being probabilistic (based on Bayes' theorem), LDA expected performs better than EWMA in most of the metrics. However, like EWMA, LDA also struggled with distinguishing between high volume legitimate traffic and malicious traffic. This problem becomes more pronounced when low traffic windows(s) is/are followed by window(s) with slightly higher traffic counts. In such instances, the succeeding window(s) would be classified as malicious even if there are not.

4.6 Prediction

As stated earlier, three prediction models were considered, and their results are summarized on Table 5. Of the three models compared, LGR performed the best, with a prediction accuracy of 98.6%. It was closely followed by KRR at approx. 98%. SVR was the least accurate of the lot at 94.64%. For R2, values closer to 1 are desirable, and depicts the "closeness" of predicted values to the actual values. For the three models, the same trend is observed with R2 scores, as LGR led with a score of approx. 0.94, followed by KRR at 0.91. SVR scored 0.76, implying that its prediction curve differed greatly from the actual curve. Finally, for RMSE, values closer to 0 are desirable as they indicate lower prediction errors. Once again, LGR was the least error prone as it had the lowest RMSE values, followed by KRR with a score of 0.1439. However, both models were less error prone than SVR with a RMSE value of 0.2314. We can thus conclude that LGR is the best predictor, while KRR is a close alternative. With such high RMSE value, SVR is a less than ideal predictor in our use case.

Table 5. Comparison of Results of the Prediction Models

Metric	KRR	LGR	SVR
Accuracy	97.93%	98.60%	94.64%
R^2	0.9054	0.9361	0.7555
RMSE	0.1439	0.1183	0.2314

Overall, these results show that LGR and KRR are better prediction models than SVR for our use case. With attack prediction accuracies of approximately 98% for both LGR and KRR models, it can be inferred that regression models can be used to predict potential DDoS attacks in IoT networks. For both LGR and KRR, the inaccurate predictions were in instances where they assumed that attacks would occur when none occurred. These wrong predictions or false alarms, though leading to unnecessary deployment of defensive mechanisms, are preferable to the reverse case. In the reverse case, as observed with SVR, the model gives a false sense of security by predicting that no attack would occur, when imminent threats abound. We therefore consider the wrong predictions of KRR and LGR as "erring on the side of caution".

5   Conclusion

In this study, the accuracy and timeliness of supervised, unsupervised, and semi-supervised machine learning techniques for detecting Distributed Denial of Service (DDoS) attacks in Cyber Physical-Internet of Things Systems (CPS-IoT) were explored. CPS-IoT systems often rely on two well-known protocols for data transmission, namely HTTP and MQTT, both of which are built upon TCP/IP, hence vulnerable to TCP/IP targeted attacks. DDoS attacks are common to TCP/IP, thus pose a potential threat to the security, dependability and safety of CPS-IoT systems. In this work, five machine learning models (ML) and two statistical models were considered for modelling DDoS attacks in IoT networks (TCP/IP-based). These are Logistic Regression (LGR), Artificial Neural Networks (ANN), K-Means, Kernel Ridge Regression (KRR), Support Vector Regression (SVR), Exponentially Weighted Moving Average (EWMA) and the Linear Discriminant Analysis (LDA).

In distinguishing between normal traffic and bogus (attack) traffic, two supervised ML classifiers were used - LGR and ANN (and two slight variations of ANN based on slicing). LGR gave a classification accuracy of 99.19%, a false positive rate of 1.62%, and an average detection latency of 51 s from the initiation of the attack. The ANN model, on the other hand, had better accuracy at 99.41% and lower false negative value of 0.67%, but was extremely slow at 130 s. We introduced slicing, and split the traffic into fixed windows sizes, before applying ANN. This slicing improved the false negative values and significantly cut down the detection time to just 11 s. We then considered the K-Means unsupervised ML model, which resulted in 96.76% classification accuracy. Finally, we developed semi-supervised ML models by combining the K-Means with the ANN and LGR. These combinations resulted in a classification (detection) accuracy of 100% with near zero false positives across all models. Compared to the ML models, the statistical models performed poorly w.r.t false positive and negatives.

We further examined the use of regression models to support network administrators in transiting from reactive to proactive network management approach. LGR, KRR, and SVR were investigated for their abilities to correctly predict attacks before they occur. LGR gave the best prediction accuracy at 98.6%, followed by KRR at 97.9%, while SVR had the worst performance at 94.64%. The R^2 values for the LGR and KRR were 0.94 and 0.91 respectively, representing closeness to actual values, while their RMSE values were respectively 0.12 and 0.14. SVR was significantly off the mark for these metrics. In essence, LGR and KRR are both capable for predicting imminent threats, with LGR being slightly better.

This work only considered traffic counts, time and status in determining DDoS attack. In future works, other features such as source and destination IP addresses or ports can be considered. Similarly, only the possible future attack times were considered, potential future research could consider the target machine or subnet. Finally, in CPS-IoT systems, attack detection and prediction using network topology graphs could be another avenue for future research work.

References

1. Ajayi, O.O., Bagula, A.B., Maluleke, H.C., Odun-Ayo, I.A.: Transport inequalities and the adoption of intelligent transportation systems in Africa: a research landscape. Sustainability **13**(22), 12891 (2021)
2. Bagula, A., Mandava, M., Bagula, H.: A framework for healthcare support in the rural and low income areas of the developing world. J. Netw. Comput. Appl. **120**, 17–29 (2018)
3. Ismail, A., Bagula, B.A., Tuyishimire, E.: Internet-of-Things in motion: a UAV coalition model for remote sensing in smart cities. Sensors **18**(7), 2184 (2018)
4. Ma, K., Bagula, A., Nyirenda, C., Ajayi, O.: An IoT-based Fog computing model. Sensors **19**(12), 2783 (2019)
5. Zennaro, M., Bagula, A.: Design of a flexible and robust gateway to collect sensor data in intermittent power environments. Int. J. Sens. Netw. **8**(3–4), 172–181 (2010)
6. Bagula, A.B.: Hybrid traffic engineering: the least path interference algorithm. In: Proceedings of the SAICT 2004, ACM International Conference Proceedings Series, pp. 89–96 (2004). ISBN: 1-58113-982-9
7. Ahmad, R., Alsmadi, I.: Machine learning approaches to IoT security: a systematic literature review. Int. Things **14**, 100365 (2021)
8. AMQP: CloudAMQP. https://www.cloudamqp.com/docs/amqp.html
9. Pardo-Castellote, G.: Omg data-distribution service: architectural overview. In: Proceedings of IEEE Military Communications Conference (MILCOM), pp. 200–206 (2003)
10. Anonymous "MQTT FAQ." https://mqtt.org/faq/
11. Millard, P., Saint-Andre, P., Meijer, R.: "No title," XEP-0060: Publish-Subscribe, XMPP Standards Foundation
12. Bagula, A., Ajayi, O., Maluleke, H.: Cyber physical systems dependability using CPS-IOT monitoring. Sensors **21**(8), 2761 (2021)
13. Garber, L.: Denial-of-service attacks rip the Internet. Computer **33**(04), 12–17 (2000)
14. Zargar, S.T., Joshi, J., Tipper, D.: A survey of defense mechanisms against distributed denial of service (DDoS) flooding attacks. IEEE Commun. Surv. Tutorials **15**(4), 2046–2069 (2013)
15. Khan, F.I., Hameed, S.: Understanding security requirements and challenges in internet of things (IoTs): a review. arXiv preprint arXiv:1808.10529
16. Singh, K., Singh, P., Kumar, K.: Application layer HTTP-GET flood DDoS attacks: research landscape and challenges. Comput. Secur. **65**, 344–372 (2017)
17. Hosseini, S., Azizi, M.: The hybrid technique for DDoS detection with supervised learning algorithms. Comput. Netw. **158**, 35–45 (2019)
18. Wang, M., Lu, Y., Qin, J.: A dynamic MLP-based DDoS attack detection method using feature selection and feedback. Comput. Secur. **88**, 101645 (2020)
19. Chaudhary, P., Gupta, B.B.: Ddos detection framework in resource constrained internet of things domain. In: Proceedings of IEEE Global Conference on Consumer Electronics (GCCE), pp. 675–678 (2019)
20. Wehbi, K., Hong, L., Al-salah, T., Bhutta, A.A.: A survey on machine learning based detection on DDoS attacks for IoT systems. In: Proceedings of the IEEE Southeastcon, pp. 1–6 (2019)
21. Polat, H., Polat, O., Cetin, A.: Detecting DDoS attacks in software-defined networks through feature selection methods and machine learning models. MDPI Sustain. **12**(3), 1035 (2020)
22. Lichman, M.: DARPA intrusion detection evaluation dataset. DARPA Intrusion Detection Evaluation Dataset—MIT Lincoln Laboratory (2000)
23. Machaka, P., Bagula, A.: Statistical properties and modelling of DDoS attacks. In: Vinh, P.C., Rakib, A. (eds.) Context-Aware Systems and Applications, and Nature of Computation and Communication. ICCASA ICTCC 2020 2020. Lecture Notes of the Institute for Computer Sciences, Social Informatics and Telecommunications Engineering, vol. 343. Springer, Cham (2021). https://doi.org/10.1007/978-3-030-67101-3_4

24. Morissette, L., Chartier, S.: The k-means clustering technique: general considerations and implementation in Mathematica. Tutorials Quant. Methods Psychol. **9**(1), 15–24 (2013)
25. Roberts, S.W.: Control chart tests based on geometric moving averages. Technometrics **1**(3), 239–250 (1959)
26. Theodoridis, S.: Classification: a tour of the classics. In: Theodoridis, S., Ed. Machine Learning, pp. 275–325. Academic Press, London (2015)

Application of 4IR in Environment and Agriculture Monitoring

Towards a Microservice-Based Middleware for a Multi-hazard Early Warning System

Adeyinka Akanbi(✉) iD

Centre for Sustainable Smart Cities (CSSC), Central University of Technology,
Bloemfontein 9300, Free State, South Africa
aakanbi@cut.ac.za

Abstract. Environmental hazards—like water and air pollution, extreme weather, or chemical exposures—can affect human health in a number of ways, and it is a persistent apprehension in communities surrounded by mining operations. The application of modern technologies in the environmental monitoring of these Human-made hazards is critical, because while not immediately health-threatening may turn out detrimental with unwanted negative effects. Enabling technologies needed to realize this concept is multifaceted and most especially involves deploying interconnected Internet of Things (IoT) sensors, existing legacy systems, enterprise networks, multi-layered software architecture (middleware), and event-processing engines, amongst others. Currently, the integration of several early warning systems has inherent challenges, mostly due to the heterogeneity of components. This paper proposes transversal microservice-based middleware aiming at increasing data integration, interoperability, scalability, high availability, and reusability of adopted systems using a containers orchestration framework for a multi-hazard early warning system. Devised within the scope of the ICMHEWS project, the proposed platform aims at improving known challenges.

Keywords: Microservices · Kubernetes · Middleware · Containers · Interoperability · Integration · Early Warning Systems

1 Introduction

Natural hazards can be defined as *"a serious disruption of the functioning of a community or a society causing widespread human, material, economic or environmental losses which exceed the ability of the affected community or society to cope using its own resources"* [1]. The preparedness towards natural hazards is a key factor in the reduction of their impact on society. Natural hazards/disasters are mostly from compromised hydro-meteorological origins resulting in pollution and chemical exposure to naturally occurring ones from extremes of temperature, wind and rainfall. An important part of a holistic approach to disaster risk reduction (DRR) management of natural hazards or disasters is the set-up of early warning systems, with several international initiatives towards the development and promotion of early warning systems for all natural hazards [3–5].

© ICST Institute for Computer Sciences, Social Informatics and Telecommunications Engineering 2023
Published by Springer Nature Switzerland AG 2023. All Rights Reserved
M. Masinde and A. Bagula (Eds.): AFRICATEK 2022, LNICST 503, pp. 179–191, 2023.
https://doi.org/10.1007/978-3-031-35883-8_12

Early warning systems (EWS) can be defined as information systems with the ability to detect and provide warnings in the form of timely and effective information through identified institutions that allow individuals exposed to a hazard to take action to avoid or reduce their risk and prepare for effective response [1]. Several studies have illustrated the effectiveness of an early warning system (e.g., [8, 9, 12, 13]) (Fig. 1).

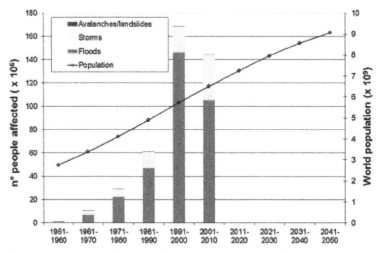

Fig. 1. Mean yearly number of people affected per decade (stacked bars) and comparison with global population for global water-related disasters in the world in the last 60 years, including trend for the future 40 years [6]

In previous studies, EWS(s) are primarily constructed to target a particular natural hazard – this approach is widely used, especially those concerning natural hazards [7, 10, 14–16]. However, the world's climate is changing [17–19], and natural hazards are now intertwined with environmental phenomena leading directly/indirectly to natural hazards occurring concurrently with cascading effects; the failure to integrate EWS could affect their effectiveness and reach. Thus, it is important to devise the integration of new and existing EWS for an integrated climate multi-hazard early warning system (ICMHEWS[1]). The specifications and requirements of existing EWS are extremely different depending on the application area, leading to ad-hoc implementations of monolithic software applications and cumbersome legacy systems. The integration of several related EWS has inherent challenges, which are mostly data incompatibility and system interoperability due to heterogeneity, reliability, availability, transparency and abstractions to applications [2, 20, 21, 34, 35], inhibiting the possibility of harnessing an integrated MHEWS.

In recent years, the field of cloud computing has shown rapid growth, and a variety of virtualization technologies have emerged, such as microservices, with immense application characteristics for monolithic heterogeneous systems or applications. Monolithic

---

[1] https://urida.co.za/icmhews.

applications components are tightly coupled, having been developed, deployed and managed as one entity. This results in increased rigidity and complexity of the system. On the other hand, microservices are loosely coupled, independently deployed, cloud-native small services [22]. The cloud-native microservices exploit containerization orchestration framework and container management systems such as Google Kubernetes to deploy software components or applications separately, without compromising the application life cycle [23, 26]. Containers encapsulate a microservice environment, abstracting the hardware and software infrastructure and provide application portability across platforms as a resource-isolated process. This provides the ability to break down monolithic applications into software components, and run them as a node on a variety of Infrastructure as a Service (IaaS) or Platform as a Service (PaaS). Therefore, containerization enables a paradigm shift from machine-oriented to application-oriented orchestration, resulting in easier and faster deployment, improved scalability, increased utilization of computing resources, data integration and system interoperability. To automatically manage applications with containers, several orchestration frameworks are developed, such as Kubernetes [26], Docker SwarmKit [25] and Apache Mesos [11].

In this paper, we develop a formal model towards the decomposition of monolithic EWS components as containerized microservices managed by Kubernetes. This allows the deployment of EWS software components towards an integrated MHEWS under several configurations to be explored at the modelling level before deployment to production. Thus, the analysis of the performance, suitability, and usability of Kubernetes in a decoupled monolithic EWS is an interesting and relatively new research area. We aim to facilitate the expediency of the Kubernetes container orchestration tool in MHEWS and highlight the limitation therein (Fig. 2).

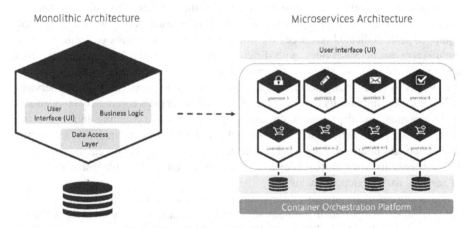

Fig. 2. Monolithic vs Microservice Architecture

More specifically, the contributions of this research study can be summarized as follows: (i) describing the model for the distribution of containerized EWS software applications; (ii) proposing a model for the application of Kubernetes container scheduling techniques for the deployment of reliable and scalable MHEW distributed systems; (iii) validation in EWS is conducted, more especially, in drought forecasting domain, (iv) discussing the limitation of current Kubernetes container orchestration design for EWS.

The rest of the paper is organized as follows. In the next Section, the background is discussed. Section 3 presents the proposed experimental framework architecture, the implementation in a test environment and performance results. Finally, conclusions are presented in Sect. 4.

2 Background

In this section, we present the relevant background of our work; we start by presenting an overview of microservices and container management. Then we present the containerized orchestration framework for the study.

2.1 Microservices and Containers Management

In a monolithic software application, all components and services are highly coupled, preventing scalability and reusability of these systems or even integration with new or existing ones. However, to overcome these challenges, a microservices-based architecture is used. The application principle of microservices is all about modularization and decoupling capabilities into components that are easily adapted to distributed hardware. This emanates from service-oriented architectures (SOA) [24]. In a nutshell, microservice-based architecture is the evolution of classical SOA [21, 22]. The adaptability of the SOA approach to a transversal microservice-based middleware is to ensure seamless implementations of the various software component such as APIs, extensions, heterogeneous technologies or clusters in the monolithic software application or systems.

Microservices are independent components conceptually deployed in isolation and equipped with dedicated resources for utilization. The components of a microservice architecture are microservices, with different behaviour derives from the composition and coordination of its decoupled software components. Microservices manage growing complexity by functionally decomposing large systems into a set of independent services [22]. This takes modularity to the next level by making services completely independent in development and deployment, through emphasis on loose coupling and high cohesion. This approach delivers all sorts of benefits in terms of maintainability, scalability, integration and interoperabilty. Containers encapsulate the execution environment providing the ability to develop, deploy and scale applications as multiple instances or a set of services without dependencies [22].

In literature, there are several container orchestration tools developed by different companies or open-source communities, typical examples such as Google Kubernetes [26], Apache Mesos [11], OpenShift [27], Nomad [28], Docker Compose [29], Cloudify [30], etc. Google Kubernetes is an open-source container orchestration tool for managing containerized applications across multiple hosts [23]. It provides automatic deployment, scaling and management of container-based applications or software components. Figure 3 depicts a logical representation of Kubernetes instances. The architectures follow a master-slave model or Pods concept, where a master node manages the worker nodes (slaves) – set up as a cluster consisting of Kubernetes-master and a

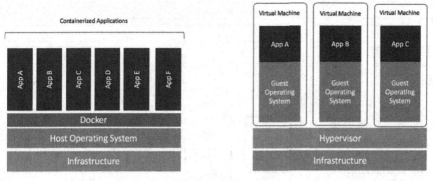

Fig. 3. A comparison of model of containerized application and VMs.

set of Kubernetes-workers. As consequence, these nodes can be executed on-premises, in public cloud or hybrid infrastructure. The communication between microservices is possible only through interfaces using APIs.

There are four master processes in a Kubernetes-master node, namely: the *API server*, *scheduler*, *controller manager* and *etcd*. The Kubernetes-worker node has three processes, the *container runtime, Kubelet* and the *KubeProxy*. The container runtime needs to be installed on every node. The smallest unit of a Kubernetes cluster is a pod, which is an abstraction over the container runtime; usually, one application is dedicated to running in pod. The communication between pods is possible through virtual networks, with each pod having its own internal IP address. Within one pod, containers can reference each other directly. The access to the executed applications is through external service in the form of the node IP address and the service's port number e.g., http://124.95.101. 2:8080. The external request goes to Ingress, which passes the request to the services residing in the container node.

Services are an integral part and another component of Kubernetes; services comprise a static or permanent IP address attached to each pod and act like a load balancer between pods. Each app in a pod has its own respective service with a disjointed life cycle. The two sub-types of services are the internal service and the external service. The internal service received request from ingress to access running containerized applications via respective endpoints. The orchestration of requests is possible with the help of *ConfigMap*, which contains the external configuration of applications, they are connected to the pods for integrated applications. Configuration of secured external applications makes use of *Secret*, which is similar to the *ConfigMap* to store access credentials for secured infrastructure. Volumes are another important feature that allows saving of persistent data required by applications running in the pods. These data are available through external storage attached physically to the infrastructure in an on-prem environment or remotely to the cloud infrastructure (Fig. 4).

2.2 Container Orchestration

Containerization expedites the feasibility of running applications that are containerized over multiple hosts in different service models [31]. Kubernetes has grown into container

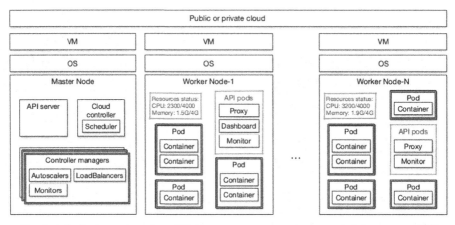

Fig. 4. A logical representation of Kubernetes components in a generic infrastructure [36].

orchestration standards by simplifying the deployment and management of a container-ized application. The Kubernetes-master provides the API server – a cluster gateway for scheduling various deployments and managing the overall cluster. This is achieved through RESTFul interface, which allows control point for managing the entire Kuber-netes cluster. The interactions with the clusters or configuration of the Kubernetes-worker nodes are through *Kubectl* – a built-in Kubernetes Command Line Interface (CLI). The *scheduler* receives validated requests from the API server to start pods in the cluster. The *container manager* detects the state changes and notifies the *scheduler* if a con-tainer has to be restarted. *Etcd* is a key value pair store of the cluster state, used for coordinating resources and sharing cluster configuration; it acts as the brain of the clus-ter. In the Kubernetes-workers node, The *Kubelet* is a process that interfaces with both the container and the node and is responsible for starting a pod within a container and assigning resources from the node to the container. *KubeProxy* forwards service requests intelligently to available replicas in the cluster.

A cluster orchestration platform should be able to have fully automated, self-managed and self-healing capabilities. It also provides the ability for scalability and integration of containerized applications, promoting interoperability and eliminating the isolation of applications and systems. Among various available orchestration platforms in this paper, we have used Kubernetes for monitoring and managing EWS software components or applications (Fig. 5).

3 Proposed Experimental Framework

In this study, we presented an experimental framework towards the integration of sev-eral EWS for an integrated MHEWS using microservices. The objective is to address and eliminate the rigidity of monolithic EWS application for an ICMHEWS by imple-menting Kubernetes in a hybrid infrastructure. The infrastructure design consists of on-premises workstation and VMs in the cloud. The study adopts Microsoft Azure[2] cloud

---

[2] https://www.portal.azure.com.

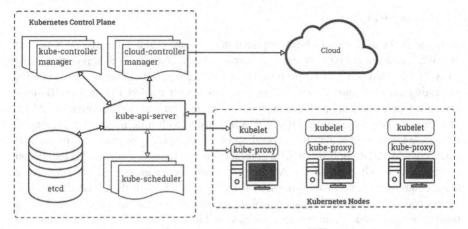

Fig. 5. Components of Kubernetes [37].

services to host the VMs with Azure Kubernetes Services, which are accessible via a public endpoint. Azure Kubernetes Services[3] (AKS) provides automated management and scalability of Kubernetes clusters for our container orchestration with the ability to deploy containerized Windows and Linux applications in the cloud. Kubernetes orchestrates clusters of VMs and schedules containers to run on those virtual machines based on available resources and the resource requirements of each container. The presented solution suggests the ability of Kubernetes to implement containerized EWS applications using it load-balancing capabilities to respond to requests.

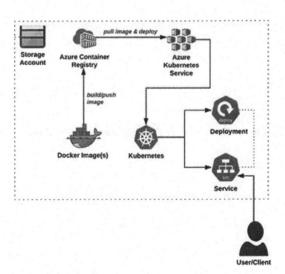

Fig. 6. Experimental framework of EWS application as microservices in AKS.

---

[3] https://azure.microsoft.com/en-us/products/kubernetes-service/.

3.1 Cluster Setup

To replicate the execution of EWS application, we converted a software component of an EWS into a docker base image to be deployed as a containerized application using AKS. Our testbed is a VM in the Azure cloud, using a preset cluster configuration for the testing/dev environment. The VM configurations utilize a 4 vCPUs and 16GB memory with a primary node pool for size 10. All nodes run Kubernetes version 1.23.12. The cluster name is given as MHEWS_KB_Cluster with a default scaling setting at Autoscale for prompt scalability depending on the computing requirement of the executed containerized application. The complete environmental variables for the cluster are available on GitHub at [33]. After creating the docker images now to orchestrate these containers created using installed Kubernetes 1.23.12 in the cloud cluster. The master node is the principal node controlling the rest of the machines which run as container execution nodes. Kubernetes provides the tools that automate the distribution of applications across the cluster. Next, we configure Kubernetes to deploy the application for conducting the experiment and compare the performance result. Figures 7, 8 and 9 below depicts the pods in the cluster nodes, the up-running services that facilitate communication and provision of requested services through the endpoints and the external service endpoint to access the cluster through the BASH shell.

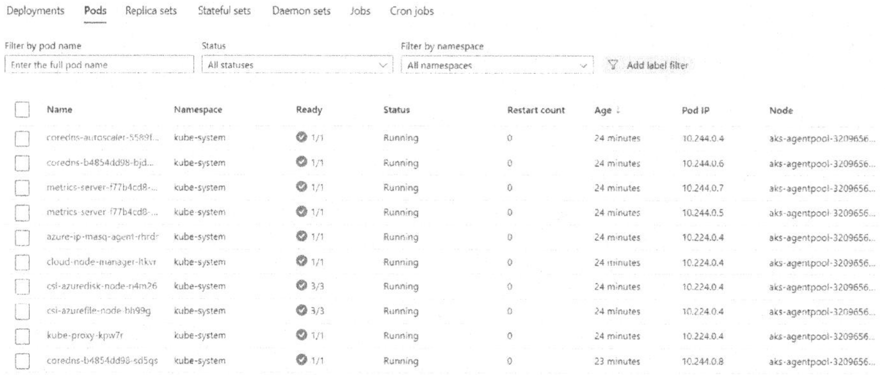

Name	Namespace	Ready	Status	Restart count	Age	Pod IP	Node
coredns-autoscaler-5589f...	kube-system	1/1	Running	0	24 minutes	10.244.0.4	aks-agentpool-3209656...
coredns-b4854dd98-bjd...	kube-system	1/1	Running	0	24 minutes	10.244.0.6	aks-agentpool-3209656...
metrics-server-f77b4cd8-...	kube-system	1/1	Running	0	24 minutes	10.244.0.7	aks-agentpool-3209656...
metrics-server-f77b4cd8-...	kube-system	1/1	Running	0	24 minutes	10.244.0.5	aks-agentpool-3209656...
azure-ip-masq-agent-rhrd	kube-system	1/1	Running	0	24 minutes	10.224.0.4	aks-agentpool-3209656...
cloud-node-manager-ltkvr	kube-system	1/1	Running	0	24 minutes	10.224.0.4	aks-agentpool-3209656...
csi-azuredisk-node-n4m26	kube-system	3/3	Running	0	24 minutes	10.224.0.4	aks-agentpool-3209656...
csi-azurefile-node-bh99g	kube-system	3/3	Running	0	24 minutes	10.224.0.4	aks-agentpool-3209656...
kube-proxy-kpw7r	kube-system	1/1	Running	0	24 minutes	10.224.0.4	aks-agentpool-3209656...
coredns-b4854dd98-sd5qs	kube-system	1/1	Running	0	23 minutes	10.244.0.8	aks-agentpool-3209656...

Fig. 7. Running nodes' pods in the deployed cluster

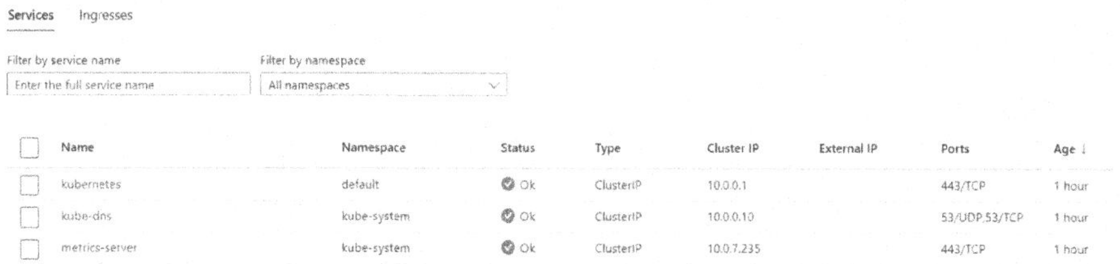

Name	Namespace	Status	Type	Cluster IP	External IP	Ports	Age
kubernetes	default	Ok	ClusterIP	10.0.0.1		443/TCP	1 hour
kube-dns	kube-system	Ok	ClusterIP	10.0.0.10		53/UDP,53/TCP	1 hour
metrics-server	kube-system	Ok	ClusterIP	10.0.7.235		443/TCP	1 hour

Fig. 8. Deployed Kubernetes services and ingresses

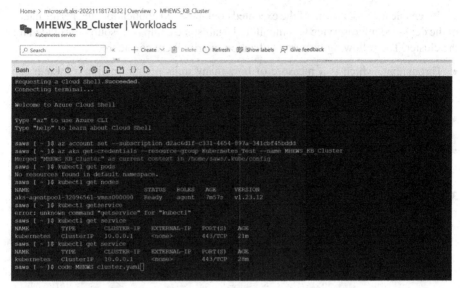

Fig. 9. Verification of the external service endpoint to access the cluster through the BASH shell.

A pod is defined by the YAML file that consists of the parameters of the container image for the EWS application. Code snippet 1 shows the example of variables for creating a microservice pod for Fig. 6.

```
apiVersion: apps/v1
kind; Deployment
metadata
  name: MHEWS cluster
spec:
  replicas:1
  selector:
    matchLabels:
      app: MHEWS Cluster
  template:
    metadata:
      labels:
        app: MHEWS Cluster
```

To enable the monitoring of the executed containerized application, the performance of the deployed microservice was monitored against the compute resources provided for the cluster. The following resource utilization metrics were considered:

- Throughput, which is a measure of how many units of information a system can process in a given amount of time is measured as a performance metrics of the cluster. It is measured in bits / second.
- Cluster performance is the CPU utilization when interacting with the cluster. It is measured in CPU core usage in milliseconds and percentages.
- Other metrics obtained are memory usage, network utilization in bytes and statuses for various node conditions.

3.2 Results

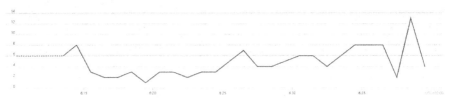

Fig. 10. Average Throughput for deployed microservice.

Fig. 11. CPU usage utilization.

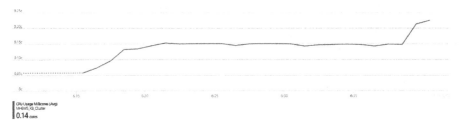

Fig. 12. Average CPU usage Milli-cores.

Figures 10, 11 and 12 show the effect of executing the containerized application as a microservice in the cluster. The figures reveal the throughput and CPU usage on average during execution, which are not overloaded or above the median threshold for the cluster

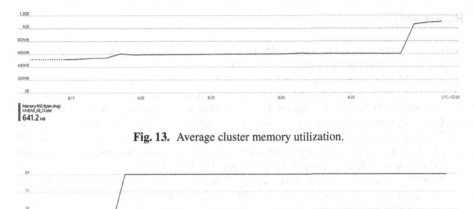

Fig. 13. Average cluster memory utilization.

Fig. 14. Status of various node conditions

configuration resources. This is important as it shows the ability of Kubernetes to run EWS applications as a containerized microservice. Figures 13 and 14 show a minimum memory utilization of the cluster – all within limits. From the results shows, we can conclude that Kubernetes microservices is an excellent choice for decoupling monolithic EWS applications towards integration of several EWS for an integrated climate-driven multi-hazard early warning system.

The experimental results discussed above show that containers enabled with Kubernetes are capable of running the EWS application as a microservice, which will foster integration and interoperability towards a fully-fledged integrated climate multi-hazard early warning system. The experimental setup to validate the proposed framework proved to be advantageous.

4   Conclusion

In this study, we presented an experimental framework towards a middleware that integrates several EWS for an integrated climate-driven multi-hazard early warning system using Kubernetes microservices. The experiment shows proper execution of the deployed EWS docker image in the pod. The deployed pods were monitored based on the throughput and CPU utilizations to verify the ability of pods to run containerized applications and has performed optimally. Preliminary tests carried out on the platform are encouraging, but there are still much work to do in many aspects. This study is advantageous in light of a research study that predicts over 75% of global organizations are expected to run containerized applications in production by 2022–2023 [32]. The work reported in this paper is a subset of a bigger project aimed at increasing data integration, interoperability, scalability, high availability, and reusability of EWSs for an integrated climate-driven multi-hazard early warning system.

References

1. ISDR: Terminology Basic Terms of Disaster Risk Reduction (2004). http://www.unisdr.org/eng/library/lib-terminology-eng%20home.htm
2. Zeng, M.L.: Interoperability. Knowl. Organ. **46**(2), 122–146 (2019)
3. IDNDR: Yokahoma strategy and plan for action for a safer world. Yokahoma, Japan, United Nations (1994). https://www.ifrc.org/Docs/idrl/I248EN.pdf. Accessed 2 Sept 2021
4. UNISDR: Developing early warning systems, a checklist: third international conference on early warning (EWC III), 27–29 March 2006, Bonn, Germany. Geneva, Switzerland: UNISDR (2006). http://www.undrr.org/publication/developing-early-warning-systems-checklistthird-international-conference-early-warning. Accessed 01 Mar 2021
5. UNFCCC: Paris Agreement. Paris, France: United Nations Framework Convention on Climate Change (2015). https://unfccc.int/sites/default/fles/english_paris_agreement.pdf. Accessed 2 Sept 2021
6. CRED, E.: EM-DAT: The OFDA (2011)
7. Guzzetti, F., et al.: Geographical landslide early warning systems. Earth Sci. Rev. **200**, 102973 (2020)
8. Rogers, D., Tsirkunov, V.: Costs and benefits of early warning systems. Global assessment rep. (2011)
9. Teisberg, T.J., Weiher, R.F.: Benefits and Costs of Early Warning Systems for Major Natural Hazards. Background Paper. World Bank (2009)
10. Liu, C., Guo, L., Ye, L., Zhang, S., Zhao, Y., Song, T.: A review of advances in China's flash flood early-warning system. Nat. Hazards **92**(2), 619–634 (2018). https://doi.org/10.1007/s11069-018-3173-7
11. Apache Mesos. https://mesos.apache.org/. Accessed 14 Nov 2022
12. Braimoh, A., Manyena, B., Obuya, G., Muraya, F.: Assessment of food security early warning systems for East and Southern Africa (2018)
13. Šakić Trogrlić, R., van den Homberg, M., Budimir, M., McQuistan, C., Sneddon, A., Golding, B.: Early warning systems and their role in disaster risk reduction. In: Golding, B. (eds.) Towards the "Perfect" Weather Warning. Springer, Cham (2022). https://doi.org/10.1007/978-3-030-98989-7_2
14. Xu, Q., et al.: Successful implementations of a real-time and intelligent early warning system for loess landslides on the Heifangtai terrace China. Eng. Geol. **278**, 105817 (2020)
15. Kafle, S.K.: Disaster early warning systems in Nepal: institutional and operational frameworks. J. Geogr. Nat. Disasters **7**(2), 2167–2587 (2017)
16. Masinde, M., Bagula, A.: ITIKI: bridge between African indigenous knowledge and modern science of drought prediction. Knowl. Manag. Dev. J. **7**(3), 274–290 (2011)
17. Jiménez, L., et al.: Ecosystem responses to climate-related changes in a Mediterranean alpine environment over the last ~ 180 years. Ecosystems **22**(3), 563–577 (2019)
18. Auffhammer, M.: Quantifying economic damages from climate change. J. Econ. Perspect. **32**(4), 33–52 (2018)
19. Edmonds, H.K., Lovell, J.E., Lovell, C.A.K.: A new composite climate change vulnerability index. Ecol. Ind. **117**, 106529 (2020)
20. Akanbi, A.K., Masinde, M.: Towards semantic integration of heterogeneous sensor data with indigenous knowledge for drought forecasting. In: Proceedings of the Doctoral Symposium of the 16th International Middleware Conference, pp. 1–5, December 2015
21. Akanbi, A., Masinde, M.: A distributed stream processing middleware framework for real-time analysis of heterogeneous data on big data platform: case of environmental monitoring. Sensors **20**(11), 3166 (2020)
22. Newman, S.: Building microservices. O'Reilly Media, Inc. (2021)

23. Burns, B., Beda, J., Hightower, K., Evenson, L.: Kubernetes: Up and Running. O'Reilly Media, Inc. (2022)
24. Xiao, Z., Wijegunaratne, I., Qiang, X.: Reflections on SOA and microservices. In: 2016 4th International Conference on Enterprise Systems (ES), pp. 60–67. IEEE, November 2016
25. Docker SwarmKit. https://docs.docker.com/engine/swarm/key-concepts/. Accessed 15 Nov 2022
26. Google Kubernetes. https://cloud.google.com/kubernetes-engine. Accessed 15 Nov 2022
27. Redhat Open Shift. https://www.redhat.com/en/technologies/cloud-computing/openshift/container-platform. Accessed 15 Nov 2022
28. Nomad. https://www.nomadproject.io/. Accessed 08 Nov 2022
29. Docker Compose. https://github.com/docker/compose. Accessed 15 Oct 2022
30. Cloudify. https://cloudify.co/. Accessed 10 Nov 2022
31. Muralidharan, S., Song, G., Ko, H.: Monitoring and managing IoT applications in smart cities using kubernetes. Cloud Comput. 11 (2019)
32. Global Application Container Market - Industry Trends and Forecast to 2029. https://www.databridgemarketresearch.com/reports/global-application-container-market. Accessed 14 Nov 2022
33. GitHub. https://github.com/yinchar/MHEWS-Kubernetes-Cluster-EnvPram/blob/4b54786fa54b677b433f1aee1007c91875cf558f/cluster-environment-parameters. Accessed 18 Nov 2022
34. Akanbi, A.: Development of Semantics-Based Distributed Middleware for Heterogeneous Data Integration and its Application for Drought (Doctoral dissertation, Central University of Technology, Free State) (2019)
35. Amará, J., Ströele, V., Braga, R., Dantas, M., Bauer, M.: Integrating heterogeneous stream and historical data sources using SQL. J. Inf. Data Manag. 13(2) (2022)
36. Turin, G., Borgarelli, A., Donetti, S., Johnsen, E.B., Tapia Tarifa, S.L., Damiani, F.: A formal model of the kubernetes container framework. In: Margaria, T., Steffen, B. (eds.) Leveraging Applications of Formal Methods, Verification and Validation: Verification Principles. ISoLA 2020. Lecture Notes in Computer Science(), vol. 12476. Springer, Cham (2020). https://doi.org/10.1007/978-3-030-61362-4_32
37. Bisong, E.: Containers and google kubernetes engine. In: Building Machine Learning and Deep Learning Models on Google Cloud Platform, pp. 655–670). Apress, Berkeley, CA (2019)

Indigenous Knowledge Mobile Based Application that Quantifies Farmers' Season Predictions with the Help of Scientific Knowledge

John Nyetanyane[(✉)]

Central University of Technology, Bloemfontein, Free State, South Africa
`tadojohnson2@gmail.com`

Abstract. This paper presents the development of the indigenous knowledge (IK) mobile based application that quantifies farmers' season predictions with the help of weather data, satellite imagery data and the Single Exponential Smoothing (SES) model. The system facilitates the indigenous knowledge indicators' collection and processing to compute farmers' certainty level of an oncoming rainy season behaviour which is mainly categorized into abundant, droughts and floods. Despite the value of IK indicators, they can only tell the behaviour of the season without stressing on valuable scientific information such as rains onset, distribution, magnitude and cessation. To solve this problem, the researcher integrates the use of IK indicators with farmers' historic data of periods when they have experienced abundant(normal) rains, less rains (below normal) and excessive rains (above normal). For each period, weather data (rains and average temperature) and satellite imagery data were collected, processed and stored in the database for use by the application. For each satellite image, the following land cover features: vegetation, soil moisture and waterbodies area cover were computed. The indigenous knowledge indicators were also systematically structured to enable certainty level computation of an oncoming season. Based on farmers' predictions of the oncoming season behaviour, the system extracts historic data with respect to the predicted season and send the data to the SES model. The SES model will predict the next season's weather data, vegetation, soil moisture and waterbodies cover data to help the farmer to have robust knowledge on the possible season outcome. The data is also downscaled to provide meaning to the farmers.

Keywords: indigenous knowledge · alpha · single exponential smoothing · vegetation · waterbodies · soil moisture

1 Introduction

Climate change continuous to demoralize the livelihood of many people particularly in Sub-Saharan Africa where rain-fed agricultures underpin food production for many Africans. The IK is a primary shield many local farmers use to adopt and or mitigate the

M. Masinde and A. Bagula (Eds.): AFRICATEK 2022, LNICST 503, pp. 192–205, 2023.
https://doi.org/10.1007/978-3-031-35883-8_13

impacts of climate change. Farmers use IK indicators which are classified mainly into environmental (e.g. trees, birds, insects etc.), meteorological (e.g. wind, temp, rains pattern etc.) and astronomical (e.g. shape of moon, pattern of stars etc.) to predict oncoming season behaviour which is mainly classified into abundant rains, droughts and floods. From their predictions, farmers, can be able to execute their cropping plans accordingly such as cultivation of drought tolerant crops when there is expectation of less rains during the season. The farmers' certainty level is built through an observation of multiple indicators. These indicators are also associated with weights based on their precision towards season prediction. Some are more reliable or trusted than others. Even though IK indicators are well trusted to predict the season behaviour, they are failing to signify exact rains onset, distribution, magnitude and cessation to enhance farmers cropping decisions. To address this problem, the researcher integrates the IK indicators and farmers' historic data of the seasons when they have experienced abundant rains, less rains and excessive rains to be able to quantify the farmers' predictions. For each period, weather data (weekly rains and average temperature) collected from the weather station close to the farmers' location and weekly satellite imagery data collected within the farmers' location are extracted. For each satellite image, the researcher computes the vegetation cover pixel values using Normalized Difference Vegetation Index (NDVI), soil moisture cover pixel values using Normalized Difference Moisture Index (NDMI) and waterbodies cover pixel values using Mc Feeter's Normalised Difference Water Index (NDWI). The data is stored in the database for use by the mobile application. The IK indicators are also systematically structured to enable computation of certainty level of an oncoming season. Based on farmers' predictions of the season, the system extracts the historic data with respect to the predicted season and send the data to SES model which will predict the next season's weather data and satellite imagery data to enable farmers to foresee possible movement of precipitation and temperature to enhance their cropping decisions. The motivation behind the use of satellite images, is to complement mainly the rains data which is not scaled down to the region of interest. These predictions are also scaled down to the range of 1 to 4 for simplicity purposes, where 1 represents no change, 2 below normal change, 3 represents normal change, and 4 represents above normal change.

2 Literature Review

Climate change is a predator that feeds in agricultural sector leaving billions of people under nutrition especially in Sub-Saharan Africa (SSA) that is characterized by inadequate technological, economical and financial resources to tackle the climate change impacts particularly in rain-fed agricultures that underpin the livelihood of many people [9]. The aggressiveness of climate change impacts is exacerbated by increase in human population, pollution, land degradations, industrialization, deforestation and many more putting sustainability of land, water and food in an imbalanced situation.

The indigenous knowledge is the primary shield many local farmers relying on to tackle harsh realities brought by the change in climate [3, 6, 8]. It is known as a body of knowledge existing within or acquired by local people over a period of time through accumulation of experiences, society nature relationships, community participations and handed down through generations [8]. The IK indicators are fundamental phenomena that make up the IK system and are mainly used to predict the weather patterns to enable farmers to implement key cropping decisions to improve and sustain crop yield [3]. The IK indicators are mainly categorized into environmental, meteorological and astronomical. Despite the value of the IK indicators, they cannot emphasize valuable information about precipitation such as rains onset, distribution, magnitude and cessation. The seasonal climate forecasts provided by the meteorologists, can only tabulate total rainfall for the oncoming season. This also creates problems given that farmers are interested in more than just total rainfall and they need the forecasts to stress duration and distribution of rains over time and space to be most valuable [2, 6]. Further, the seasonal climate forecasts are not well supported by many local farmers since they do not incorporate the knowledge of the farmers, they have credibility, legitimacy, scale, cognitive capacity and institutional barriers [2, 3].

With respect to the fact that farmers are the main custodians of historic weather events occurred in their environment, the use of remote sensing techniques collaborated with statistical methods can assist farmers at the local level with season predictions. The remote sensing is a technology of acquiring knowledge about the earth surface without coming into contact with it. The satellite imagery is a remote sensing technique that is equipped with powerful sensors and cameras used to collect images of the world surface [5]. This technology is extensively applied in agricultural sector to track and monitor vegetation cover, soil moisture cover and surface water bodies cover to assist the decision makers to effectively and timely device mainly drought planning and mitigation strategies to lessen the effect and reduce the economic loss [7]. Given that these land cover features (soil moisture, vegetation cover, waterbodies cover) are sensitive to precipitation and are good proxy of it, they can be utilized to downscale the precipitation data to allow increase in spatial resolution [4].

The time series models are statistical models that are used to learn from the past observations and predict the future. They are used to forecast change of the variable over time by first analyzing its historical movement and extracting hidden patterns such as seasonality effects and the mean of the variable. The Long Short-Term Memory (LSTM) deep learning networks and Autoregressive Integrated Moving Average (ARIMA) family models are among powerful and sophisticated time series models that are used mainly to predict weather parameters and with remarkable effects.

To specifically address the communities in their localities, IK can be integrated with the scientific knowledge for as long as the IK is systematically modelled accordingly. According to [1] measuring of IK indicators' weights based on the impact they have towards season behaviour predictions is among good approaches in quantifying their processing. This is motivated by the fact that some indicators continue to lose value while others gain it towards season predictions.

3   Methodology

The action based-research methodology was adopted with an intention to get the depth ground information on farmers' historic data of the past weather events, information on how IK indicators are collected and processed to build farmers' certainty level and then come up with mobile-based application that will facilitate the IK collection and processing with the help of weather data, remote sensing and machine learning techniques to enhance farmers' cropping decisions. The qualitative research paradigm was adopted where focus group interview was selected to get the depth and variety of knowledge from the phenomena. The purposive sampling technique was used to sample 20 respondents on the basis that they reside in a study area (Hennenman, Whites Village Free State, South Africa) for over 10 years, known to be the primary custodians of the IK, doing crop farming, and rely heavily on rains to sustain the development of their crops. The sample consist of 13 male and 7 female farmers aged between 50 and 70. During the focus group interview, farmers were requested to measure the IK indicators based on their accuracy towards the predicted rainy season behaviour. Farmers also emphasized that the indicators are no longer precise and therefore, their weight must be complemented with the frequency of their observations. Farmers further elaborated on rules associated with the IK indicators' collection and processing. These rules will be discussed later. Lastly, farmers were requested to tabulate historic data of periods they could remember where they have experienced abundant rains, less rains and excessive rains during the rainy periods categorized in to warm rainy season (starts from September to February) and cold rainy season (starts from March to May). All these data were documented for further processing.

The Sentinel 2 weekly satellite images with spatial resolution of 10 m were extracted from United States Geological Survey (USGS) Earth Explorer database for the periods tabulated by the farmers. An approximate of 300 images ranging between 2013 to 2022 were extracted. Cloud masking and image mosaic were performed with the help of Semi-Automatic Classification Plugin (SCP) tools from Geographic Information System (GIS) software to smooth noisy images by mapping and replacing cloudy pixels of one image with non-cloud pixels from another images. Given coarse spatial resolution and high synoptic view of the satellite images, the BaseMap and SCP tools were utilized to locate and extract pixels that covers the region of interest. The atmospheric effects were removed by converting images from calibrated digital numbers (DN) to reflectance pixel values to enable quantitative analysis. The raster calculator was used to compute the vegetation cover using NDVI, soil moisture cover using NDMI and surface waterbodies using Mc Feeters' NDWI.

3.1 NDVI

It is a vegetation index utilized to analyze the changes in vegetation cover. It is computed by manipulating the Red and near infrared(NIR) spectral bands of the satellite image as shown below.

$$NDVI = \frac{\text{Re}d - NIR}{\text{Re}d + NIR} \qquad (1)$$

Its normalized values ranges between −1 to 1, where values close to 1 reflect high vegetation greenness and values close to −1 indicates stressed or non-vegetated areas.

3.2 NDWI

Introduced by Mc Feeters, is one of the most commonly used water index to detect open surface waterbodies or waterlogged areas and is computed by manipulating green and NIR spectral bands as shown below.

$$NDWI = \frac{Green - NIR}{Green + NIR} \qquad (2)$$

Its normalized values ranges between −1 and 1, where 1 represents high surface water reflectance and values close to −1 represents non-waterbodies area.

3.3 NDMI

This type of an index quantifies water content in vegetation leaf canopies and soil moisture using NIR and Short-Wave Infrared (SWIR) spectral bands computed as:

$$NDMI = \frac{NIR - SWIR}{NIR + SWIR} \qquad (3)$$

Its normalized values ranges between −1 to 1, where values close to 1 represents high moist or saturated soil or high water content in leaves and the values close to −1, represent dry soil or water stressed vegetation.

For each satellite image, the vegetation (NDVI) spectral values greater than 0.3, soil moisture (NDMI) spectral values greater than 0 and waterbodies (NDWI) spectral values greater than 0 were classified and pixel intensity values representing their coverage in m^2 were recorded.

3.4 Mobile Application Development

The Entity Relationship Diagram (ERD) presented in Fig. 1 shows the relationship between an indicator, observer and observation entities.

From the diagram above, an observer can observe one or many indicators. An indicator can be observed once or many times by either one or many observers. Below is set of rules stipulated by the farmers regarding the validity assessment of the indigenous knowledge indicators:

- All indicators should be observed and registered strictly in the farmers' location.
- An indicator should only be environmental, meteorological and astronomical in nature. Hence, indicators of spiritual type are not considered.
- For an indicator observation to be valid, it must be observed more than once and by different observers.
- For an observation of environmental indicator, the location, time stamp and image of the indicator need to be recorded.
- For an observation of either meteorological or astronomical indicator, only the time stamp will be recorded. There are limited restrictions regarding the two (meteorological or astronomical indicator) because they can be witnessed by everyone in the area.

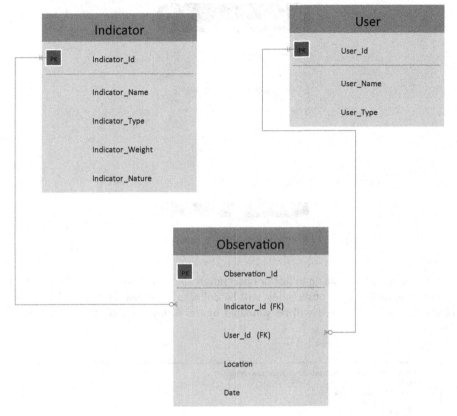

Fig. 1. Relationship between Indicator, User and Observation entities

- No duplicate entries should be allowed. For instance, one environmental indicator can be observed many times in a day by one or many observers for as long as they are observed at different locations (at least 1 km apart).
- An environmental indicator can be observed once or many times in one location for as long as they are observed at different time stamps (days)
- This also goes to meteorological and astronomical indicators that can be observed in different days.

The above-mentioned rules were utilized in the development of a mobile application that will facilitate registration and authentication of the IK indicators' observations.

Initially, the user will be requested to register before making use of the application.

A registered user will be displayed with the following screen to select the IK type (drought, floods or abundant) that they have observed. Based on the user's selection, list of indicators will be displayed as shown in the Fig. 2 below.

A user will select an indicator that they have observed, and based on the nature of the indicator, the following operations will be performed when the Register button is clicked. If the nature of the indicator is environmental, the observer information (username and Id), Global Positioning System (GPS) coordinates and date of observation

Fig. 2. List of indicators that represents Rainy Season

will be collected to create an indicator observation object. Otherwise, only the observer information and date of observation will be collected to create indicator observation object. The object created will be validated by the following algorithm presented in Fig. 3.

```
boolean ValidateAndInsertObservation(Observation observation)
    Declarations
      num timeStampDistance
      num locationDistance
      boolean flag = false
      Collection observations = conn.readObservationsForIndicator(observation.getIndicator())
    if observation.getLocation().toLowerCase().contains( "hennenman")
AND observation.getLocation().toLowerCase().contains( "whites ")  then
        flag=true
      if observations.size() = 0 then
        flag = conn.createObservation(observation)
      else
        if (NOT)observation.getIndicator().getNature().equals("environmental") then
          for num count = 0, count < observations.size(), count++
            timeStampDistance= getTimeStampDistance(observations.get(count).getCreated(), observation.getCreated())
            if timeStampDistance = 0 then
                flag = false
            endif
          endfor
        else
          for num count = 0, count < observations.size(),count++
            timeStampDistance= getTimeStampDistance(observations.get(count).getCreated(), observation.getCreated())
            locationDistance = getLocDistance(observations.get(count).getLatitude(),
                        observations.get(count).getLongitude(),
                        observation.getLatitude(), observation.getLongitude())
            if timeStampDistance = 0 AND locationDistance < 1000 then
                flag = false
            endif
          endfor
        endif
      endif
    endif
    return flag
```

Fig. 3. Validation of an IK observation

The algorithm in Fig. 3 receives the tested observation object passed as a parameter. It will first check if the observation was made in the region of interest. If so, it will extract all observations of the same indicator object from the cloud storage. If there are no observations made for that indicator, the tested observation will be declared valid and it will be registered. Otherwise, the algorithm will first check the nature type of an observed indicator. If it environmental, it will compute the timestamp distance and location distance of a tested observation against all extracted observations of the same indicator with the aim to avoid duplicate entries. For meteorological or astronomical indicator observation, only the timestamp distance will be computed. The observation will be registered only when its location or timestamp parameters meet the stipulated criteria tabulated by farmers.

The Harvesine equation presented below is utilized to compute the shortest location distance between two points on an earth surface using their latitudes and longitudes.

$$d = 2r \sin^{-1}(\sqrt{\sin^2(\frac{x_2 - x_1}{2}) + \cos(x_1)\cos(x_2)\sin^2(\frac{y_2 - y_1}{2})}) \quad (4)$$

Where:

r represents the radius.

x_1 represents latitude of point A.

x_2 represents latitude of point B.

y_1 represents longitude of point A.

y_2 represents longitude of point B.

The time distance is computed as a days' difference between two dates.

The observation images collected for the environmental indicators will be assessed by an administrator. An image is declared valid if it corresponds with the observation made, otherwise the image together with its observation object will be removed.

3.5 Season Prediction

Before computation of season predictions, the system will first compute the farmers' certainty level of the predicted season behaviour using the weights of all the observed indicators. If the certainty level is greater than the threshold set by the farmers, then it means farmers are certain of the oncoming season behaviour.

3.6 Certainty Level Computation

To compute the certainty level, the indicators observed will be extracted from the observations table inside the database. Distinct indicators will be identified, their frequency (how many times they were observed) and the number of observers. This is illustrated on a Table 1 below.

Table 1. List of indicators, their frequency and frequency of observers

Indicator Id	Count of Indicators	Count of observers	Valid ?
1	5	3	☑
2	3	1	☒
3	1	5	☒
7	3	2	☑

The certainty level will be computed for only the indicators that qualifies based on the following farmers' rule:

- An indicator observation is declared valid if it was made 3 times or more by 2 or more observers at different locations and or time stamps depending on the indicators' nature.

The qualifying indicators will be grouped based on their type (rains, drought and floods). The system will compute which group has a maximum total of certainty weights. This is motivated by the fact that any indicator of any type can be observed by the farmers. The group considered as a winner will be selected and will be utilized to compute the certainty level (CL) which is a total weight of observed indicators divided by the sum of weights of all indicators of the same type as shown below.

$$CL = \left(\frac{1}{\sum_{i=1}^{n} F_i} * \sum_{b=1}^{k} L_b \right) * 100 \tag{5}$$

Where L_b represents sum of observed indicators and F_i represents sum of all indicators.

3.7 Next Season Prediction

If the certainty level is greater than the threshold set by the farmers, the system will extract the farmers' historic data based on the indicators' type that was declared as a winner and also the season type (warm rainy season and cold rainy season) that will be selected by the user. These data will be sent to the SES model which will predict every record of the historic data as shown in the Table 2 below where $t + 1$ is the forecast that will be generated from the historic data (past observations indicated as t, $t-1$, $t-2$, $t-3$......$t-n$).

The weekly predictions will be made from September to January for warm rainy season and March to May for cold rainy season.

Table 2. Example of historic, current and future data points

	t-5	t-4	t-3	t-2	t-1	t	t+1
Week 1	0	24	13	12	10	5	?
Week 2	12	0	0	34	44	0	?
.	.	.	.	.	.	.	?
.	.	.	.	.	.	.	?
Week 20	21	34	0	23	50	121	?

3.8 SES Model

The SES model is among powerful and simple to use time series smoothing and prediction model that works well with time-series data that does not have a trend or seasonality effects. It is an extension of moving(rolling) average model where more recent observations get higher weight. It utilizes the learning rate mechanism known as alpha(α) which is a constant value ranging between 0 and 1. The formula is generalized as.

$$f_{t+1} = \alpha F_t + \sum_{i=1}^{n} a(1-a)^i F_{t-i} \tag{6}$$

Where f_{t+1} represents the next forecast,

F_t represents the today's forecast,

α represents the learning rate parameter that takes value of 0 to 1

n represents number of observations

The weighting scheme of this model assigns high weight to recent data and it exponentially decays as observations gets older. The accuracy level of SES depends on the selection of the learning rate based on a cost function that needs to be optimized. In simplest form, the optimum alpha value is the one that has less error rate. The extreme values of alpha (0 and 1) are ignored to avoid under-smoothing and over-smoothing where the model doesn't learn.

The function in Fig. 4 runs through the learning rate candidate values and the farmers' historic data arranged into rows and columns with the motive to find the optimum learning rate parameter.

The function presented above in Fig. 4 invokes the SES model's fit() function presented below in Fig. 5. This fit() function receives every farmers' historic data record and the candidate alpha value. It will perform the learning process and return the error rate for the candidate alpha value. This function will be repeatedly called to evaluate every candidate value on farmers' historic data records. The fit() function is sectioned into three iterations. In the first iteration, predictions are performed starting from the old observations towards the recent observations. The model predicts the next forecast as a today's forecast plus an error term of today adjusted by the learning rate. The second iteration computes the error by comparing the model's predictions and the actual values.

```
Collection fitting(num[][] weeklyRecords)
     Declarations
          num error = 0, alpha, col, row
          Collection errors=new Collection(), colElements = new Collection(), errors =new Collection()
          ExponentialSmoothing model = new ExponentialSmoothing()
     for alpha = 0.1, alpha < 1, alpha += 0.1
          for col = 0, col < weeklyRecords[0].length, col++
               for row = 0, row < weeklyRecords.length, row++
                    colElements.add(weeklyRecords[row][col])
               endfor
               error += model.fit(colElements, alpha)
               colElements = new Collection()
          endfor
          errors.add(error)
     endfor
     return errors
```

Fig. 4. Evaluation of different model parameters

The error rate is computed as an absolute difference between the predicted value and the actual value. The third iteration sum all errors for a given record and the learning rate. Finally, the model will return the average of absolute errors.

```
num fit(Collection dataPoints, num alpha) {
     Declarations
          num error, actual,count,prediction
          Collection predictions=new Collection(), errorList=new Collection()
     for num count = 1, count < dataPoints.size(),count ++
          if count = 1 then
               prediction = dataPoints.get(0)
          else
               prediction = prediction + alpha * (dataPoints.get (count - 1) -
prediction)
          endif
          predictions.add(prediction)
     endfor
     for num count = 0, count < predictions.size(), count++
          actual = dataPoints.get(count + 1)
          prediction = predictions.get(count)
          error = Math.abs(actual - prediction)
          errorList.add(error)
     endfor
     for num count = 0, count < errorList.size(), count++
          sum += errorList.get(count)
     endfor
     return sum / errorList.size()
```

Fig. 5. Model's fit function

The model's predict() function is shown in Fig. 6. This function receives an optimum alpha computed during the training phase and every historic data record to perform next prediction.

```
num predict(Collection dataPoints, num alpha)
    Declarations
        num count,prediction
    for count = 1, count <= dataPoints.size(), count ++
        if count = 1 then
            prediction = dataPoints.get(0)
        else
            prediction = prediction + alpha * (dataPoints.get(count - 1) -
prediction)
        endif
    endfor
    return prediction
```

Fig. 6. Next season predictions using best alpha

3.9   Downscaling of Predictions

At this stage the predictions are still in pixel cover values for remote sensing data, in millimetres(mm) for rain data and in degree Celsius for temperature data. Hence, they are not presentable to the farmers. To scale down the predictions, the system extracts the historic data and perform mathematical computations to scale the predictions to the range of 1 to 4, where 1 represents no change, 2 represents below normal change, 3 represent normal change and 4 represents above normal change. For instance, to scale down the satellite imagery data, the system will first compute the average pixel values of periods when floods were received, when abundant rains were received, and when drought were received. The researcher's expectation is that during excessive rains periods, average pixel values will be high than during abundant and drought seasons, however, that is what the system will figure out using its algorithms. From this data, the system will create the following values *min, middle* and *max* pixel values. The median will be computed as the average between the corresponding small and large values. As shown in the Fig. 7 below.

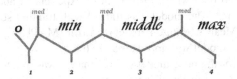

Fig. 7. Scaling down of predictions

The unknown pixel value will be categorized based on the range to which it falls. For instance, it will be assigned 1, if it is between 0 and median, it will be assigned 3, if it is greater than median between min and middle and less than the median between middle and max and so forth. The rains data will be computed in the same manner. To scale the temperature values, the system will compute the average of temperature during warm rainy seasons and cold rainy seasons. The middle value will be computed as the average between the computed values.

Finally, the data will be presented in a form of a graph as shown in Fig. 8 below. From this data, farmers will be able to identify possible rains pattern by analyzing weather data predictions and remote sensing data predictions.

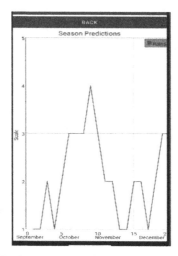

Fig. 8. Rains predictions using rains data

4 SES Model Evaluation

The farmers' historic data were split into two subsets (training and testing sets). The data from 2013 to 2019 was used for training set while the remaining portion (2020 to 2022 data) was used for testing set. The training was performed on both cold and warm rainy seasons' collected data where farmers have experienced abundant rains, scarce rains and excessive rains. The model was trained with training set and was validated with testing set. The Mean Absolute Percentage Error (MAPE) was computed and the overall accuracy of the model was approximately 60%.

The main reason for the poor model's performance was due to scarcity of historic data. However, this can be improved as years progress for as long as farmers document every season behaviour.

5 Conclusion

This paper presented the development of the IK mobile based application that quantifies farmers' season predictions with the help of scientific data to enhance farmers' cropping decisions. The development of this application was motivated by the under-resourced and overlooked IK system that many local farmers rely on to tackle the impacts of climate change. This paper emphasized that the IK indicators can be systematically collected and processed to compute the farmers' certainty level of the oncoming season. The results are also integrated with farmers' historic knowledge of different weather events with the aim to quantify the season predictions.

Given the fact that the application is decoupled from the cloud database holding the IK indicators and farmers' historic data, this implies that the same system can be adopted by other farmers from different regions where they will inject their own IK indicators and their own historic data. However, the challenge will only be when the rules governing the collection and processing of the indicators varies from region to region.

The system is equipped with SES model that is automatically evaluated with different learning rate parameters to come up with the optimal learning rate parameter to optimize the predictions. However, the model cannot accurately predict the data that has trend and seasonality effects. This can be addressed by adopting more sophisticated algorithms such as Double Exponential Smoothing (DES) model that can handle data with trend, and Holt-Winter's Model that can handle data with both trend and seasonality effects.

Although, farmers' predictions can be quantified, they still need to be integrated with scientific forecasts to come up with robust predictions that can address the harsh realities of climate change.

References

1. Akanbi, A.K., Masinde, M.: A framework for accurate drought forecasting system using semantics-based data integration middleware. In: Glitho, R., Zennaro, M., Belqasmi, F., Agueh, M. (eds.) e-Infrastructure and e-Services. AFRICOMM 2015. Lecture Notes of the Institute for Computer Sciences, Social Informatics and Telecommunications Engineering, vol. 171. Springer, Cham (2016). https://doi.org/10.1007/978-3-319-43696-8_12
2. Andersson, L., Wilk, J., Graham, L.P., Wikner, J., Mokwatlo, S., Petja, B.: Local early warning systems for drought–Could they add value to nationally disseminated seasonal climate forecasts? Weather Clim. Extremes **28**, 100241 (2020)
3. Basdew, M., Jiri, O., Mafongoya, P.L.: Integration of indigenous and scientific knowledge in climate adaptation in KwaZulu-Natal, South Africa. Change Adapt. Socio-Ecol. Syst. **3**(1), 56–67 (2017)
4. Ezzine, H., Bouziane, A., Ouazar, D., Hasnaoui, M.D.: Downscaling of open coarse precipitation data through spatial and statistical analysis, integrating NDVI, NDWI, elevation, and distance from sea. Adv. Meteorol. (2017)
5. Gupta, R.P.: Remote Sensing Geology. Springer (2017)
6. Jiri, O., Mafongoya, P., Mubaya, C., Mafongoya, O.: Seasonal climate prediction and adaptation using indigenous knowledge systems in agriculture systems in Southern Africa: a review (2015)
7. Shashikant, V., Mohamed Shariff, A.R., Wayayok, A., Kamal, M.R., Lee, Y.P., Takeuchi, W.: Utilizing TVDI and NDWI to classify severity of agricultural drought in Chuping, Malaysia. Agronomy **11**(6), 1243 (2021)
8. Smith, L.T., Maxwell, T.K., Puke, H., Temara, P.: Indigenous knowledge, methodology and mayhem: what is the role of methodology in producing Indigenous insights? a discussion from mātauranga Māori (2016)
9. Chhibber, A., Laajaj, R.: Disasters, climate change and economic development in sub-Saharan Africa: lessons and directions. J. Afr. Econ. **17**(suppl_2), ii7–ii49 (2008)

Weed Identification in Plant Seedlings Using Convolutional Neural Networks

Samuel Damilare[1], Chika Yinka-Banjo[1(✉)] ⓘ, and Olasupo Ajayi[2] ⓘ

[1] Department of Computer Science, University of Lagos, Lagos, Nigeria
cyinkabanjo@unilag.edu.ng
[2] Department of Computer Science, University of the Western Cape, Cape Town, South Africa

Abstract. Agriculture is essential for the continuous survival of man, however, the adverse effect of weeds in agronomy cannot be ignored. These weeds compete with crops for nutrients and sunlight, hence resulting in low crop yield. It is therefore necessary to identify and remove them at an early growth stage for effective weed control and maximum farm produce. This study focuses on distinguishing between crops and weeds at their infancy, using images processing. To achieve this, three convolutional neural networks (CNNs) architectures, ResNet, MobileNet and InceptionV3, were evaluated using a transfer learning technique on a dataset of 5,339 RGB plant images containing 12 different species of plants. Comparing their performances from experiments carried out, the results revealed the Inception V3 model as the best for crop identification with an accuracy of 82.4%, while ResNet and Mobilenet both achieved average accuracies of 71.1% and 75.4% respectively. ResNet however gave the best performance in terms of identifying weeds. Overall, Inception v3 was the best as other performance metrics including the recall, precision, and F1-score also corroborated the superiority of Inception v3 in distinguishing between crops and weed.

Keywords: Precision Agriculture (PA) · Deep Learning · Convolutional Neural Network (CNN) · Weed Control · Plant Seedling Classification · Transfer Learning

1 Introduction

Food is a necessity for human survival. The continuous increase in world population and corresponding increase in demand for food, places immense strain on farmers. There is the need to meet up with the ever-increasing demand of food while maximizing profits. According to reports from Food & Agriculture Organization of the United Nations (FAO) [1], the population of the world is estimated to be 7.7 billion and this is expected to grow to almost 10 billion by the year 2050. To feed this population, the FAO estimates that global food production must increase by at least 70%, moreover, food production in developing countries must be at least twice that of the developed countries [1]. Since the challenges before farmers goes beyond meeting the demands of the increasing human populace to maximizing their farm produce, there is an important need to eliminate or

M. Masinde and A. Bagula (Eds.): AFRICATEK 2022, LNICST 503, pp. 206–224, 2023.
https://doi.org/10.1007/978-3-031-35883-8_14

reduce weeds in farmlands, as they can cause up to 100% loss of farm produce. Weeds are simply undesired plants that compete with crops for land, sunlight, water, and other resources. According to [2], weeds are said to be any unwanted biological vegetation or plant which interferes with man's activities and goals. Weeds are one of the most cogent and significant factors affecting agricultural production, as they affect crop productivity and sometimes harm livestock [3].

Smart farming is key to the future of agriculture. It can be referred to as the use of modern technologies to increase the quantitative and qualitative output of agricultural products. In recent years, Artificial Intelligence (AI), Machine Learning (ML) and technologies of the fourth industrial revolution (4IR) have been applied in agriculture to improve crop quality and yield. The impact of the 4IR on the agricultural sector has led to the birth of terminologies such as Precision Agriculture or Precision Farming or Smart Agriculture. Precision agriculture (PA) enabled farmers to capture and analyze data related to their farms, using technologies such as Global Positioning System (GPS), sensors, weather tracking etc. [1, 6]. The goal of PA is to ensure sustainability, profitability, and protection of the farming environment. PA leverages on several technologies including software applications (mobile and web), robots, drones, and cloud computing. With the help of PA, farmers can automate irrigation and harvesting processes, easily identify and control weeds, as well as get powerful insights about farmlands and produce that can help them make informed decisions.

A standard agricultural practice is the use of chemicals to improve farm output and crop yield. The use of herbicides constitutes about two-third of the chemical applications to agricultural lands globally. However, despite the use of modern techniques and changes in the composition of these chemicals, there are growing concerns, both biologically and environmentally, of the use of these chemicals on crops. Recent studies have shown that glyphosate, which is a prevalent herbicide in use since the early 1970s, contains harmful carcinogenic toxicities that are dangerous to man [4]. There is therefore a need for a better and more balanced approach in the use of herbicide on crop fields. Coupled with this challenge of using chemicals in farmlands, farmers encounter the problem of distinguishing between weeds and native plant species. Traditionally, the differentiation is done by farm personnel while walking or driving around the farm. This process is difficult and strenuous due to the resemblance and/or similarities between the weeds and some crops, particularly at the early stages of growth. Recent studies have applied PA to solve this challenge. One of such study is [4], where PA was deployed for weed identification using field mapping. Field mapping assumes that the crops are planted in rows, hence uses line detection to classify crops by assuming that plants outside the seedling lines are weeds. Similarly, in [5], three models (4 convolution layers, 6 convolution layers, 8 convolution layers, and 13 convolution layers) were built to identify the weeds that grow alongside crops. The network with 8 convolution layers resulted in the highest accuracy of 97.83% for training and 96.53% as test accuracy.

It is important to know that the successful cultivation of plants in large numbers is directly proportional to the weed control efficacy, especially as weeds compete with the crops for space, nutrients, and water during the first eight weeks of seeding, i.e., the critical period. Weed identification is therefore pertinent for ample crop yield. Image analysis or "computer vision" can be impactful in this regard, as it can precisely identify weeds with minimal negative impacts to the crops or the environment. This paper aims to investigate the efficacy of image analysis models, specifically convolutional neural network (CNN), in distinguishing weeds from crop seedlings. The contributions of this paper are to explore the application of CNN in distinguishing between weeds and crop seedlings based on their images, and to compare the performance of three CNN models i.e., ResNet, MobileNet v2 and Inception v3 for the above task as recommended.

The remainder of this paper is organised as follows, related works in literature are reviewed in Sect. 2, while Sect. 3 presents the research methodology. Section 4 discusses the experimental setup and obtained results, while Sect. 5 concludes the paper and provides suggestions for future work.

2   Related Works

Over the years, there have been several applications of computer vision techniques to solve classification issues at various levels. In [6], the authors reviewed the application of drones in agriculture, including their use in crop monitoring, irrigation, and weed control through identification and spot spraying. A unique advantage of drones in spot spraying is their ability to cover a large area in a short amount of time. Once images are captured using cameras mounted on drones or from satellite images, image detection algorithms are then used to distinguish crops from weeds. For instance, in [7] the authors used histograms based on color indices to distinguish between soybean, soil, and broadleaf (weeds). The representation of the features was tested with Support Vector Machine (SVM) and Back-propagation Neural Network (BPNN) and obtained total accuracy of 95% and 96% respectively. The authors in [12] aimed at ascertaining the growth levels of paddy crop while applying CNN to the paddy dataset which was gotten from FAO repository. According to them, paddy should be well monitored to help farmers know when to water, when to harvest and know the growth level of the paddy. They obtained an 82% accuracy with their used metrics which was better than SVM.

Though supervised ML algorithms such as SVM and Random Forest (RF) have been successful in the past, most recent research work favour deep learning and neural networks. [11] presented a deep learning algorithm that could perform image segmentation and classification. They used a convolutional network to separate maize plants from the weeds in real time. The network performance was then analyzed with various models such as LeNet, AlexNet, cNet and sNet using metrics such as processing time and accuracy. cNet performed the best and had huge potential for autonomous weed control in real world systems. Likewise, authors presented in [9] displayed a system that autonomously detected milkweed plants by placing cameras on top of vehicles. The authors used faster region-based CNN and aggregated channel features (ACF). While the latter was used on embedded systems with central processing units for running the detectors, the former was used with ResNet and graphics processing units for optimized processing. These detections were mainly used to estimate the milkweed plant densities in geo-referenced areas, which were dependent on the GPS point that corresponds to the recorded images. In [10] a pipeline based on deep learning was developed that localized and found the total number of agricultural pests in various images. A combination of Zeiler & Fergus model, region proposal network, and non-maximum suppression were used to handle overlapping detections.

The researchers in [8] focused on an agricultural robotics system that addressed weeding problem by means of selective spraying or mechanical removal of the detected weeds. They described a deep learning-based method that enabled a robot to perform an accurate weed/crop classification using a sequence of two Convolutional Neural Networks (CNNs) applied to RGB images. The first network was based on an encoder-decoder segmentation model and performed a pixel-wise, plant-type agnostic segmentation to distinguish crops from soil. The second network was then used to classify crops from weeds. Similarly, in [13] the authors investigated the influence of input image resolution on the classification performance and proposed a patch augmentation strategy. Radhika et al. proposed the classification of paddy and weed using colour features in [14], while [15] studied different tools and techniques which are necessary for the assessment of weeds development using four major procedures, i.e., pre-processing, segmentation, feature extraction and classification. Ref. [16] implemented an Encoder-Decoder based architecture for weed classification.

In [17], a field weed and crop classification algorithm based on CNN and SVM was proposed. The model used VGG16 + SVM for classification and achieved an accuracy of 96.4%. Ref. [18] also used a CNN model to differentiate between weeds and crops on a farm field. The work then suggested the best type of herbicide to apply based on the classification result. Ref. [3] used a combination of CNN and Long-Short-Term Memory (LSTM) for the identification and classification of weed plants. The CNN had a unique structure to get discriminative features for the input images, while the LSTM allowed to jointly optimize the classification. To validate the proposed model, nine species of weeds were classified using the proposed method including vine weeds, three-leaf weeds, spiky weeds, and invasive creeping weeds. After several extensive experiments, they achieved an average classification accuracy of 99.36%.

From the research papers surveyed, it was observed that there are different approaches to achieving plant image recognition and weeds/crops classification. While some researchers tend to segment the images before classification, others-built hybrid models from ground up. Moreover, most authors used datasets containing RGB images of plants obtained from online repositories or captured from drone mounted cameras or mobile phones.

This paper aims to investigate and implement a ResNet model similar to that proposed in [1], then compare it with two models using plants image dataset.

3 Materials and Methods

In this paper, the power of CNN is adopted and applied to classify weeds and crops on a plant-seedling image dataset. This work builds on the work done in [1] by comparing the proposed ResNet model with two CNN models i.e., MobileNet and Inceptionv3. In this section, a brief description of the architectures used is done before an overview of the methodology is given.

3.1 System Architecture

a. ResNet Overview. The Residual Network as presented in [19] by some researchers at Microsoft allows for successful training of networks with hundreds of layers. This was very difficult hitherto the novel architecture came to existence as previous models suffered from the problem of vanishing gradients. Vanishing gradient can simply be summarized as a problem that occur when the gradients of an artificial neural network (ANN) become smaller as they are being applied to the previous layers during back propagation. This will in turn influence the performance as well as the accuracy of the network. A neural network's depth is paramount to performing visual recognition tasks. Unlike a traditional neural network (see Fig. 1), ResNet works by using "skip connections" to connect components in different layers of the network to an identity mapping as illustrated in Fig. 2. This essentially feeds the original input to the output, thus allowing easy flow of information from previous layers to later layers in the network. The flow of information can also be sent through alternate paths if the need arises.

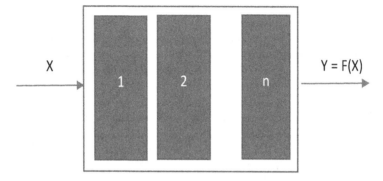

Fig. 1. Classic Neural Network Architecture

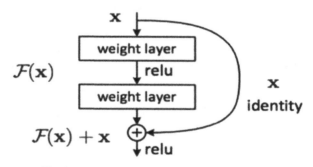

Fig. 2. Basic building blocks of a residual module

The residual learning building block in Fig. 2 is defined in Eq. 1

$$y = F(x_i\{W_i\} + x)$$ (1)

where input (x) and output (y) are vectors of the considered layer, while the function $F(x, \{W_i\})$ depicts the residual mapping that the model needs to learn.

b. MobileNet Overview. The MobileNet V2 was developed by Howard *et al.* [20] and was pre-trained using the ImageNet dataset (with about 1.4 million images and

1000 categories of web images). They were built as a unit of mobile-first models for computer vision for Tensorflow [21]. MobileNet aims for effectiveness and maximum accuracy while being frugal on resources, as it is meant to run on embedded or mobile devices. MobileNet can be used for classification, segmentation, and detection tasks. The architecture works based on a depth-wise separable convolutions. Unlike traditional CNNs which adds filters and the input into the next class of outputs in one stride, MobileNet's convolution is divided into two layers i.e., a 3x3 depth-wise convolution and a 1x1 pointwise convolution. Equation 2 shows a depth-wise convolution which has a single filter per channel:

$$GK, i, n = \sum_{ij,m} Ki, j, m.Fk + i - 1, l + j - 1, m \tag{2}$$

where K represents the depth-wise kernel with magnitude Dk x Dk x M and the mth filter in the kernel is used on the mth channel of **F**, which gives an output of mth channel with a filtered feature map **G**. The cost of computation is given in Eq. 3 as:

$$Dk.Dk.M.DF.DF \tag{3}$$

The depth-wise convolution does not combine the input channels but rather filters them. For it to bring new attributes, an extra layer which computes progressively the output of the pointwise (1×1) and depth-wise convolution is done. The combination of these two convolutions is known as Depth-wise Separable Convolution and is highly efficient compared to the standard convolution. The computation is shown in Eq. 4 defined as:

$$Dk.Dk.M.DF.DF + M.N.DF.DF \tag{4}$$

It is paramount to note that the Rectilinear Linear Activation Function (ReLu) and batch normalization (BN) are applied after each convolution. While there are other activation functions, these two were selected as they can solve the vanishing gradient problem. The ReLu is simply a non-linear function that returns a value as input directly, or the value 0.0 if the given input is 0.0 or negative. It is given as:

$$f(x) = \max(0, x) \tag{5}$$

Figure 3 shows a standard convolutional layer using BN and ReLU on the left, and a MobileNet convolutions with the depth-wise layers and pointwise layers respectively followed by BN and ReLU.

c. Inception Overview. Also known as GoogleNet was developed 2014 during ImageNet visual recognition challenge. It uses a 1×1 convolution technique in the middle of the architecture and global average pooling to create deeper neural networks. The idea behind the inception model is to set up a deep NN while reducing the outputs. In a typical deep learning network, certain operation(s) need to be performed on each layer, such as addition of a pooling layer, a convolution operation, or filter size adjustment. The inception model allows all three to be performed in parallel. Though this would normally lead to an extreme large output, the introduction of the 1 x 1 convolution in

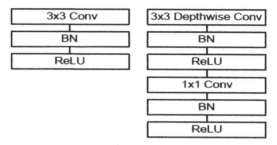

Fig. 3. Illustration of neural net layers using ReLu and Batch normalization.

the layer before the 3 × 3 and 5 × 5 layers solves this problem. Thus, providing a form of dimension reduction in the numbers of output to be passed to the next layer [22].

The architecture is built progressively in steps of factorized and the smaller convolutions. The factorized convolutions help to decrease the inefficiency of computations, as it reduces the size of parameters involved in each network. It also serves as a guard on the efficiency of the network. Furthermore, by replacing bigger convolutions with smaller convolutions, there is an increment in the speed of training. For instance, a 5 × 5 filter consist of 25 parameters, but if two smaller 3 × 3 filters are used instead of the 5 × 5 filter, the parameters are reduced from 25 to 18 (3*3 + 3*3) (Fig. 4).

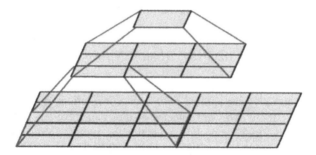

Fig. 4. Mini-network replacing the 5 × 5 convolutions

3.2 System Methodology

This subsection discussed the methodology applied in this work, including data collection, processing, transfer learning and tools used, as illustrated in Fig. 5.

i. Data Collection. The need for a large data cannot be overestimated when performing deep learning tasks. This is because it aids the neural network (NN) to better learn the relationships and patterns in each dataset. The dataset used in this paper contains images created from the department of Engineering and Signal processing at the University of Southern and Aarhus University. It contains a total of 5,539 images of crops and weeds seedlings. The dataset is grouped into 12 classes of plant species common in Denmark.

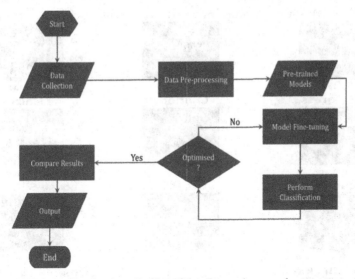

Fig. 5. Flow diagram of the proposed approach

The images are in PNG formats, and are pictures of plants of different sizes, and growth stages (Fig. 6).

ii. Data Pre-processing. The first step was to remove the non-segmented label class found in the dataset. This ensured that the total number of classes were 12, as summarized on Table 1. Other data pre-processing techniques such as transforms, resize, converting the images to float tensor were done using the PyTorch [23]. Using PyTorch's random split method, the dataset was split into 4,539 training samples and 1000 test samples.

iii. Pre-trained Model. The PyTorch framework provides out of the box deep learning pre-trained models which was utilized. A pre-trained model is a model which has been trained already on a large dataset such as ImageNet which is a very large dataset with many parameters and weights with more than 1 million labels and 1000 different categories [24]. The pre-trained models neural network models from PyTorch were utilized for the purpose of this research [25].

iv. Transfer Learning. The idea behind this is that we can use pre-trained model or an architecture which was trained differently on a particular dataset and task, then make it suitable for our own task. By doing this, we avoid having to build our NN from scratch and spending hours (or days) training it. The technique of feature extraction was used in the implementation of the project. This simply involves the reduction in numbers of resources to describe a large data. In PyTorch, the pre-trained models contain the fully connected layers. In applying it to our work, we froze the early convolutional layers of the models and trained only the last few layers which make the actual predictions or classification. We also reshaped the final layers to output twelve classes, corresponding to the number of classes of our dataset. In essence, though a pre-trained model was used, not all the layers were trained (Fig. 7).

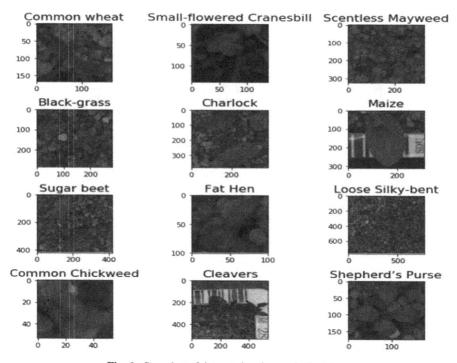

Fig. 6. Snapshot of dataset showing each plant type.

Table 1. Partitioning of plant species

Specie	Number of elements	Plant Type
Black grass	309	Weed
Charlock	452	Weed
Cleavers	335	Weed
Common chickweed	713	Weed
Common wheat	253	Crop
Fat hen	538	Weed
Loose silky-bent	762	Weed
Maize	257	Crop
Scentless mayweed	607	Weed
Shepherd's purse	274	Weed
Small-flowered cranesbill	576	Weed
Sugar beet	463	Crop
TOTAL	5539	

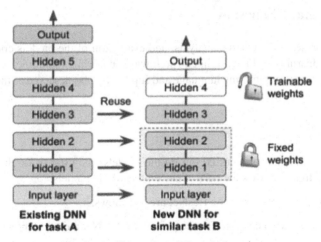

Fig. 7. An illustration of Transfer learning

3.3 Performance Metrics

Evaluating a CNN model is a major part of deep learning tasks. For the implementation done in this paper, performances were evaluated using the average accuracy, average f1-score, average recall, average precision, and the confusion matrix, and its corresponding TN (True Negative), FP (False Positive), FN (False Negative), and TP (True Positive). These metrics are described as follows:

i. Accuracy. This is the number of accurate predictions made by the model divided by the total predictions made. It is a good measure when the target variables or the target classes are nearly balanced.

$$Accuracy = \frac{(TN + TP)}{(TN + TP + FP + FN)} \quad (6)$$

ii Precision. This is a measure that tells if the number of predicted classes are correct. As an example, it determines if the proportion of plants which the model classifies as weeds are actually weeds.

$$Precision = \frac{TP}{TP + FP} \quad (7)$$

iii. Recall (or sensitivity): In the example, recall is a measure which tells the proportion of actual weeds versus those the model predicted as being weeds.

$$Recall = \frac{TP}{TP + FN} \quad (8)$$

iv. F1_Score (or F-measure): It is the harmonic mean between the recall and the precision. It is used to get a balance between the precision and the recall.

$$F1\_Score = 2 * \frac{(Precision * Recall)}{(Precision + Recall)} \quad (9)$$

4 Results and Discussion

This section presents the results, analysis, and evaluation of the models compared. As stated, a deep learning framework in PyTorch was used, while the implementation was done using Python programming language and Jupyter notebook served as the integrated development editor (IDE).

4.1 Results

Extensive experiments were carried out on the models using the PyTorch framework. The following figures shows the performance plots of the models.

ResNet Result. The results of the ResNet are as follows.

i. Accuracy and Loss: The performance plot of the ResNet model is shown in Fig. 8.

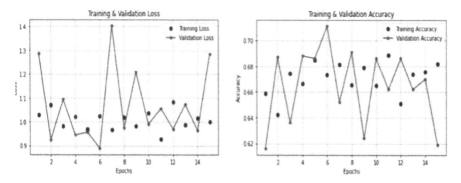

Fig. 8. ResNet performance plot

From the above plot, it can be observed that the model obtained an accuracy of 71.1% and 68.9% on the testing and training samples after 15 epochs, representing an increase of 2.2%. Similarly, the loss is shown to dropped from 1.02% in the training sample to 0.88% in the testing sample.

ii. Confusion matrix: The confusion matrix that shows the predicted classes versus the true classes is shown in Fig. 9.

The confusion matrix in Fig. 9 depicts twelve rows and columns of the actual and predicted classes respectively. The diagonal record tells the result of the true positives i.e., the correctly predicted classes.

iii. Classification Report: The classification result below shows the F1-score, recall and the precision of the model for the twelve classes of the plants.

Table 2 shows the classification report of the ResNet model using other performance metrics. Of all the 12 plants, Cranesbill, Charlock, and Maize had the highest F1-Scores at 83%, 79% and 85% respectively. The model struggled slightly with identifying weeds,

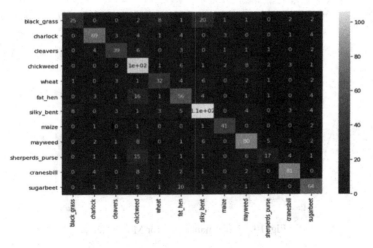

Fig. 9. Confusion matrix for ResNet mode

Table 2. Classification report for ResNet model

Class	Species/Metrics	Precision (%)	Recall (%)	F1-Score (%)
1	Black grass	74	40	52
2	Charlock	81	78	79
3	Cleavers	72	68	70
4	Chickweed	60	81	69
5	Wheat	65	62	63
6	Fat-hen	60	64	62
7	Silky-bent	72	77	75
8	Maize	80	89	85
9	Mayweed	75	74	75
10	Shepherd's purse	61	35	45
11	Cranesbill	84	82	83
12	Sugar beet	73	71	72
Average Values		71.4%	68.4%	69.2%

with the F1-Scores of Chickweed and Mayweed being 69% and 75%. There is therefore a very high probability that the model would mistake these weeds for crops.

MobileNet Result. The results of the ResNet are as follows.

i. Accuracy and Loss: The performance plot for the MobileNet is shown below (Fig. 10).

The above plot shows the performance of both training and validation samples. It is seen that the testing accuracy of the model is 75.4% improving on the 68.4% accuracy it

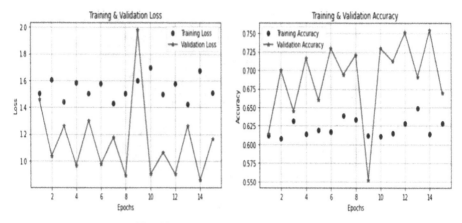

Fig. 10. Performance plot for MobileNet

achieved during training. This is a 7% increase on the training sample without overfitting. The loss accuracy also showed a progress from 1.67 to 0.61.

ii. Confusion matrix: The confusion matrix of predicted versus true values is depicted in Fig. 11.

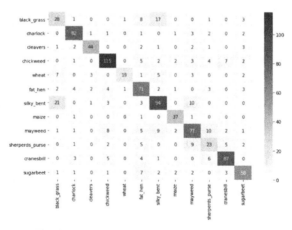

Fig. 11. Confusion matrix for MobileNet model

The confusion matrix in Fig. 11 depicts twelve rows and columns of the actual and predicted classes respectively. The diagonal record tells the result of the true positives i.e., the classes that the model correctly predicted.

iii. Classification Report: The classification result below shows the F1-score, recall and the precision of the model for the twelve classes of the plants for the model.

Table 3 shows the classification report of the MobileNet model using the performance metrics. For F1-Scores, in addition to Charlock (86%), Maize (87%) and Cranesbill

Table 3. Classification report for MobileNet model

Class	Species/Metrics	Precision (%)	Recall (%)	F1-Score (%)
1	Black grass	46	47	47
2	Charlock	85	88	86
3	Cleavers	86	79	82
4	Chickweed	83	82	82
5	Wheat	90	47	62
6	Fat-hen	63	76	69
7	Silky-bent	71	71	71
8	Maize	82	93	87
9	Mayweed	46	49	47
10	Shepherd's purse	90	96	93
11	Cranesbill	84	82	83
12	Sugar beet	76	75	76
Average values:		75.2%	73.8%	73.8%

(83%) for which ResNet performed well, MobileNet was also able to achieve good F1-scores of 93% for Shephard's purse and 82% for Cleavers. For the weeds, MobileNet performed well for Chickweed (82%), but very poorly with Mayweed at just 47%.

Inception Result. The results of the Inception model are as follows.

i. Accuracy and Loss: The performance plot for the inception is shown below.

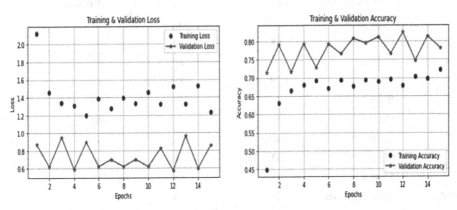

Fig. 12. Inception performance plot

Figure 12 shows testing and training accuracies of 82.4% and 67.9% respectively, while the training and testing losses were 1.5% and 0.7% respectively. This shows a significant improvement in the accuracy between the training and test sample sets. With a testing accuracy of 82.4%, Inception produced the best result of the three models.

ii. Confusion matrix: The confusion matrix showing the number of true positives in the diagonal is shown Fig. 13.

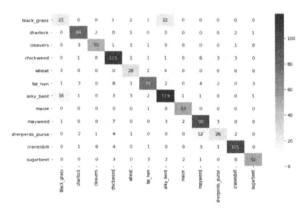

Fig. 13. Confusion matrix for the inception model

iii. Classification Report: The table below shows the classification report of the model using the metrics F1-score, precision, and recall.

Table 4. Classification report for Inception model

Class	Species/Metrics	Precision (%)	Recall (%)	F1-Score (%)
1	Black grass	50	45	47
2	Charlock	88	93	91
3	Cleavers	94	88	91
4	Chickweed	79	88	83
5	Wheat	74	76	75
6	Fat-hen	87	76	81
7	Silky-bent	78	81	79
8	Maize	91	98	95
9	Mayweed	78	86	82
10	Shepherd's purse	74	54	63
11	Cranesbill	93	91	92
12	Sugar beet	91	83	87
Average values:		81.4%	79.9%	80.5%

Table 4 shows the classification report of the Inception model using other performance metrics. Again Cranesbill, Maize and Charlock had good F1-Scores at over 90% each. Inception performed well in identifying the weeds with 83% and 82% F1-Scores for Chickweed and Mayweed respectively. Like the other models, Inception also struggled with Black grass.

4.2   Comparative Performance Evaluation

Figure 14 shows a graphical comparison of the average performance of the 3 models. It can clearly be seen that Inception performed the best across board, followed by MobileNet.

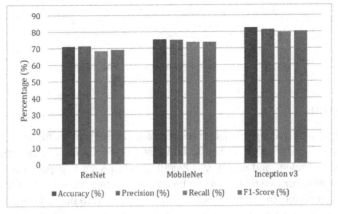

Fig. 14. Summary of Results – ResNet vs MobileNet vs Inception v3

4.3   Weed Detection

Figure 15 shows the performance of the three models in weed identification. This result is important because it shows how well the models perform in weed detection, which is vital step in weed control on farmlands. For this result we considered "Black-grass", "Chick-weed", and "Mayweed" as weeds. The graph shows the Precision, Recall and F1-Score of the three models – ResNet, MobileNet, and Inception v3.

The figure reveals that all three models performed relatively well with regards identifying Chick-Weed Inception v3, however, their performance was poor for black-grass, with only ResNet managing a precision of over 70%. A possible explanation for the poor performance w.r.t black-grass could be because of the blades / leaves of the black-grass are relatively slim compared to all other crops in the dataset. Finally, for all 3 weed samples, ResNet achieved an overall average Precision of 69.7%, followed by Inception v3 at 69% and MobileNet with a score 58.3%.

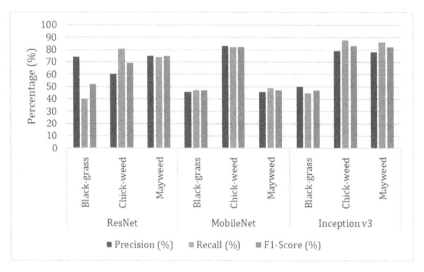

Fig. 15. Comparative Performance in Weed Detection

4.4 Discussion

In this section, inclusive arguments for the realized comparison results are summarized. From the overall results seen, it can be said that the proposed methodological system was relatively efficient and effective. Overall, ResNet seems to perform the poorest compared to the other two models while Inception is seen to have the best results of the three. The high results of the Inception could be attributed to the auxiliary classifier of the model which improve convergence during the training process. It is important to note that, though ResNet seemed to perform poorly, on closer examination, especially w.r.t to weed detection, ResNet was almost at par with Inception v3 and even outperforming it in detecting black grass.

5   Conclusions

In this paper, three CNN architectures were studied and evaluated on a plant seedlings image dataset to classify weeds from crops. The dataset which contains 9 crop plants, and 3 weed plants were in their early growth stage. It contains a total of 5539 images to which 4539 was set for training and 1000 plant images set for the test or validation samples. This dataset was divided into 12 classes of different plant species at different growth stages. Using a transfer learning technique and a popular deep learning library - PyTorch, the models which are pre-trained were evaluated on the dataset. Comparing the results of the three models, the ResNet model achieved an average classification accuracy of 71.1% on the testing sample while, the MobileNet and Inception v3 achieved accuracy scores of 75.4% and 82.4% respectively. When their performance in term of weed identification alone was considered, ResNet performed the best with a score of 69.7%, but was closely followed by Inception v3 (69%), and MobileNet (58.3%).

There is a need to develop datasets for local farm produce and crops. The curation of such datasets might be another avenue for expanding this work. Once such datasets are in place, the deployment of pre-trained models via transfer learning on localized dataset for weed control might be considered. Furthermore, the development of a web-based platform via which farmers can access the solutions might also be considered. It would be interesting to note the performance of these neural network models on embedded and mobile devices.

References

1. Binguitcha-Fare, A., Sharma, P.: Crops and weeds classification using convolutional neural networks via optimization of transfer learning parameters. Int. J. Eng. Adv. Technol. (IJEAT). **8**(5), 2249–8958 (2019)
2. Iderawumi, A., Friday, C.: Characteristics effects of weed on growth performance and yield of maize (zea mays). Biomedical J. **1**(4) (2018)
3. Wu, Z., Chen, Y., Zhao, B., Kang, X., Ding, Y.: Review of weed detection methods based on computer vision. Sensors **21**(11), 3647 (2021)
4. Asad, M., Bais, A.: Weed detection in canola fields using maximum likelihood classification and deep convolutional neural network. Inf. Process. Agric. **7**(4), 535–545 (2020)
5. Gothai, E., Natesan, P., Aishwariya, S., Aarthy T., Singh G.: Weed identification using convolutional neural network and convolutional neural network architectures. In: 2020 Fourth International Conference on Computing Methodologies and Communication (ICCMC), pp. 958–965 (2020)
6. Yinka-Banjo, C., Ajayi, O.: Sky-farmers: applications of unmanned aerial vehicles (UAV) in agriculture. Auton. Veh. 107–128 (2019)
7. Petit, S., Boursault, A., Le Guilloux, M., Munier-Jolain, N., Reboud, X.: Weeds in agricultural landscapes. A review. Agron. Sustain. Dev. **31**(2), 309–317 (2011)
8. Fawakherji, M., Youssef, A., Bloisi, D., Pretto, A., Nardi, D.: Crop and weeds classification for precision agriculture using context-independent pixel-wise segmentation. In: 2019 Third IEEE International Conference on Robotic Computing (IRC), pp. 146–152. IEEE (2019)
9. Ozcan, K., Sharma, A., Bradbury, S., Schweitzer, D., Blader, T., Blodgett, S.: Milkweed (Asclepias syriaca) plant detection using mobile cameras. Ecosphere **11**(1), e02992 (2020)
10. Li, W., Chen, P., Wang, B., Xie, C.: Automatic localization and count of agricultural crop pests based on an improved deep learning pipeline. Sci. Rep. **9**(1), 1–11 (2019)
11. Dyrmann, M., Karstoft, H., Midtiby, H.: Plant species classification using deep convolutional neural network. Biosys. Eng. **151**, 72–80 (2016)
12. Neforawati, I., Herman, N., Mohd, O.: Precision agriculture classification using convolutional neural networks for paddy growth level. J. Phys. Conf. Ser. **1193**(1), 012026 (2019)
13. Brilhador, A., Gutoski, M., Hattori, L., De Souza Inácio, A., Lazzaretti, A., Lopes, H.: Classification of weeds and crops at the pixel-level using convolutional neural networks and data augmentation. In: 2019 IEEE Latin American Conference on Computational Intelligence (LA-CCI), pp. 1–6. IEEE (2019)
14. Kamath, R., Balachanra, M., Prabhu, S.: Paddy crop and weed classification using color features for computer vision-based precision agriculture. Int. J. Eng. Technol. (UAE) **7**(4), 2909–2916 (2018)
15. Mishra, A.M., Gautam, V.: Weed species identification in different crops using precision weed management: a review. In: 2021 ISIC, pp. 180–194 (2021)

16. Khan, A., Ilyas, T., Umraiz, M., Mannan, Z., Kim, H.: Ced-net: crops and weeds segmentation for smart farming using a small cascaded encoder-decoder architecture. Electronics **9**(10), 1602 (2020)

17. Haichen, J., Qingrui, C., Zheng Guang, L.: Weeds and crops classification using deep convolutional neural network. In: 2020 the 3rd International Conference on Control and Computer Vision, pp. 40–44 (2020)

18. Grace, R.: Crop and weed classification using deep learning. Turkish J. Comput. Math. Educ. (TURCOMAT) **12**(7), 935–938 (2021)

19. He, K., Zhang, X., Ren, S., Sun, J.: Microsoft Research: Deep Residual Learning for Image Recognition. arXiv preprint 2015:1512.03385 (2015)

20. Howard, A., Zhu, M., Chen, B., Kalenichenko, D., et al.: Mobilenets: efficient convolutional neural networks for mobile vision applications. arXiv preprint 2017:1704.04861 (2017)

21. Abadi, M., Agarwal, A., Barham. P., Brevdo, E., et al.: TensorFlow: large-scale machine learning on heterogeneous systems. www.tensorflow.org. Accessed 21 June 2022

22. Szegedy, C., Vanhoucke, V., Ioffe, S., Shlens, J., Wojna, Z.: Rethinking the inception architecture for computer vision. In: 2016 Proceedings of the IEEE Conference on Computer Vision and Pattern Recognition, pp. 2818–2826 (2016)

23. Paszke, A., Gross, S., Massa, F., Lerer, A., et al.: Pytorch: an imperative style, high-performance deep learning library. In: Advances in Neural Information Processing Systems, vol. 32 (2019)

24. Deng, J., Dong, W., Socher, R., Li, L., et al.: Imagenet: a large-scale hierarchical image database. In: 2009 IEEE Conference on Computer Vision and Pattern Recognition, pp. 248–255. IEEE (2009)

25. Cadene, et al.: pre-trained ConvNets for pytorch: NASNet, ResNeXt, ResNet, InceptionV4, InceptionResnetV2, Xception, DPN etc. (2017)

Author Index

Printed in the United States
by Baker & Taylor Publisher Services